Post-war British theatre

Post-war British theatre

John Elsom

Routledge & Kegan Paul
London, Henley and Boston

First published in 1976
by Routledge & Kegan Paul Ltd
39 Store Street, London WC1E 7DD
Broadway House, Newtown Road,
Henley-on-Thames, Oxon RG9 1EN and
9 Park Street, Boston, Mass. 02108, USA
Set in Baskerville
and printed in Great Britain by
Unwin Brothers Ltd.

ISBN 0 7100 8350 5

Contents

Illustrations

Acknowledgments

The illustrations in this book are reproduced by kind permission of Bristol Old Vic Company (no. 1); Royal Court Theatre (no. 2); Chichester Festival Theatre (no. 3); Royal Shakespeare Company (nos 4 and 7); National Theatre (nos 5 and 8) and photographers Alex Agor (no. 6), and Zoë Dominic (nos 5 and 8).

The author would like to thank Brian Southam and John McLaughlin, without whom this book would not have been written; and Sue Rolfe and Benedict Nightingale without whom it would have been written with more mistakes.

Introduction

A short history of post-war British theatre is almost impossible to write. It has to be very short or very long. There is an anecdote, concerning the late Pope John XXIII who was asked by a friend visiting Europe whether he could see Rome in a day. The Pope answered casually, 'Yes.' His friend then looked guilty, 'I'm sounding just like an ordinary tourist. Of course I can't see Rome in a day. I'll take a week.' At that, the Pope looked doubtful, 'You won't be able to see much of Rome in a week.' 'Then,' said his friend heroically, 'I'll cancel my business appointments, I'll send a telegram to my wife and I'll stay here for a whole month!' The Pope threw up his hands in horror, 'You can see nothing what-soever of Rome in a month!'

The situation is similar if we pay a historical visit to the theatre of the past thirty years. We can summarise what has happened in a few phrases; or we can pursue accuracy down every theatrical by-way leading to an enormous and probably unreadable com-pendium of minutiae. Fortunately, such a tome is not really needed. This period, a fruitful one for British theatre, has been almost equally prolific in reference books, guides and substantial critical surveys. Lists of most professional productions can be found (firstly) in the *Stage Yearbooks* (from 1948 to 1969) and then in the *British Theatre Directories* (from 1972 to 1974); the gaps in these lists, of course, are irritating. Biographies of contemporary dra-matists can be found in several reference works, notably *Mid-Cen-tury Authors* and *Twentieth Century Authors*, *Contemporary Dramatists* and the *Authors' and Writers' Who's Who*. *Who's Who in the Theatre* gives career summaries of actors, dramatists, directors. John Russell Taylor's three books, *Anger and After* (1962), *The Decline and Fall of the Well-Made Play* (1969) and *The Second Wave* (1971), manage to combine useful critical introductions to the work of major British dramatists from the mid-1950s onwards, together with a comprehensive, if necessarily brief, list of the minor ones. Bamber Gascoigne's *Twentieth Century Drama* describes some developments in the theatre until the end of the 1950s. Richard Findlater's *The Unholy Trade* and Ronald Hayman's *The Set-Up* pro-vide good accounts of the different stages in the re-organisation of post-war British theatre, thus supplementing two other detailed surveys on *Theatre Ownership in Britain* (1953, a report prepared for the Federation of Theatre Unions) and *The Theatre Today* (1970, published by the Arts Council). Michael Billington's *The Modern Actor* provides a description of the conditions facing actors today, together with some studies of individual performers, while Findlater's *The Player Kings*, with two volumes of interviews, *Great Acting* and *Acting in the Sixties* (1967 and 1970, published by the BBC), give illuminating accounts of the work of certain selected 'star' actors. For those who require short but surprisingly detailed general studies of the different phases in the development of drama since the war, there have been four chronicles published for the British Council: Speight's *Drama Since 1939*, Trewin's *Drama, 1945–50* and *Drama in Britain, 1951–64*, and Lambert's *Drama in Britain, 1964–1973*. There have been many studies of individual movements, such as Martin Esslin's *The Theatre of the Absurd* and *Brecht: A Choice of Evils*. Even fringe theatre is acquiring a bibliography. There is a quick guide to the origins of fringe theatre in the magazine, *Theatre Quarterly* (volume III, no. 12), compiled by Jonathan Hammond, while Peter Ansorge's *Disrupting the Spectacle* (1975) considers the five years of fringe theatre from 1968 onwards.

With these and other lists, why do we need a short history of post-war British theatre at all? What should be the scope of this book? I am attempting two main tasks: first, to provide a general introduction to post-war theatre which deliberately does not concentrate on any one aspect (such as the dramatists concerned or the directors) but which tries to relate the many different facets; the second aim is to consider the evolution of the theatre, particularly in such matters as critical standards. Our current standards, while not necessarily 'better' than those of the past, do seem to have evolved from them in a distinct progression. Thus, I do mean 'evolution' and not just 'change'. To consider (and possibly evaluate) such developments, however, requires a certain critical stance of one's own. It would be misleading to pretend that my standards are the same as other people's, or even generally accepted. This history therefore begins in a personal, subjective way, so that the reader can guess at my predilections and (during the course of the book) modify his consideration of my judgments accordingly.

This book is dedicated to my many friends at the City Literary Institute, Marylebone Institute and the Kensington and Chelsea Institute, who heroically sat through some very long lectures.

Chapter 1

Language and money

W. H. Auden once remarked that the prime duty of a poet was 'to maintain the purity of the language'. My instinct (hunch or prejudice—as you will) tells me that a similar duty rests on the shoulders of those who belong, even indirectly, like critics, to the theatrical profession. Their first task is to maintain the purity of the theatrical language.

Auden was not suggesting that languages should be racially or ethnically 'pure', that British poets should only be permitted to use good British words. Nor was he implying that words should be kept in convent isolation until they can be properly mated with a true Master of Language. He did mean that the words chosen by poets should be pure in the sense of 'authentic', a term much employed by the German philosopher, Karl Jaspers, whose brand of existentialism greatly influenced Auden.

Language evolves from the human need to discover effective symbols which can correspond to and communicate experiences. They should reflect a vital response to life, not as a mirror flashes off the sun but as a token, given in love, reflects the feelings of the lover. These symbols, these tokens, contain a core of meaning which does not, or ought not to, fluctuate too wildly from individual to individual. Totally accurate communication is, of course, impossible. We experience life as individuals and our impressions are neither identical nor interchangeable. To one person, the taste of salt may be nauseating; to another invigorating. But when we use the word salt, we don't mean pepper or the army. To that extent, communication is possible, and by using words with as much accuracy as we can muster, we are maintaining the purity of the language.

Languages can easily become defiled. Clichés are phrases which have lost some authenticity by being used too often and too carelessly. Jargon is language which buries its meaning under a pile of other intentions, such as the desire to impress, seduce or otherwise falsely to persuade. Sometimes, languages are simply incapable of expressing certain experiences, perhaps because their vocabularies are limited in one direction or another. The quest for pure language also implies overcoming the deficiencies of an inherited language by borrowing, resurrecting or inventing words to convey experiences which would otherwise have been hard or impossible to express.

This is also the poet's task, one which is often fraught with social and political implications, for societies, governments, ruling and non-ruling classes can restrict their languages deliberately in order to prevent people from thinking and communicating in inexpedient ways. George Orwell's nightmare of governmentally restricted language, in his novel *1984*, has never been too far from daylight reality. The Edwardian dramatist, Edward Garnett, had to use a French word, 'enceinte', to explain in 1909 that the heroine of his play, *The Breaking Point*, was pregnant, because the English word was considered vulgar and likely to inflame lascivious thoughts. The unofficial and sometimes unconscious restrictions can be worse than the official ones, expressed (say) through censorship. Class and racial loyalties, political and religious beliefs, can have the effect of outlawing those words (and through them those experiences) which do not seem to belong within their schemes of commitments. The poet who knowingly allows the language to be restricted like this has perpetrated the worst literary crime of all, 'the treason of the clerks', but avoiding this treachery can require moral, mental and sometimes physical courage of a high order.

A language is, of course, more than the sum of its words. It is also the organisation of these words, the formation of sentences and paragraphs, the general technique whereby one idea or impression is related to the next. The same test of authenticity can be applied here. Some syntactical rules are mere pedantry, providing contorted sentences if rigidly observed and more of an obstacle than a help to thought and expression. Other rules contain the origins of all logic. Without them we would have difficulty in thinking rationally at all, or at least through the medium of words.

Not all verbal organisation is so cerebral. The poet who chooses to write in verse organises the natural stresses and sounds of language into metrical patterns, thus in a sense dancing with words. Pattern can have many purposes. It may simply be a way of holding together many impressions in the mind: when the pattern is broken, an impression has been lost or deliberately dropped. Pattern can be useful in this way, or decorative, or establish musical rhythms with definite beats and pitches, or even mimic life after a fashion. When the Narrator in Dylan Thomas's *Under Milk Wood* (1954), a radio play afterwards staged, describes Llaregyb harbour at night, he talks about the 'sloeblack, slow, black, crow-black, fishing-boat-bobbing sea', a phrase which captures the sound of the lapping waves.

Patterns which shape entire works and may include subsidiary patterns change their characteristics. The actual meaning of a poem may be lost without that consecutiveness and order which an overall pattern can provide. We require another word, form. A leaf which is seen as part of a tree has pattern: the tree itself has form. If we examine the leaf by itself, plucked from the tree and placed on a sheet of white paper, then its overall shape is its form, whereas an intricate vein from this leaf has pattern. In literature, patterns can be closely linked with overall forms, as in French neo-classical drama; or, as in Jacobean drama, the relationship between the patterns and the forms can be a tenuous one. The form can be like a travelling bag into which all kinds of different objects, each with its own pattern, can be quickly, if not carelessly, thrown.

Vocabulary, syntax, pattern and form: these are the main attributes of language and the poet's job is to maintain their authenticity. His work is life-enhancing in two respects. He is trying to maintain the close contact between the symbol and the experience, so that his transitory experience can be retained in symbolic shape and contemplated. He is thus affirming the value of his impressions of life by his efforts to hold on to them. By his choice of public rather than private symbols, he is also insisting that such experiences can and should be passed on to others, thus affirming the value of human relationships.

The theatre can be said both to *have* and to *be* a language.

It obviously has a language in that ordinary words are used for dialogue. But it is also a language in itself, by providing a vocabulary of symbols which need not be verbal at all. The rising of a curtain tells us that the action is about to begin. The lowering of lights may indicate that a scene (but not an act) has ended. In theatres with open stages and no curtains, some other action may take place (a fanfare, the dimming of house lights) to tell us that something is about to happen, while the director who chooses not to provide us with such a signal, may be indicating that the theatrical action has no beginning, but springs from the infinite origins of life.

Traditional genres provide their own symbols. If the curtain rises on a box set, a living room with a couch and cocktail cabinet, the audience will probably guess that the play will be a 'middle-class' comedy or drama, 'well-made' and 'naturalistic'. If we see an open stage with a prop or two instead of a set, we anticipate a play with a looser structure, perhaps a documentary or an 'epic', with many changes of locale and not 'naturalistic'.

The vocabulary of the theatre is, on one level, exceptionally precise and, on another, vast and cumbersome. A glance between two good actors on stage tells us more about their (fictional) relationship than a page of verbal description in a book. But there are almost too many ways in which information can be theatrically conveyed. The medium extends in all directions. A tune can be a theatrical symbol, as in Tennessee Williamss' *The Glass Menagerie* (1944). The visual appearance of the stage can be symbolic, not only in such matters as sets and props but in the structure of the stage itself, the presence or otherwise of a proscenium arch, or a forestage, whether the audience looks up or down to the playing area, whether the stage is circled by seats, or half-circled, or kept separate from the audience by an orchestra pit. The nature of the theatre itself may be symbolic. We expect a different type of production from a basement fringe theatre than we do from the West End. A theatre may be, in Yeats's phrase, just 'a rug at the end of a room', or it might be a Palace or an Alhambra. Before the curtain goes up on a first night, we have probably guessed something about the type of production we are going to see, except that we haven't exactly *guessed*: we have been given information through a variety of conscious and unconscious symbols, from the atmosphere of the theatre to the style of the programmes.

Methods of acting also contain symbols. To signify anger in Balinese dance drama, the actor must flicker his lower eyelids. European acting contains many styles, often jumbled together but still recognisable. They range from improvisation to 'naturalism' to 'alienation' to the shock tactics of Artaud and his school. Acting styles can be added to the theatrical vocabulary, together with directorial and writing styles. All these different symbolic ways of conveying impressions, thoughts and the logic connecting them would add up to a monstrous dictionary, if one could be compiled. But, of course, it can't, despite John Russell Taylor's brave attempt with the *Penguin Dictionary of the Theatre*. This is perhaps the first weakness of the theatrical language. Whilst the symbols exist, with their surrounding syntaxes, patterns and forms, many survive as remnants of long-lost traditions which have been built into the very processes of theatre-going. Some retain their original relevance, many do not. The theatre has a vast vocabulary and a wide range of organisational methods; but it has always lacked that continual, rigorous and patient assessment of aims and usages which characterises verbal (and often less complete) languages. There have been plenty of theatrical poets and demagogues, but very few grammarians and philologists. This was why Brecht, when formulating his own theories, felt the need to attack Aristotle first, which is rather like a twentieth-century astronomer having first to debunk Ptolemy.

These telling absences can be explained to some extent historically. For centuries the theatre was regarded either as a popular art or as a courtly indulgence, and as thus beyond the concern of academics—just as before Dr Johnson appeared, the vulgar English tongue was not considered worthy of a formal dictionary. Most people knew what the words meant and so why bother? 'A play either works or doesn't work', one director said to me. 'Why waste time on considering the structure of its language?' The answer to this rhetorical question is that without some academic discipline, the theatrical language has a tendency to spread, to become so loose and floppy that it is virtually unusable; at which point some theatrical fashion comes along which imposes a very rough discipline indeed, cutting out many effects which might otherwise seem naturally to belong to the theatre.

This pendulum swing, 'anything goes' followed by 'only that is allowed', has characterised the development of the theatre and it derives partly from the lack of study of the theatre as a language. The past thirty years have offered a classic illustration. In the early 1950s the theatre was afflicted by all kinds of inhibitions. There was an unhealthy concentration of theatrical power in the hands of a few impresarios, whose influence (though not necessarily philistine) helped to prevent other ideas from being expressed. The writing of plays was constricted by an unthinking dependence upon the 'naturalistic well-made play' formulae, popularised by Ibsen, Shaw, Rattigan and others. It could also be argued that these formalised techniques were directed towards a particular class outlook on the part of the audiences. The shapes of theatre buildings were constricting, the picture-frame stages, the rows of seats stretching backwards and upwards into the cavernous recesses of Edwardian auditoria, the too rigid endings to acts with quick or slow 'curtains', the gulf of the orchestra pits, the rows of formal lighting which never quite prevented unwelcome shadows, the fixed entrances and exits from the wings.

By the mid-1960s, much of this had changed, in that few people at all knowledgeable of the theatre assumed that theatres had to be built like *this* or plays written like *that*—or even that impresarios were necessarily fat men with cigars. A play could be a Happening, or a sensory experience along the lines of the Living Theatre or the Liquid Theatre, or a sustained Marxist polemic, or whatever. Although the majority of plays in the West End could still have been characterised as farces, comedies, musicals or Society Dramas, we could justifiably feel that the West End no longer dictated the standards to the theatre as a whole. A much greater variety of theatrical experiences had replaced the old uniformity.

With this diversity, however, there came a certain loss of precision. There was a time in the late 1960s and early 1970s when it seemed that anything could happen in the theatre, but nothing seemed quite right. Individual productions were marvellous, but they did not lead to a fruitful genre. There were many interesting new plays, at least in typescript, but few seemed actually to work in the theatre. Dramatists got bored with their incapacities to write satisfying plays consistently and drifted off in other directions. The re-organisation of the theatre as a profession had led to a strong repertory movement, a much weaker touring network, a mixed economy of subsidised and commercial theatre with the balance tilting year by year in favour of the subsidised, an active and sometimes positively anarchic fringe, a more forceful Equity (the actors' trade union) and some very tentative managements, so frightened of getting their fingers burnt that they wouldn't warm them by the fire.

If we consider both the constricted theatre of the 1950s and the fruitful, diverse, but eventually dissatisfying, theatre of the late 1960s, we are confronted by one main question: how can we combine an exact use of the theatrical language with that wonderful comprehensiveness which is that language's greatest asset?

This approach, however, may seem pedantic. It is all very well to talk idealistically about 'maintaining the purity of the language' but this is not much comfort to the actor or dramatist speaking this language superlatively well who cannot get a job. The theatre is an industry, as well as a language, and how the industry is run, who employs whom and why, occupies much of that money-grabbing time which nearly everyone in the Profession would prefer to be dedicated to Higher Matters.

After the Second World War, the theatre industry, notoriously unstable at best, was in a state of approaching chaos. About a fifth of the theatres in London had been destroyed or badly damaged by bombing; others were battered or just neglected. There was inevitably a shortage of actors, some still in the forces, others on ENSA tours. Comparatively wealthy pre-war managements had gone out of business. In 1942, the entire Stoll Theatres Corporation, which owned six London theatres, four regional ones, a music hall and a film company, was sold for only £140,000. Unlike the situation during the First World War, when soldiers returning on leave and families re-uniting kept the theatres thriving, the Second World War dealt a body blow to the theatre which (many feared) could have been followed by a total knock-out.

Even without the war, the theatre would have faced harsh problems. It had been confronted for thirty years by the challenge of the mass media. Many theatres had been converted into cinemas. Of seventeen live theatres owned by the Abrahams Group before the war, only four were functioning as theatres by 1949. Films were the challenge in the 1940s; radio indirectly helped the theatre by publicising its stars. The greatest challenge, however, was yet to come, that of television. The spectre of widespread television haunted everyone in the theatre, from impresarios to small-time rep managements alike, because it was assumed that post-war television (like the pre-war variety) would be run by the BBC, a national corporation. In the 1920s, theatre managements had protected themselves against the growing film industry by taking shares in film companies. They were not able, until commercial television was established in 1956, to hedge their bets similarly against the possibility of the small-screen taking over the drama industry.

The aftermath of war and the mass media, together with Entertainments Tax at 10 percent of gross receipts, provided a packaged nightmare to post-war theatre companies. They would chase the future down one blind alley, only to backtrack and run along another. They could have coped more successfully if the industry had been in a better shape initially. Since the 1920s, however, the theatre had undergone a tortuous transition from the many small, competing, independent managements of Edwardian theatre to a supposedly more streamlined industry, in which groups of companies controlled chains of theatres.

This 'streamlining' had half taken place when the war struck, so that sections of the theatre industry were in the hands of business combines, while other sections were still struggling along in the old ways. There had emerged an 'absentee' landlord class in British theatre, men who had bought a theatrical chain, then let individual theatres to managements who ran them and who in turn sub-let to producing managements. Through this process of letting and sub-letting, the costs of hiring West End theatres steeply escalated. Richard Findlater, in *The Unholy Trade* (1952), calculated that in the years which separated the heyday of the actor-managers (c. 1880) from 1949, theatre rents had increased by up to 1000 percent, production costs by 600 percent, while admission prices had risen by only 50 percent.

Sometimes nearly half the gross receipts from a West End production would disappear in rents, rates and taxation, before an independent impresario could start to pay off his production costs and, of course, his actors. Under these circumstances, the independents were naturally cautious: most would only risk cheap, 'sure-fire' productions, of mystery plays, light comedies and revues. Some paid for a limited theatrical ambitiousness through exceptionally careful housekeeping. Henry Sherek balanced the profits from intimate revues staged at the Dorchester Hotel and elsewhere against the risks entailed in launching the plays of T. S. Eliot. But the days of great personal gambles, such as those which distinguished Sir Charles Cochran's career, were almost over. Cochran died in 1951, the end of an era indeed.

One method of cutting down the risks was to try out a play in one of the many 'little theatres' around London, or with a play-producing society (such as the Repertory Players, who staged Sunday night productions in West End theatres), or in a small rep in the regions. Norman Marshall, in his book *The Other Theatre* (1947), has described the honourable history of the 'little theatres' in the years between the wars, when they pioneered the work of new playwrights (such as Pirandello, Cocteau and even Coward), introduced new theatre genres (such as documentary drama and expressionism) and unfamiliar methods of acting and directing. Komisarjevsky brought the methods of Stanislavski to Britain via a cramped cinema stage in Barnes, while Terence Gray at Cambridge anticipated the sort of production ideas (slow-motion fights, open stages with props, actors on stilts) now inevitably associated with the Royal Shakespeare Company. 'I seek', stated Gray in 1931, 'the unexpected reaction, the unanticipated pleasure, the irresponsible wrath, the readjustment of values.' Such remarks remind one irresistibly of Peter Brook, who was then too young (at six) even to be an *enfant terrible*.

Most little theatres after the war were self-financed (thus avoiding high rents) and operated as clubs (thus avoiding direct censorship). The leading ones in London included the

Arts, Boltons, Lindsay, Mercury, Players and the Unity: less
noted were the Chepstow, Gateway, Irving, Torch, Twentieth Century and Watergate. At Swiss Cottage, there was the
Embassy, while in the suburbs were the Alex, Stoke
Newington, the 'Q', Kew Bridge, the Intimate, Palmers Green
and the Granville, Waltham Green. These clubs had different
reputations. The Boltons and the Lindsay were known for intimate revues, written by (say) Peter Myers or Eleanor Far-
jeon; the Unity was the leading left-wing theatre club, while
the Alex was linked with a Jewish company, the New Yiddish
Theatre. The most prestigious club of all was the Arts, run
after the war by Alec Clunes, whose seasons would now be
compared to the best provided by the leading subsidised
reps. The 1950 season included a rare Chekhov (*Ivanov*),
Chiarelli's *The Mask and the Face*, *Lady Precious Stream* and *Mrs
Warren's Profession*. Clunes staged Fry's first major success, *The
Lady's not for Burning* (1948), which transferred in a full Tennent Production to the West End, with John Gielgud,
Richard Burton, Claire Bloom and Pamela Brown. Among
his casts were Alec McCowen and Michael Hordern: his
directors included John Fernald.

The atmosphere at the lesser clubs, however, was often
depressing, a mixture of wan hopefulness and despairing
energy. The club members took advantage of the bar, eyeing
warily those eager directors and writers who had hired the
theatre, painted the scenery and were now expecting them to
drift into the auditorium, glasses in hand, to witness the
triumphant débâcle of another first night. Burrowing
through the lists of now-forgotten productions, the archivist
must be impressed, however, by the familiar names whose
early careers were interred there. Brook, fresh from Oxford,
directed *Dr Faustus* at the Torch (1943) and Cocteau's *The In-
fernal Machine* at the Chanticleer (1945). In one year, 1950,
Frank Marcus's first play, *Minuet for Stuffed Birds*, was produced at the Torch, Giles Cooper's first two plays were produced at the Torch and the Lindsay, while Paul Scofield and
Donald Sinden appeared at the Twentieth Century. If our
fringe theatres nowadays can produce such a crop from such
seeds, they will not have struggled in vain.

The independent impresarios searched for their next productions among the little theatres: they also went talent-spot-

ting among the reps, where there was a similar gap in prestige between the leading ones (at Birmingham, Bristol, Cambridge, Liverpool, Sheffield and, in Scotland, Glasgow) and the 250 lesser ones, tactfully described in the 1949 Stage Year Book as the 'nursery of dramatic art'. The lesser reps were often barely professional, hopelessly overworked with sometimes two separate productions a week and two perfor- mances a night. Established actors regarded them with a hor- ror normally reserved for Devil's Island. The prestigious reps, however, carried with them a reputation for high- minded seriousness and lofty anti-commercialism. Bir- mingham Rep, under Sir Barry Jackson, was one of the most adventurous theatres in the country, renowned for discover- ing new actors (among them, in generation order, Felix Aylmer, Laurence Olivier, Greer Garson and Albert Finney), new playwrights and directors. The Bristol Old Vic, with its glorious Georgian auditorium, can be regarded perhaps as the first major success of state subsidies, since it was partly financed and encouraged by CEMA (the Council for the En- couragement of Music and the Arts) during the war. In 1948, Basil Dean (who founded the Liverpool Playhouse in 1911) staged a season of productions from regional reps at the St James's, astonishing London critics by their high quality.

Among the independent impresarios were the last of a venerable breed, the actor-managers. It was still regarded as the peak of a successful actor's ambition to run and star in his own company. Sir Donald Wolfit was one, who had run an independent company throughout the war, still toured the regions and occasionally took over large theatres on the fringes of London's main theatre areas to present mammoth seasons. In 1949, he took over the Bedford (Camden Town) to present a repertoire which included *King Lear*, *Hamlet*, *Macbeth*, *Othello*, *Twelfth Night*, *Much Ado*, *The Merry Wives of Windsor* and *The Master Builder*. Sir Laurence Olivier became an actor-manager in 1950, presenting two seasons at the St James's which included the première of Fry's *Venus Observed*, *Antony and Cleopatra* and Shaw's *Caesar and Cleopatra*. Sir John Gielgud ran two seasons as an actor-manager, at the Queen's Theatre in 1937–38 and at the Haymarket in 1944–55. Jack Buchanan went into partnership with Bernard Delfont to manage and run the Garrick Theatre, a régime which was distinguished by his appreciation of the needs of other independent impresarios.

From what were these impresarios 'independent'? What would be meant by a 'dependent' impresario? They were mainly independent from a consortium of business/theatrical interests, popularly known as The Group. After the Second World War, many feared that the concentration of large sections of the theatre industry into a few people's hands was approaching the proportions of an outright monopoly. The best example of this tendency towards monopoly was the growth of Prince Littler's theatrical interests. In 1940, he was the Chairman or Managing Director (or both) for a wide range of companies, including six theatre chains, a catering firm, a theatre insurance company and a property company. During the war, with so many theatre firms becoming bankrupt, his Prince Littler Consolidated Trust bought up theatres at rock-bottom prices, including the Stoll Theatres Corporation, Moss Empires and the General Theatre Corporation, and Littler became the Chairman of Howard and Wyndham Ltd, which had a majority holding in H. M. Tennent Ltd, the leading play-producing management in London. By the late 1940s, the Prince Littler Consolidated Trust directly owned with its affiliated companies 18 out of the 42 functioning West End theatres and 57 (70 per cent) of the main out-of-London touring theatres. If we consider simply the Number 1 touring circuit, which then consisted of 53 theatres, 34 were owned by The Group. Indirectly, The Group's influence was also great, for members of Prince Littler's board also sat on the boards of other supposedly independent companies. I have mentioned Jack Buchanan's régime at the Garrick where he held a sublease from the Abrahams company who owned the theatre. The Abrahams company with its chain of theatres was not considered to be part of The Group, but Charles Gulliver, a member of Prince Littler's Board, also sat on the board of the Abrahams company.

There was an obvious danger of a 'horizontal' monopoly emerging, in which most London and regional theatres would be controlled by The Group. Of equal danger was the possibility of 'vertical' monopoly, in which every facet of the entertainments industry, from real estate, actors' agencies, sheet music and records to play production and wardrobe design, would be controlled by The Group: and at the centre of this patchwork empire sat Prince Littler.

Critics of the theatre system blamed The Group for all kinds of post-war theatre evils. Actors not employed by The Group complained that they were being victimised: actors who were objected that they were paying for this privilege through agency fees. Many felt that the theatrical tastes of their generation were being moulded by a not particularly enlightened élite. Inevitably, left-wing critics drew telling political morals. Under a dog-eat-dog capitalistic system, powerful companies increased in strength, weaker ones went to the wall, until finally a small group of owners dominated the profession, controlling the people, the places and the expressivity of the medium alike. Who in 1950 was unsuccessfully directing a season of Victorian melodramas at the Bedford, Camden Town? That 'romantic Marxist', Kenneth Tynan. Who was struggling to establish a people's theatre, first in Manchester, then at Stratford-atte-Bowe? The Mother Courage of community theatre, Joan Littlewood. If (as has been suggested) a substantial section of the Profession wheeled politically to the left in the late 1950s, the origins of this movement can perhaps be traced to the trials and frustrations of the early 1950s which were blamed on The Group.

The Group was not without its problems, however, nor its advocates. It was generally agreed that the industry needed streamlining and whatever else The Group had or had not done, it was certainly prepared to 'streamline'. It also required courage, not to mention patriotism and a readiness to gamble, to buy London theatres in 1942, when everyone else was scrambling to sell. Their assets may have been extensive, but their commitments were equally so. One of the most telling criticisms of The Group was that directed against it by other business men, that it was simply over-extended. The Group could not afford to renovate the properties it had acquired, and the burden of post-war theatre reconstruction fell on its shoulders. In the mid-1950s, The Group faced the challenge of television and tried to sell off its assets, diverting the capital raised into record companies and television. Unprofitable touring theatres on valuable property sites were sold; others were run as dance halls and (later) bingo parlours. The touring circuits shrank from 150 theatres to about 30 within fifteen years. In Leicester, there were three theatres during the early 1950s, two of them belonging to The Group; by 1956, all had closed.

If we glance through the programmes at London theatres connected with The Group during one year, 1949, the impression is not that of an all-pervading philistinism. Tennessee Williams's *A Streetcar Named Desire*, directed by Laurence Olivier and starring Vivien Leigh, was playing at the Aldwych; Arthur Miller's *Death of a Salesman* was at the Phoenix; the year at St James's included Rattigan's *Adventure Story* and Paul Scofield in *The Seagull*; Tolstoy's *Power of Darkness* was produced at the Lyric, and John Clements and Kay Hammond appeared in *The Beaux Stratagem* at the Phoenix. Sid Field was in Mary Chase's *Harvey* at the Prince of Wales, while the musicals included *Annie Get Your Gun* at the Coliseum and *Brigadoon* at His Majesty's. A better farce of the period, John Dighton's *The Happiest Days of Your Life*, was at the Apollo. Other shows aimed at the popular market included Novello's *King's Rhapsody*, *Song of Norway* and an intimate revue, *Sauce Tartare*, with Ronald Frankau and Claude Hulbert. Cicely Courtneidge starred in a new, though rather faded, British musical, *Her Excellency* at the Hippodrome. By glancing through this selection, and those of the surrounding years, we can begin to understand the theatrical, as opposed to commercial, strengths of The Group.

Through H. M. Tennent Ltd, and its subsidiary 'non-profit distributing' company, Tennent Productions Ltd, The Group encouraged classical revivals and some plays by new dramatists. H. B. Beaumont, the managing director of Tennent Productions Ltd, was an austere, self-contained man, a literary purist and confident of his judgments. On his board sat Sir John Gielgud, Sir Ralph Richardson and George Rylands, the Cambridge don, an expert on verse-speaking, who through the Marlowe Society trained several generations of students, among them Peter Hall, John Barton and Trevor Nunn. Beaumont was prepared to champion new writers, although by the end of the 1950s his standards came under attack for being too narrowly literary, too 'middle-class' and concerned with the behaviour of the genteelly rich. He would not sidle a play into London cheaply, but with star names and lavish sets, perhaps by Oliver Messel. The dramatists he sponsored included Christopher Fry, N. C. Hunter, John Whiting and Enid Bagnold.

The strength of The Group, however, never lay in its links with the Tennent companies. Its main interest lay in the field of light entertainment, particularly musicals. The 1950s was as outstanding period for musicals. After *Annie Get Your Gun* and *Oklahoma* came *Guys and Dolls*, *Kiss Me Kate*, *Call Me Madam*, *Porgy and Bess*, *Pal Joey* and eventually *West Side Story* and *My Fair Lady*, still running in 1963. These came from the States, but they were staged and marketed mainly by companies connected with The Group with great efficiency and zest. No other theatre genre since the war has achieved the same degree of mass popularity. For every teenager who was attracted to the theatre by an Old Vic production, there must have been a thousand who were hypnotised by these great show-business spectaculars. Connected with the success of the musicals was the whole marketing operation of The Group which it alone could tackle because it had achieved such dominance, in so many fields, from sheet music to regional tours. If we talk about a revival of theatre in the late 1950s, we must remember that in one area at least, that of major musicals, there has been a steady decline. The effect of the dearth during the late 1960s and early 1970s was nearly catastrophic, both upon major West End theatres, built for spectaculars, and upon major regional touring theatres, which either went dark for long periods or were forced to stage deplorable replicas of former glories, such as John Hanson's touring operettas.

Most of The Group's successes were imported. British musicals (such as *Salad Days* and *The Boy Friend*) paled beside those from the States. The new plays of merit, encouraged by the Tennent companies, were few and far between, constricted moreover by a wan gentility. The most successful British genre (in light entertainment) was that of intimate revues with their patter songs, quick sketches and irreverent jibes against authority, but ten years later, with the arrival of *Beyond the Fringe* (1962), these lighthearted miscellanies seemed soft and soporific. The inability to discover and encourage new talents points to one structural flaw in The

Group. The pyramid of power tapered so narrowly towards the top, that the peak did not appreciate the importance of its foundations. Even the stars at the Palladium were mainly imported.

No theatre system is ideal, for there are so few ways of trying to arrange that the people with talent also have the opportunities. It was argued in the mid-1950s that theatrical capitalism has led to pop commercialism on the one hand and a stiltedness of expression, with an inhibited lack of questioning about fundamental values, on the other. Sources of money and the loyalties implied in them, can and do profoundly alter the nature of productions. We would be shocked if, say, the National Theatre presented the same sort of productions as those at the Palladium. We now expect that where public money is involved, the results should be somehow 'better' than those where the object is solely to gain box-office income, for the benefit eventually of the impresario and his shareholders. Whether these expectations are justified or not, is another matter.

This subject is dogged with predictable left- and right-wing attitudes. Let us suppose (although the situation is more complex) that the 'commercial' élite dominating the theatre after the war was replaced during the 1960s by another kind of élite, which directly or indirectly influenced the theatre through subsidies. Such an élite could be the result (say) of appointments to the Drama Panel of the Arts Council, which advises the standing officers. The temptation is to evaluate this change according to one's political beliefs. The right-winger would probably argue that this is an inherently dangerous development, leading at worst to a totalitarian control of culture and, at best, to a certain do-gooding in art, where the wishes of the public are subordinated to a desire to educate. Commercial companies may be crass, they may be greedy, they may even exploit emotions and frustrations to drag people (perhaps against their better natures) through the turnstiles. But at least they only survive by bringing the public to the theatre. To that extent, the commercial theatre is inherently more 'democratic' than the subsidised, and more honest perhaps, in that the public is not taxed to pay for productions which they may not wish to see.

The left-winger might retort that in a society where wealth

is fairly distributed, the box-office system might indeed be an honest way of financing the theatre; but we do not live in such a society. Where wealth is unjustly distributed, commercial companies will simply direct their productions towards those with money. Subsidies help to redress the balance. They have kept seat prices low, particularly among the regional reps, so that more sections of the community can visit the theatre—and thus widened the range of subjects which can be tackled through the theatre but which previously had been barred by class prejudice. Subsidies have built theatres in neighbourhoods which could not otherwise have afforded to have them and have supported companies (such as 7.84) whose declared intention is to attack the capitalistic system.

This ideological battle simmered rather than raged throughout the 1950s, even before grants became a significant factor in financing theatres. Terence Rattigan attacked the whole idea of State intervention in the arts, flippantly, in *Harlequinade* (1948). 'Good citizenship and good theatre don't go together.' '(Actors) are entirely self-centred, entirely exhibitionistic and entirely dotty...they make no compromise whatsoever with the outside world.' Jack in *Harlequinade* describes the 'social purpose' of the Arts Council like this:

> As far as I can see, it means playing Shakespeare to
> audiences who'd rather go to the films; while audiences
> who'd rather go to Shakespeare are driven to films
> because they haven't got Shakespeare to go to. It's all got
> something to do with the new Britain and apparently it's
> an absolutely splendid idea.

To protect the embryonic Arts Council against such criticism, the late Sir Ernest Pooley, who led the Arts Council until his retirement in 1953, described the role of the Arts Council as providing State support for the arts without State control, a formula which satisfied few critics, since, while it absolved the Council from the charge of State interference, it also acquitted them from responsibility for the changes which might unwittingly be brought about.

How did the influence of The Group, and the commercial

principles it embodied, affect the theatre as a *language?* In various ways, some of which I have mentioned. By marketing first to London audiences, and then sending productions out on tour, The Group encouraged the dominance of metropolitan tastes. Many new plays seemed to be set in opulent houses in Sussex or Kent. The prevalence of musicals, and the ability to market them, was another symptom of their interests. There was also the dependence on the star system, which was not invented by The Group but which nevertheless assisted the easy marketing of plays. Sometimes plays were re-written to throw more attention towards the star part, or to make it more attractive. The star system is not necessarily a bad one, for many plays do require outstanding single performances, but it may have discouraged the growth of permanent companies and thus those plays which depend on good teamwork. In such ways, money and its sources influence language, which is not to suggest that this influence is harmful or that we can do without it, but that we should be aware of its effects.

Chapter 2

Actors, stars and changing styles

A 'star' is best defined as someone whose presence in a production helps to guarantee a commercial success. 'Stars' are
those whom the public are prepared to pay to see, almost in
any production anywhere. This definition may seem unfair,
by not distinguishing between those with exceptional talents
(thus, star quality) and those who are the products of good
publicity machines. I am not, of course, denying that there
are actors and actresses whose emotional power and skill lick
into the corners of the minds of all who are lucky enough to
watch them; but the star system can operate without such
exceptional performances, just as outstanding talents can be
found in companies whose intention is not to operate the
star system. It is possible for a clever agent or impresario to
groom someone for stardom, to anticipate a fashion and provide an acting product for it: it is not possible in the same
way to cultivate a great actor.

The star system has been regarded with very mixed feelings by actors and impresarios since the end of last century.
The rules of Sir Frank Benson's company in 1880 specified
'No stars'. For impresarios, stars could provide their main
assets, but they could also be quickly de-valued by incautious
handling. Television in the mid-1950s absorbed and dis-
carded stars with remarkable rapidity, particularly those of
light entertainment. Whereas Sid Field in the 1930s had
toured the halls for years with a few sketches, comedians in
the 1950s would find that their best-rehearsed acts were use-
less after one television series. One month's star was next
month's has-been.

Some actors like the thought of being a star. Noël Coward
never wanted to use too much make-up in his early days, for
fear of not being recognised on a bus, one sign of a star. This
was not just vanity, for, in an insecure profession, stars are
those who can expect to be employed, not in dull jobs but

exciting ones. The pursuit of excellence also provides its own arrogance. Actors compete. However much they may rightly and honestly insist that the production as a whole is what matters, they are quick to note, imitate and (if possible) out-do the talents of others. The belief persists that the winner in these innumerable, barely conscious contests is the 'star'. To be a star, however, can be intolerably exhausting. The burden of a production rests on one's shoulders, including the employment of perhaps a hundred fellow professionals. The roles are often so demanding. Sir Laurence Olivier was convinced after playing Othello that Shakespeare had set out to write a part which neither Burbage nor anyone else could play. One type of climax is so quickly succeeded by another that the actor has no time to call upon his resources of men-tal, emotional and physical energy. To be a star, and par-ticularly to be an old-fashioned actor-manager star, meant that this strain had to be carried night after night, with critics sniping at you and envious actors waiting in the wings. Sir Donald Wolfit used to fortify himself by changing his shirt in the interval and drinking a pint of Guinness. Others were less resilient.

The star system, however, prevailed in the 1950s, as it does to a lesser extent today; and if I have conveyed the impres-sion that this was solely due to the pressures of commercial-ism, I must hasten to add that these were only one factor among many. There was a general tendency among Western plays to personalise great issues. If a play was written about atomic warfare, the central character would probably be someone who didn't want to build the bomb. This presented the individual in a semi-heroic light; hence, required a star performance. The Marxist would argue, as Brecht did, that Western individualism misunderstood the forces of history, which crush the private person within waves of largely im-personal class and economic warfare. To pretend otherwise might lead to the cult of the Individual, providing the first step towards a reactionary dictatorship. The Westerner might retort that it was vitally important to present great issues in terms of private moral choices, for in the last resort the real obstacles to totalitarianism of one sort or another lay in the consciences of individuals. The struggle for and against the star system was partly a political one. There were other factors. The technique of dramatists in the 1950s partly depended on the Aristotelian idea of 'empathy', which meant audience identification with 'heroes'; while on the level of day-to-day culture, an almost domestic affection prevailed for certain stars—Gracie Fields for example. Husband and wife teams were popular: Laurence Olivier and Vivien Leigh, Michael Denison and Dulcie Gray, John Clements and Kay Hammond, Jack Hulbert and Cicely Courtneidge, Nan Kenway and Douglas Young.

Stars personalised the theatre, but there were different kinds of stars. If we concentrate first on the actor-stars (as opposed to light entertainment ones), useful distinctions can be made, which also indicate priorities in acting styles. Harold Hobson in *Theatre Now* (1953) borrowed two terms from M. Quéant, the French critic: *acteur* and *comédien*. An *acteur* was someone who imposed his own character on the part: the *comédien* was someone who imposed the role upon himself. Thus, Sir John Gielgud was commonly regarded as being an *acteur*, in that he possessed an elegant personal presence, marvellous voice control and an ability to extract inner meanings from difficult lines. But he, like Noël Coward, could rarely be mistaken for anyone else: his Trigorin and Hamlet were both identifiably 'Gielgud'. Alec Guinness, on the other hand, was 'decidedly a comédien', renowned for his physical and vocal transformations, as revealed in the film, *Kind Hearts and Coronets*. Olivier was a borderline case. Hobson placed him with the *acteurs* because of his highly individual physical vibrancy and attack. Other critics would have dubbed him a *comédien* because of his physical transformations, from the blond hero-king in *Henry V* (1945) to the deformed dwarf usurper in *Richard III* (1948). Indeed, one of the slighter reasons for visiting a production with an Olivier performance was to find out what the man would look like next. He played Puff in Sheridan's *The Critic* and Oedipus in *Oedipus Rex* in a double bill with the Old Vic in 1945; and in the same year played Hotspur and Shallow, the fiery young rebel and the doddering old sycophant, in the two parts of *Henry IV*. Among the younger actors, Paul Scofield, Alan Badel and Richard Burton were *acteurs*, while Antony Newley was a *comédien*, at that time, although later, of course, Newley proved to have a remarkable capacity to impose himself upon any material around.

I would add another category to these two, the hero stars, by which I mean, first, those stars who attempted 'heroic' acting (so highly praised by Kenneth Tynan in his first book, *He that Plays the King*, 1950) and second, those who had become during the war somehow representative of national aspirations. Tynan, in an appreciation of Olivier (*Observer*, 12 December 1965), listed the 'cards' which 'great actors' had in his opinion to hold: 'complete physical relaxation, powerful physical magnetism, commanding eyes that are visible at the back of the gallery, a commanding voice that is audible *without effort* at the back of the gallery, superb timing, which includes the capacity to make verse swing, *chutzpah*—the untranslatable Jewish word that means cool nerve and outrageous effrontery combined, and the ability to communicate a sense of danger.' This is a fine description of what I would call 'heroic' acting, although I doubt whether 'great' acting need necessarily be 'heroic'. I do not believe that all great actors dominate the stage with their physical presence, or necessarily convey a sense of danger, or necessarily startle, for all these 'cards' belong to the aesthetics of Romanticism. There can be urbane, civilised, persuasive actors as well, who are not less great because they belong to a different social (as well as aesthetic) viewpoint. Olivier, Wolfit, Richardson and the late Frederick Valk (the exiled Czech actor) were stars who attempted 'heroic' acting; but there were others who were elevated to some kind of heroic status for other reasons, perhaps because they had appeared in patriotic war films. Eric Portman represented diplomatic Britain, John Mills—amiable, tenacious Britain, Gordon Harker—cheeky Cockney Britain. If this emphasis on Britishness sounds excessive, we must remember the post-war context. Greer Garson was 'Mrs Miniver': Anna Neagle, Nell of Old Drury.

By the mid-1950s, the patriotic appeal of these stars had worn thin. The war had been over ten years. The actors who had been elevated to national symbols, now found themselves relegated to stock types, ones moreover which represented the kind of class-dominated society from which Britain was eager to escape. Gielgud and Mills were able to rise above change of social attitude: others sank hopeless beneath it. Michael Wilding, who during the war represented the happy, sensitive, ex-public schoolboy (with unexpected powers of leadership in battle), re-emerged in stage farces (such as *The Geese Are Getting Fat*) only to meet with a cruel battery of sarcastic criticism. Cecil Parker, a prime minister by presence, became the tetchy civil servant in innumerable comedy films.

When we use terms like *acteur*, *comédien* or hero star, we are adopting the jargon of the age, for few actors or critics would use them now. We would use words like 'Method' or 'Alienated' acting. The early 1950s were years when increasingly the traditionally English styles of acting were starting to be thought either old-fashioned or philistine. The acting careers of some major stars indicate that they either fell out of favour or felt that West End theatre was no longer the place for them. Noël Coward, for example, did not appear in the West End from 1953 to 1966, from his performance as King Magnus in Shaw's *The Apple Cart* to his final stage appearances in *Suite in Three Keys*. His absence can be explained away easily: he was growing old, perhaps he was trying to avoid tax or was earning more money in films and cabaret elsewhere. But one has the sneaking suspicion that he would have appeared more often in the West End if he had felt that there would be the remotest possibility of repeating his former triumphs. Gielgud's career also showed signs of a decline in the mid-1950s. After his triumphant season at Stratford in 1950, his knighthood in 1953, a recognition that he developed from the best Hamlet of his age to the best Leontes, he found it hard to find exactly the right parts for his acting style. His King Lear (1955) was good, but less than triumphant, slightly ill-at-ease in a setting by the Japanese designer, Isamu Noguchi. His Prospero (1957) was musical but not magical, while his Othello (1961) was a qualified disaster. In modern plays, he simply lacked the roles which could test him, reduced to playing Sebastien in Coward's *Nude with Violin* (1956) or James Callifer in Greene's *The Potting Shed* (1958).

Younger actors who had modelled themselves upon the styles and even the appearances of their former idols, either found themselves out of work or had to change their images. On John Neville's shoulders the mantles of the younger Gielgud seemed in the early 1950s to have fallen. His lean handsome appearance was equally romantic: his voice had something of Gielgud's musical quality, and in the six years which he spent at the Old Vic (from 1953 to 1959), he played most of the leading romantic and younger Shakespearian roles, acquiring a matinée idol following. His Hamlet was regarded, as Gielgud's had been, as the best of the age; and in *Othello* (1956) he alternated the parts of Othello and Iago with Richard Burton, an experiment which mirrored the famous dual performances of Gielgud and Olivier in *Romeo and Juliet* in 1935. But Neville left the Old Vic in 1959, brusquely abandoned that Shakespearian image and returned to London in 1963 as the Cockney wide-boy in Bill Naughton's play, *Alfie*. The qualities which had distinguished Neville's work previously appeared in Alfie, but with their moral and social values reversed. His eloquence was just quick-talking, his style—vulgar and flashy, his romanticism—a gigolo seductiveness. He had also changed from being an *acteur* to a *comédien*. Other actors were not able to change their styles so dramatically. They stayed as matinée idols at a time when matinées usually meant audiences of twenty old women. Beautiful and elegant male leads (John Justin, Jeremy Brett, Alan Badel) who had all played Romeo in their times, were cast aside in favour of the Albert Finneys, Tom Courtenays and Alan Bateses of this world.

This was partly but not solely a class reaction. After the war—and despite the rightly acclaimed performances of Olivier, Richardson and others at the Old Vic during the 1940s—English acting was associated with a particular type of elegance, a natural 'upper-classness' which so prevailed that the Royal Academy of Dramatic Art was used as a finishing school when the other finishing schools were closed. This elegance particularly belonged to the *acteurs*, such as Coward, and involved an approach towards drama diametrically opposed to that of the American 'Method' school. The clash between these views dominated discussions about acting in the early 1950s, often leading to an unreal polarisation of outlooks. Method actors dressed and talked like Method actors: traditional English actors licked down their hair and tilted their cigarette holders at a vaguely defiant angle. Everyone expressed opinions about the Method, from Tyrone Guthrie to the humblest contributor to *Stage*; and the real theatrical issues were often buried beneath polemic.

The prototype 'English actor' was Noël Coward, which is not to suggest that he was the 'best' but that he was regarded as being the most representative of a particular tradition. To many of his contemporaries he was the Master. John Gielgud as a young man had understudied for Coward in *The Vortex*, eventually taking over from him on tour, with trepidation, realising how much the play depended on Coward's technical precision. In *Private Lives*, Coward cured Olivier's bad stage habit of giggling; and even Richard Burton, that shy and secluded man, turned to him for advice after Burton's very successful seasons at Stratford in the early 1950s. Coward played none of the great classic parts. The roles for which he was chiefly famous were those which he wrote for his own stage personality which merged into his private one: he explored the dramatic possibilities of that clipped accent, inimitable and yet always imitated, hair brushed back, lips tight yet full, a playboy manner concealing an honest heart. This presence appeared in all his leading roles, as Nicky Lancaster in *The Vortex* (1924), Elyot Chase in *Private Lives* (1930), Leo in *Design for Living* (1933) and even Hugo Latymer in *Song at Twilight* (1966). He could take 'character parts', such as Henry Gow in *Fumed Oak* (1936) with that 'terrible moustache', or the Captain in *In Which We Serve*; but, curiously enough, he found 'character' parts almost a self-indulgence—an easy way of acting.

Coward once stated that he had learnt practically everything about comedy acting from Sir Charles Hawtrey, the Edwardian actor-manager. Hawtrey directed and starred in the first production in which Coward appeared, as a pageboy in *The Great Name* (1911). Many critics considered Hawtrey to be scarcely an actor at all, since he always seemed to be his own charming, lazy and caddish self. Coward knew otherwise. The familiar Hawtrey trademarks concealed a very precise and controlled technique. 'Every time he went on stage, he raised his voice half a tone to pitch.' Hawtrey knew exactly how to make the slightest verbal nuance effective throughout the theatre, to the back row of the gallery. It was not just a question of good voice projection, but of timing and clarity as well, a refusal to muddle different effects by trying to convey too much.

He taught me how to laugh. I remember him standing over me at rehearsal, in front of the whole company, and saying 'Now, boy, you've got to laugh. Now start like this. Ho, ha, ha, ha, ha, ha. But put your breath right.' And he stood over me till I did it. He said, 'Now smile with it a bit', and I'd go, 'Ha, ha, ha, ha.' That was entirely technical and, of course, it was an enormous help. He could laugh on stage indefinitely. He taught me also to use my hands and my arms and swing them without looking as if I were acting at all (Noël Coward, interview in *Great Acting*, 1967).

Edwardian handbooks on acting seem nowadays to be absurdly mechanical in their approach. Sorrow was registered by clasped hands. To cry real tears, you had to turn your face away from the audience and blink your eyelids rapidly. That was the professional method. Amateurs used onions. These books, sometimes published as supplements to games compendiums together with 'How to be a Magician' and 'Gardening for All', also stressed that you had to practise these movements until they had acquired the 'grace which comes from perfect naturalness'. Many actors saw the grace but not the mechanics, admiring the sheer styles of Hawtrey and Sir Gerald du Maurier who had perfected the different methods of lighting and stubbing out a cigarette dramatically. Coward's own long cigarette and holder can be regarded as a flamboyantly youthful vulgarism on du Maurier's art:

Gerald du Maurier, brilliant actor that he was, had the most disastrous influence on my generation, because we really thought, looking at him, that it was easy; and for the first ten years of our lives in the theatre, nobody could hear a word we said. We thought he was being natural; of course, he was a genius of a technician giving that appearance, that's all (Sir Laurence Olivier, interview in *Great Acting*, 1967).

Time had concealed, in the 1920s, two potent reasons why Edwardian actors should wish to seem 'elegantly natural'. They wanted to seem 'natural' to distinguish themselves from the old barnstorming hams and they wanted to seem 'elegant' because in the nineteenth century, as Pinero pointed out, actors were sometimes associated with rogues and gypsies.

To Method actors, this whole approach was philistine. You were being made to laugh simply by putting your breath in the right place, not because you had identified with the character who would find the situation funny. The Method was a training technique for actors, loosely based on the teachings of Stanislavski and then being taught by Lee Strasberg in New York. Strasberg, who established the Actors Studio in 1947, was an outstanding teacher. He, like Stanislavski, encouraged the actor to pursue an inner understanding of the 'character motives' before tackling the external disciplines of voice projection and set movements. He urged actors to improvise as part of their rehearsal schedules, to analyse themselves as a first step towards analysing their roles, to use memories of similar situations from their personal pasts to add reality to fictitious situations and to allow their imaginations (and their confidences) to be stimulated by physical objects, a battered cap or watch, which the fictitious characters might have possessed.

Strasberg believed that if an actor 'felt' correctly, his bodily movements would be instantly expressive. For that reason he tried to prevent actors from worrying about 'unimportant' considerations. Alone among the drama schools of the United States, the Actors Studio possessed no set schedule to its classes, imposed no rigorous restrictions upon its students (such as high fees or entry limited to those with professional experience) and banned casting directors from rehearsal sessions. The atmosphere was that of a workshop: simple, easy, relaxed and dedicated. Even Strasberg, however, was not above giving useful tips to actors, such as Coward had received from Hawtrey: recognising that relaxation was the key to authority on stage, he suggested that his actors should adopt, either standing or sitting, that position in which they could most readily go to sleep—which led to the English charge that Method actors were always lounging around. But anyone who believes the old charge that Strasberg encouraged a self indulgent approach to acting, should read *Strasberg at the Actors Studio* (Jonathan Cape, 1966), a collection of tape-recorded sessions which reveals how tough he could be, say, to an unfortunate actress who could not work without props. By reading this book, however, we can begin to appreciate what aroused the resentment of many British actors and directors. The editor, Robert H. Hethmon, describes the Actors Studio as if he were an Irish priest talking about Lourdes. Strasberg, he asserts, 'is considered by many to be *the* theatrical genius of our day'. Strasberg himself stated that nobody else could better his knowledge of the theatre and that 'the eyes of America, and really of the world, are on the Actors Studio'. Elia Kazan asserted that the Method heralded a Golden Age of American theatre, to rank up with Renaissance drama in Britain and the theatre of Molière and Racine.

What particularly irritated English actors was the suggestion that the Method school had 'discovered' Stanislavski, who had been ignored in Britain. But long before the Actors Studio had been founded, Komisarjevsky, a close associate of Stanislavski, had trained many English actors in his techniques, and his production of *The Seagull* (1936) with John Gielgud, Edith Evans and Peggy Ashcroft had transformed the appreciation of Chekhov as an author and Russian naturalism. English actors not only felt that they had been better trained in Stanislavski's methods, but also that the Method actors misunderstood them. The Method actors were too introverted in their approach, and confused by the attempt to reconcile Freud, psychoanalysis and group therapy with the business of acting. 'The Method-ists', wrote Tyrone Guthrie, who ran the Old Vic and Sadlers Wells from 1939 to 1945, 'over-prize the Search for Truth as opposed to the Revelation of Truth.'

> They have neglected the means of communication. Now the actor's principal means of expression is the voice. The expression of the eyes, of the whole body, is important too and, more particularly, the organization of sounds into, first, syllables, then words, then sentences, that the most subtle and articulate communication occurs between human creatures...none of the great classics of the theatre—the Greek tragedies, French tragedy, Shakespeare, Molière, Schiller or Goethe—can be adequately performed without a real battery of technical

accomplishments. An untrained beginner, however gifted, just cannot do justice to great rhetorical poetry any more than an untrained beginner in music can sit right down and play a Bach fugue. So far the Method has not suggested that it aims beyond a very highly developed Behaviourism (Tyrone Guthrie, *Encore*, November 1957).

If English actors were right to complain about the pretentiousness of the Methodists, the Methodists were surely justified in retorting that Guthrie was being equally lofty, with this air of patiently explaining the obvious. Guthrie later descended to criticising the personal appearance of the Methodists:

> In blue jeans, with dirty nails and wild hair, they are busy proclaiming themselves Proletarian—but members of a vintage Proletariat. While in the 1930s, it was new and even dangerous for artists to announce that they were also Proletarians, it is now cliché; especially when more than one prominent associate of the Method has been at pains to dissociate this type of Artistic Proletarianism from any taint of political subversion, from the faintest tinge of red (Tyrone Guthrie, *Encore*, November 1957).

At this point the Anglo-American debate about the Method seemed to reach deadlock. The Methodists were accused of being dirty, clichaic, Proletarian but not revolutionary, and old-fashioned. English actors were thought, on the other side, to be mechanical snobs. There is more good humour in Coward's remark to a Method actress who once asked him what was her motive for a particular move across stage. 'Your *motive*, my dear,' he replied, 'is your pay packet at the end of the week.'

This retort, a frankly commercial one, reflected Coward's dislike of the introverted approach to acting. Coward believed in learning his lines before rehearsal began, unlike most actors who prefer to read through the scenes, block them out, improvise around the situation until, finally, perhaps during the last week, the lines fall naturally into place without hard learning or having to be quickly memorised. He learnt his lines like this because characterisation was not usually one of his problems. He had written the plays and he did not need to delve into the motives and ethnic environments of his characters. His problems were different, particularly how to reach that 'silky stage' (as his friends, the Lunts, termed it) when he had so much control over the stage situation that he could manipulate it at will or according to the temper of the audience.

Coward was an expert at judging the mood of the house. He played the matador with the public as his bull:

> I nearly always play the first act of a comedy very quickly. I don't mean gabble; the difference between speed and pace. If you play quickly and articulately, it doesn't give them time, you throw away laughs; throw them away in the first act, pull them in in the last. When you've got the audience where you want them, you can then afford to take some leisurely effects. But in the first act, you've got to get their attention quickly, and therefore play it quickly. If there are big laughs, stop them, except for the very big ones. In all plays I've been in, with Gertie (Gertrude Lawrence) and with Alfred and Lynn (Alfred Lunt and Lynn Fontaine), we'd know whoever was on first, how a certain line went. If it got a laugh, we'd say, 'Ha! We're home and dry—a nice, warm audience!' If it got a titter, tricky. If it got silence, get to work, chaps (Noël Coward, interview in *Great Acting*, 1967).

These are the remarks of a professional craftsman. Through them we can hear not only echoes of the great Edwardian comic actors but also of great music-hall stars. Coward may have had a limited repertoire of emotional stances, he may have learnt them as mechanically as he had been taught how to laugh, but he had learnt them so thoroughly that he could command them at will, varying the pace of his delivery with exact precision, stifling the slight shuffles and inattentive coughs among the audience with an unexpectedly brilliant trick of the trade. His cabaret turns, happily recorded and freely available, reveal as much. When he sang 'Mad Dogs and Englishmen' for a Las Vegas nightclub, the sheer speed and accuracy of his delivery prevented those who might have regarded this song as a relic from a post-imperial twilight from laughing in the wrong places and the wrong reasons.

This personal dominance over an audience was a characteristic of Edwardian stars, who sometimes played in theatres
seating three thousand and more, and was passed on (sometimes, it seemed, through family tradition) to those of post-
war theatre. It could lead to rough, bombastic acting: Wolfit
and Sir Robert Atkins at their worst. At best, however, it
could provide an extraordinary sensitivity as to how the audience was responding, an almost hypnotic control and a
direct, near-physical rapport between the stage and the
auditorium.

Stars dominated their material almost as much as they
controlled their fans. One example, recently re-discovered, is
the theatrical command of Max Wall, a comedian who has
survived the decline of the music-halls, whose act contains
pretty old jokes and very familiar routines. But his timing, his
sense of good-humoured despair and his ability to exploit his
own indefatigable but nearly defeated grotesqueness is
theatrically riveting. At school, I went to see Robert Donat as
Becket in Robert Helpman's production of *Murder in the
Cathedral*, T. S. Eliot's play which I disliked on reading
because of its patronising tone. But Donat's presence conveyed a handsome kindliness, the ideal headmaster (stern in
his wrath, benevolent in his aims) and burdened by High
Office. When he addressed the audience in the Sermon, saying 'Now consider one thing of which you have probably
never thought...', I forgot to resent the implication that all
who listen to him must be fools. Similarly, when Laurence
Olivier as Henry V invoked 'God, for Harry, England and St.
George', he was not criticised for bombast or jingoism. He
was the Great National Leader, 'I am England', and the sudden upward inflexion of his voice indicated as much.

If we consider the English and, to some extent, the plays
translated from the French of the early 1950s, which provided the greatest successes of the period, we notice how
much they depend upon the 'star's' ability to dazzle.
Scofield's twin roles as Hugo and Frederic in Anouilh's *Ring
Round the Moon* (1950) would be one example; Olivier's performance as the Duke of Altair in Fry's *Venus Observed* (1950)
would be another. The Method approach was totally unsuitable for such plays. It was not necessary to know the psy-

chological motivation behind Perpetua's long speech in *Venus Observed* about not coming to the end of a sentence, but it was vital to have good breath control, accurate vocal inflexions, an acute sense of timing and phraseology, and above all, to have reached that 'silky stage' of supreme self-confidence. In Britain, plays were not being written which required the Method technique. Even N. C. Hunter's plays, such as *Waters of the Moon* (1951) and *A Day by the Sea* (1954), regarded as Chekhovian, were written more in the style of Society Drama, with dialogue fully expressive on a verbal level not requiring the same degree of 'acting around the line', so important in American naturalistic drama.

The plays associated with the Method school, however, were of a type which positively rejected English *bravura* acting. They were, on one level, far more serious. Arthur Miller was the modern 'Ibsen', concerned with the state of society and the individual's capacity to choose. The naturalistic logic of his plays was all important: why Keller in *All My Sons* (1948) sold defective plane parts during the war and escaped post-war punishment (except that spiritual nemesis which cannot be evaded) or why the down-trodden salesman, Willy Loman, died in *Death of a Salesman* (1949, London), or why the witch-hunt began at Salem (in *The Crucible*) and its relevance to the anti-communist witch-hunts launched by Joe McCarthy. Tennessee Williams's plays lacked some of Miller's social preoccupations, but provided instead a claustrophobic sense of atmosphere, flamboyant passions and imagery. His themes, vaguely shocking to British audiences, often presented a tortured view of sexuality, sustained by Freudian arguments and illustrated by painfully direct confrontations between the weak and the strong, the animalistic men and the yearning, tormented women. Miller and Williams, together with the two 'fathers' of modern American drama, Eugene O'Neill and Clifford Odets, required from their actors and audiences alike a painful reassessment of motives and social habits: not the 'silky stage'—more a spontaneous torment. If we regard the English acting school as being too limited, we must remember that many English actors and directors adjusted quickly and brilliantly to the new demands of American drama, and that (say) Olivier's production of *A Streetcar Named Desire*

(1949) with Vivien Leigh was in its time both shocking and persuasively successful.

Noël Coward, however, was one of those who did not adjust and had no intention of doing so. He never regarded the theatre as a means of discovering inner or social 'realities'. He would have dismissed this approach as pretentious and unbecoming for an actor who was neither a politician nor a theologian. His critics complained that he too was pretentious, putting on airs constantly as part of a one-upmanship game with the audience. His upper middle-class voice, his poised sophistication and his determination to set a style provided yet another weapon in the class war. He was teaching another generation of middle-class Englishmen how to stay on top in the battle for privilege. Of course, he could switch emotion on and off like a tap. The bourgeoisie have always been adept at laughing, crying and beating the patriotic drum when the occasion suits them. Of course, he was concerned with tone and elegance. How else can you justify privilege except by being more beautiful than others?

From the Marxist point of view, as from the Methodists, Coward was the arch-philistine, whose decadent diseases had descended to one generation (Gielgud's) and then to another (Alan Badel's). He represented establishment English acting, just as his plays (with those of Terence Rattigan) represented establishment writing. When such attacks were launched, they ran up against the curious ambivalence of the 'establishment style'. The actors, such as Coward and Gielgud, who seemed to be setting the style, were deferential about doing so. Coward was determined to underplay everything, even his genius. Even the parts they played were about establishment figures who wanted to retire from power. The scientist destroys his research papers, the prince becomes a commoner until the People recall him to his former authority, the statesman goes into retirement to sort out his matrimonial problems. It was argued, of course, that this modesty was just an establishment trick, an effort to parry criticism and class hatred. This too seemed unfair, for Coward was not cunningly modest. He could be arrogant about his craft, although very reticent at attributing more to the art of acting that it seemed to require. A Marxist could accuse him of being a brilliant tool in a capitalist's fun factory and he probably would not have denied this status. He might even have been proud of it.

English theatre in the early 1950s depended heavily upon star performances, but this very dependence led to some curious, anti-star consequences. To begin with, the great actors of the period, particularly Olivier, Redgrave and Gielgud, were highly intelligent and began to resent the frivolous parts in new drama which they were often being asked to play. Their prestige and influence was such that audiences too began to fret at the triviality of the surrounding plays—and not only the plays, but also the uneven quality of the productions. The actors sought to be part of a team of peers, thus striving towards the balance of permanent companies, which were then rare in British theatre. The performances of such stars as Michael Redgrave (as Hamlet in 1958 and Benedick) and Peggy Ashcroft laid the foundations at the Shakespeare Memorial Theatre, Stratford-upon-Avon, for the modern Royal Shakespeare Company. These foundations were not just 'artistic' but also financial. The profits from the Stratford tours to Australia, Russia and the United States left Peter Hall, when he took over the company, with useful reserve funds of $100,000, which he promptly spent on expanding the scale of the company until it could truthfully be regarded as a national theatre. Having achieved this reputation, it was thus in a position to claim large State subsidies and to be removed from the insecurities of commercial theatre altogether.

The actors, however, who had consciously or unconsciously modelled themselves upon Coward, ran into very rough times in the 1950s. The commercial theatre in which Coward had thrived was changing, and so was the British social order. Within ten years, suave actors had been replaced by rough ones as heroes, metropolitan accents by regional ones, complacent young men by angry ones, stylish decadents by frustrated, 'working-class', anti-heroes. This change in fashion had consequences for dramatists, whose techniques still depended in theory upon empathy. Actors like Paul Scofield, who could convey a sense of social superiority without seeming camp in the process, became increasingly rare, and with this loss, writers had to re-consider the whole way in which they wrote plays.

Chapter 3

Well-made plays?

There are no fixed laws about the theatre, except perhaps that the theatre is a game or a language, but not 'real life'. Sometimes, however, conventions harden into habits which feel like 'laws'. Audiences expect certain types of drama, impresarios cater to these expectations, actors and actresses are trained to tackle certain problems expertly and dramatists write for them. The act of breaking away from these habits can in itself modify the work which the rebellious dramatist or director is struggling to provide. He may start simply by being bored with the habits, with finding much of the theatre scene dull and predictable, 'deadly' (to use Peter Brook's word), but in order to justify his radicalism or iconoclasm, he concocts arguments in self-defence. The 'old' theatre (which he despises) provides 'reactionary propaganda'. His 'new' or 'living' theatre does not.

The habits governing 'straight drama' after the Second World War were rigid and limiting, but for several years no major dramatist emerged in Britain who was prepared to break them. Indeed they still linger on, providing a useful but challengeable basic technique for most dramatists. The prevailing rules can be traced back to a compromise between 'naturalism' and the 'well-made play', pioneered by Zola and Ibsen in the 1880s; and, like most compromises, it satisfied nobody completely, not even Ibsen. In the 1940s and early 1950s, most dramatists were prepared to bend the rules a little, to modify them so that they would seem less contorted and falsely theatrical; but they did not want to break them for fear that they should be left without a technique at all.

'Naturalism' was the main contribution of nineteenth-century Romanticism to the theatre. It often meant little more than those precepts voiced by Wordsworth in his *Preface to the Lyrical Ballads* (1800), that art should imitate life, and not vice-versa. Dialogue (like the language of poetry) should be drawn from the words of everyday life. The themes should come from daily experience as well, although some universal significance could be drawn from them. Zola went further. He argued that plays could construct accurate models of life, for the purpose of analysing the 'cause and effect' of human behaviour. The trend to naturalism was thus also an offshoot of scientism. For most responsive theatregoers in the late nineteenth century, however, naturalism was an exciting new style, which broke away from the sliding flats, back-drops and general staginess of the old theatre. The real tables and chairs in Strindberg's *Miss Julie* (1888) were in themselves a source of theatrical comment, while Ibsen's *The Doll's House* (1879) amazed British audiences in the 1890s by the relaxed and conversational language.

But by the 1940s, of course, the dramatic shock originally provided by naturalism had long since dwindled away. The critical language of naturalism had been generally accepted. Actors and scripts would be blamed for sounding 'artificial' or 'forced', but would be praised for being 'natural' or 'convincing', which usually meant naturalistically convincing. There were certain areas, however, where the principles of naturalism could still lead to 'shocking' or just unexpected theatrical moments. One was in the representation of sexual behaviour or bodily functions, areas of expression which were restricted by censorship. 'Bad language' was also thus restricted, whether it was in popular use or not, and the commercial theatre, centralised upon London and The Group, catered predominantly to metropolitan 'middle-class' audiences and had thus limited the naturalistic study of 'lower- or working-class' behaviour and regional sociology. In the years after the war, naturalism sometimes could still astonish and so provide lively theatre. *A Streetcar Named Desire* shocked British audiences with its 'rawness', the violent domestic brawls, the rape scene and even the bathroom, off-stage, where the lavatory could be heard to flush. There were 'forbidden' subjects which defiant naturalistic dra-matists could tackle: Homosexuality, as in Arthur Miller's *A View from the Bridge* (produced in London, 1956) and Robert Anderson's *Tea and Sympathy* (London, 1957), both of which evaded censorship through club productions. Strong hints at homosexuality provided second-act curtains in public theatres, as in Rattigan's *Ross* (1960), Shaffer's *Five Finger Exercise* and Coward's *A Song at Twilight*. On this level, with such topics, naturalism could still seem an exciting style, which sometimes meant that naturalistic writers, pursuing theatrical excitement, narrowed down their range of subjects to those which carried an aura of the 'forbidden'.

But naturalism, as Ibsen realised, did not actually provide a dramatic technique. Why should audiences be interested in imitations of life when they were surrounded by the real thing? Ibsen had gained much practical experience in the theatre before coming under Zola's influence. He helped to run a small theatre in Bergen, where his earliest plays were produced. Ibsen's *Love's Comedy* (1862) was written in the style of Scribe, the French dramatist who had simplified many existing theatrical ideas into a formula known as the 'well-made play'. Ibsen borrowed this formula, modified it to take away some of its more clumsy elements and used it to provide technical stiffening for the rather floppy concept of naturalism.

The three key features of the 'well-made play' were the Crisis, the Hero and the Unities (of Time, Place and Action). These features had all had an honourable history, which can be traced back through Boileau to Aristotle. The Crisis is that moment in a play when all the relevant information about the main story or theme has been gathered in and when the audience can guess what the outcome will be. It is not the dénouement itself, the moment of unravelling. There may be marriages to consummate, murders to commit, moral speeches to deliver. It is rather that moment just before the dénouement when the audience realises for the first time when the unravelling will start and what its outcome is likely to be. In a fever, the crisis is that pivotal moment when the patient hovers between life and death. This analogy holds for the theatre. Up to the crisis, we do not know what will eventually happen. After the crisis, we do know, although not in every detail.

From the concept of the Crisis, other technical ideas stem. The play is regarded basically as a progress from ignorance to knowledge. When the auditorium darkens and the curtain is about to rise, the audience is prepared to be transported into a situation about which they know nothing—theoretically. They are being lifted out of their normal lives and dumped—well, anywhere although in practice (from Ibsen to Rattigan, for reasons which will emerge later) it was usually a middle-class drawing room. As they learn more about the situation, the play's *pace* will accelerate: when they sense that information is being withheld, so the play will have *suspense*.

The Hero in a well-made play (particularly tragedies) was someone 'better than average', but usually with 'a flaw in his character' which circumstances (including the Fates and God) exploited. This brings about his downfall. A. C. Bradley in *Shakespearian Tragedy* (1904) applied this theory to *Hamlet*, *King Lear*, *Othello* and *Macbeth* in a highly influential work of Shakespearian criticism which was used by both actors and directors as an intellectual/academic basis for their productions. T. R. Henn, for example, who taught Peter Hall at Cambridge in the 1950s, was predominantly a 'Bradley' man. All the Shakespearian tragic heroes were 'better than average' but had character flaws—or so the argument ran. Hamlet possessed a noble mind, but suffered from indecisiveness; Othello was a great warrior, but jealous; Lear was 'every inch a king', but was pathologically proud and suspicious; Macbeth was brave, but superstitious. The flaws bring about their destructions, but because they are all 'better than average', the audience will identify with them (empathy), thus feeling the full force of their downfalls. Empathy leads to a release of emotions, the purgation or 'catharsis' of feelings, to use another Aristotelian term, borrowed by Bradley.

There were some variations on this theory. According to some students of anthropology, the Hero died for and on behalf of his audience, thus linking drama to the ritual slaughter of virgins and princes in primitive tribal societies. By 'better than average', Aristotle meant mainly a class superiority. The Hero belongs to one of a few select families and Shakespearian heroes too were usually of a superior family breed. But in Shakespeare, 'betterness' also meant 'nobility' of mind and moral insight, as well as of breeding. The question of insight came to be stressed more than the purely genealogical signs of 'betterness'. Thus, the middle-class heroes and heroines of Ibsen were better because they

knew more about the situation than the surrounding characters, not because they were aristocrats *manqués*. In the dramatic process leading from ignorance to knowledge, the
Hero is the audience's guide and they come to rely upon his
(or her) insights.

We 'identify' with the Hero because we learn through him
about the story. A simple example would be that of a detective in a routine thriller. For this reason, if a dramatist ac-
tively wishes to prevent empathy, he only has to ensure that
the audience knows more about the situation than any
character on stage, a technique well known to comedy writers long before Brecht incorporated it into his theories on
'alienation'.

Building a play towards the Crisis and encouraging (or dis-
couraging) empathy with the Hero were methods of trying to
regulate the audience's reactions. The Unities were intended
to provide plays with logical and acceptable forms. In the
strictest forms (as, say, interpreted by Boileau), the first two
Unities of Time and Place were intolerably limiting. The
fictional time span of the play was expected to correspond
with the actual time span of the performance, which meant
that the story had to be concentrated into two symbolic
hours, when the events were moving towards the Crisis. Few
dramatists came up to Boileau's expectations. In practice,
this Unity usually meant that the fictional time span might
correspond to a day, or a weekend, or a month; while its
practical usefulness was to discourage dramatists from letting their stories ramble empirically through time. The Unity
of Place was a similar restriction. It meant that the setting of
the story should stay constant throughout the play, without
wandering from place to place, country to country. In its
purest form, the dramatist was expected to set the play within one room. Dramatic events happening elsewhere could be
described through the dialogue, not shown. Murders happened off-stage.

The Unity of Action was the most important of the three
unities. It simply meant that all the events, characters and
main sequences of dialogue should contribute to the central
theme and lead eventually to the Crisis. If, as Chekhov
pointed out, you bring a gun on to the stage, it should at
some time be fired or at least significantly not fired.

Shakespeare was regarded as a barbarian by many neo-
classical critics because he sometimes introduced apparently
irrelevant clowns into sombre situations. The Unity of Action implied that no unnecessary elements should be introduced into a play and that a certain coherence of tone
should be preserved. It also sought an internal logic to
drama, so that each scene would contribute another stage in
an extended syllogism, where the major and minor premises
of the opening acts would develop towards the conclusions
of the last.

The compromise which Ibsen sought between Naturalism
and the Well-Made Play was fraught with difficulties. If you
set out to imitate life, it is almost impossible to obey the
Unities. Life does not fall easily into the syllogistic structures,
helping to preserve the Unity of Action. If you try to keep the
dramatic events all in one place or in one short span of time,
you either have to make your characters unconvincingly
knowledgeable and lucid about what is happening elsewhere
or you have to forget about that pattern of surrounding
events which gives the particular situation its wider significance. Another problem is presented by the Crisis, for is
there ever a point in life itself or the faithful imitation of life
where the dramatist and audience can truthfully say, 'I know
everything about this situation. I can anticipate exactly what
will happen'? Ibsen interpreted the Crisis in terms of old-
fashioned melodrama, usually with a symbolic additional
meaning. A Crisis was a decision or a grand gesture (such as
Nora leaving her husband or Hedda's suicide), thus leaving
himself open to pat comments from those critics who actually believed in naturalism and would echo the words of
Dr Brack in *Hedda Gabler*: 'People don't *do* things like that!'
Chekhov was more ingenious in his adaptation of the Crisis
to the demands of naturalism. He would select an entirely
plausible event with its own structure (the sale of a cherry
orchard, the arrival and departure of soldiers in a provincial
Russian town) and organise his characters and themes
around it.

It was also impossible or extremely difficult to reconcile
the so-called objectivity of naturalism with the use of the
Hero, because the Hero's dramatic function was almost to
funnel our knowledge of the situation through one

character's consciousness. You could either have empathy and not objectivity, which was Ibsen's choice, or objectivity without empathy, which was Chekhov's. You could not have both. If you didn't use 'empathy', then you had to involve the audience in some other way and, lacking this technical prop, it might be many years before audiences had learnt to appreciate your particular style. For this reason, audiences were slower to respond to the particular qualities of Chekhov's plays than they were to those of Ibsen, particularly in Britain.

The compromise between naturalism and the well-made play was thus illogical and provided self-contradictions at almost every technical level; but the persuasive example of Ibsen, backed by the slightly less persuasive Shaw, enabled the compromise to be accepted widely. Ibsen himself was moving away from naturalism during the last years of his life, while Chekhov was moving away from the well-made play. British dramatists inherited a technical approach to writing plays which required the utmost ingenuity to employ. There were many ingenious writers who skilfully adapted the compromise to their own needs: Shaw, of course, who died in 1950, Somerset Maugham and Coward, and also a host of lesser writers (such as Benn Levy) who twisted the arrangement in one direction or another with a facility which outweighed their capacity to say anything interesting. But the contradictions were always there and dramatists after the war were always trying to overcome them, usually not by breaking the rules but by bending them.

One writer who kept to the rules and was rewarded with a fair degree of commercial success was Noel Langley, a talented second-rate writer whose career illustrates the problems and opportunities of the non-experimental dramatist. Langley's best year was 1948, when he had three plays in the West End (*Edward, My Son*, written in collaboration with Robert Morley, *Cage Me a Peacock* and *Little Lambs Eat Ivy*) and one revival touring the regions, *The Farm of Three Echoes* (written in 1935). Langley, a South African, was the stand-by professional of his day. He could write in most styles then current. A poetic-historical drama? *For Ever* (1934), about Dante and Beatrice, which 'fell' (though he said it himself) 'with a pretty cadence on the ear and curiously

enough (did) not offend history'. A naturalistic comedy?
Friendly Relations, about a warm-hearted British landlady
whose daughter falls in love with a German, Hans Wierck, on
the run from communist co-patriots.

If we compare Langley's ambitious but comparatively un-
successful drama, *The Farm of Three Echoes*, with his unam-
bitious smash-hit, *Little Lambs Eat Ivy*, it is clear that his basic
technique frustrated his intentions in one play but assisted
them in the other. Both plays are set in all-purpose living
rooms, both have their problems resolved at somewhat im-
plausible crises and both have central characters who act as
focal points for the situations. Important events happen off-
stage in both plays which, fifteen years later, dramatists
would have struggled to bring on.

The Farm of Three Echoes was perhaps the first attempt to
analyse the mentality of Boer farmers (through the medium
of drama) which afterwards led to apartheid. Langley clearly
understood the peasant isolation, the rigid religiosity and dis-
trust of outsiders, the internal and spiritual war which existed within the farmer's mind and his family's behaviour. He
also understood how this could lead to bitter cruelties. He
wanted to convey the vastness of the Orange Free State: the
sense of space, distance and physical endurance. But, of
course, he had tò obey the Unity of Place and so set his story
within a farmhouse kitchen/living room. He also wanted to
show a historical distance, the way in which generations of
farmers, from the days of the Great Trek, had built up and
clung on to their farms; but the Unity of Time·did not permit
such an expansive view. He dealt simply with the problems of
one young farmer, Jan Gerart, at a critical period of his life.
Jan, whose sexual longings are powerful and passionate but
frustrated, does not want to pass on the 'bad blood' of the
Gerarts, with their history of violence, to another generation.

The 'bad blood' was a useful umbrella idea whereby
Langley could describe a number of psychological attitudes,
among them the violently maintained patriarchal system as
opposed to an increasingly more 'tolerant' outside world.
But in showing the conflict between these attitudes, and in
order to provoke a clear crisis, Langley had to invent a semi-
plausible occurrence. A commercial company selects, out of
the whole wilderness of the Free State, Gerart's farm as the

site for an airport. The company bribes Jan not with money, but with an old-fashioned vamp. The vamp only succeeds in stirring up the brutality in Jan, which had previously just been controlled by his unconsummated marriage. His grand-mother eventually shoots Jan to prevent a continuation of the family madness. This murder, the crisis, was a thoroughly unsatisfactory way of parcelling up the story: it seemed melodramatic in itself and in any case, it merely paralleled other murders from the Gerart family past without explain-ing them further. An almost comic air of doom hangs over the play, from Ouma the grandmother who sleeps in her own coffin to the latent hysteria behind the writing which sug-gests that Langley was trying to convey more than his theatri-cal story could bear.

By the early 1960s, many dramatists (such as Peter Shaffer, John Arden and even Robert Bolt) would have smiled at the difficulties which Langley's attachment to the well-made play had caused. Brechtian 'Epic' techniques had broken through the various barriers of Time and Place, not to mention the attachment to a central Hero. But Langley's craft was not al-ways so ineffective. In *Little Lambs Eat Ivy*, the very restric-tions hold a dotty, domestic, discursive farce together; and there is considerable skill at the way in which Langley con-trols the chaos, his timing of exits and entrances, the running jokes, the balance between the characters and the sudden change at the crisis from catastrophe to triumph.

Langley obeyed the rules and he was in good company, for even Shaw, who was ambitious enough for all normal pur-poses, accepted them, even thrived by them, for by necessity they concentrated his skills on the conversation between characters, his greatest asset as a dramatist.

Shaw was challenged by some of his Socialist supporters to write more about the 'workers', by which was meant the workers by hand and the minders of machines. To this, Shaw replied that in order to write plays that would be effective, the dramatist must concern himself in the main with characters who are not tied to factory hours, have some freedom to move around, and are capable of framing their opinions in sufficiently lucid conversation. Shaw practised on these lines with the result that *Candida*, his play set in the poorer reaches of the East End, is housed in a vicarage. (Ivor Brown, *Theatre 1955–6*)

It would be unfair to suggest that Shaw only set his plays in the leisured surroundings of middle-class drawing rooms. He allowed us to visit Hell on one occasion, Ireland on another. But when he strayed on to this (as I understand it) foreign territory, he had the tact to make it seem like a middle-class drawing room, thus the proper place to discuss socialism, evolution and the rights of women.

Shaw used the Places and Times of his plays, however carefully described, primarily as a background for his conversations, which were as free-ranging as he chose. This led to an awkward artificiality sometimes, for his characters would seem much more knowledgeable than from their historical situations they were likely to be. The success of his plays depended upon the liveliness and wit of the dialogue, almost abstracted from the surrounding situation. When an educated man (such as Professor Higgins in *Pygmalion*) confronted an ill-educated one, such as Doolittle, both had to be equally verbal because otherwise the dramatic debate would not take place. But what about characters who were not born debaters? They had to be relegated to the position of stooges or background furniture. Shaw also had trouble with crises, for either the decisions taken then failed adequately to summarise the preceding arguments (as in *St Joan*) or (as in *Misalliance*) they seemed concocted and somehow at a tangent from the drift of the play.

Other dramatists after the war had difficulty with the Crisis. They could often accept the Unities, and the central Hero, which was a convenient technique since it helped them to write for the stars. But the Crisis often seemed too neat and pat a device, out of tune with the difficult times and too simple-minded for a world of doubt where the old values were being questioned and new ones had not been formulated. How could one possibly describe an intricate problem and *expect* it to be resolved at the Crisis? There were no *dei ex machina* in the post-war world. Naturalism, as well as ordinary scepticism, forbade their invention.

There were several methods, however, whereby the presence of a Crisis could be practically concealed or mitigated.

One was to write a well-made play but to twist the final scene so that the play ended less than conclusively. Terence Rattigan has explained (in his preface to *Collected Plays*) how the final scene in *The Deep Blue Sea* (1952) was difficult to write and involved much heart-searching. His heroine has been deserted by her wayward, ex-RAF lover. She has ruined her marriage, although her husband, an eminent Judge, is an understanding man. She is now living in a dingy flat, poor and disillusioned. In a conventional 'well-made play', she would have taken a firm decision, probably to commit suicide. Rattigan rejected this crisis on the grounds that it was too pat and final: people don't do things like that. Instead she decides to struggle on alone, walking towards a sunset of flowery wallpaper and tattered furniture.

J. B. Priestley chose another method of avoiding the too neat Crisis. He replaced the dramatic full stop with a question mark, as in *An Inspector Calls* (1945), where we suddenly find out in the last scene that the 'inspector' who has exposed the complicity of a prosperous industrial family in the murder/suicide of a working-class girl, is not an inspector at all—but a what? A practical joker? An emanation of the world to come? Or a manifestation of the family's collective conscience? We do not know, but the curtain falls with the news that a real girl has died and a real inspector is on the way. On this level, avoiding the Crisis meant little more than those O. Henry twists at the end of short stories. Priestley dignified his unexpected endings with his theories of time and precognition, and also through a non-conformist belief that the world is so ordained that punishment pursues the miscreant. Among other writers, however, the unexpected twist became as predictable as an ordinary Crisis.

A more subtle method of preserving the dramatic shape offered by the Crisis while disguising its inexorability in the interests of naturalism was that provided by Chekhov (already described) and Chekhov's plays were particularly popular in post-war London. There were three separate productions of *The Cherry Orchard* in 1948. Chekhov's methods, although apparently simple, were extraordinarily hard to imitate, for they depended upon exact observation, a marvellous sense of social textures, accurate timing and also on an awareness of the processes of history which surrounded the apparently enclosed lives of his characters. Few British dramatists were capable of understanding these instincts, let alone matching them. Shaw's *Heartbreak House*, which refers somewhat patronisingly to Chekhov in its preface, merely showed how greatly Shaw had misunderstood the form: Shaw suggests that Chekhov was *flattering* his bourgeois benefactors! N. C. Hunter followed Chekhov in organising his plays around a plausible naturalistic incident, such as the seaside picnic in *A Day by the Sea* (1953); but the texture of his dialogue, so much explanation, so little internal change and development, indicated that Hunter was providing a hybrid genre, a cross between Society Drama and a vaguely Chekhovian naturalism. One play which did reveal some appreciation of the underlying currents within Chekhovian dialogue was Coward's *Waiting in the Wings* (1960).

The inconclusive ending, the unexpected twist and the Chekhovian incident were ways of preserving the technical usefulness of the Crisis while disguising its artificiality. There were also ways around the Unities, particularly of Time and Place. Rattigan, with other dramatists, used 'flashbacks'. His *Ross* (1960) was a biographical play about T. E. Lawrence set in an RAF depot near London, where Lawrence has enlisted as a plain Aircraftman, Ross. A surrounding incident, which culminates with his death in a motorcycle accident, takes place over twenty-four hours; but the background biography is narrated through flashbacks which span decades and continents. Sometimes, as in Christopher Fry's *A Sleep of Prisoners*, the flashbacks were presented as dreams or hallucinations. There were also methods of playing down the dominance of the Hero. Instead of being a man very much better than average, with a flaw, he could be someone like Rhodes in Graham Greene's *The Complaisant Lover* (1959) or the dry, disillusioned master in Rattigan's *The Browning Version* (1948), who were both rather stodgy and dull, and yet possessed an insight into the nature of duty and love which others lacked.

These were all methods of bending the rules without breaking them. They revealed a lack of confidence in the rules as such and also a lack of resolution (and perhaps of opportunity) to break them. The new plays of the early 1950s often seem to be half-hearted, as if the dramatists did not believe in what they were doing. Even the experimental plays, which were rare, seemed lacklustred: Tyrone Guthrie wrote a loose expressionist drama, *Top of the Ladder* (1950), with an Everyman story, about Bertie, a successful business man (played by John Mills), whose career is recreated at the moment of his death. Guthrie used props and an open stage, rather than the normal set, and dotted the story with symbols: by Bertie's bedside, an old nurse sits, embroidering Life's Rich Tapestry. This play compared badly with Auden and Isherwood's pre-war expressionist drama, *Ascent of F6*, which in turn compared rather badly with turn-of-the-century German expressionism, notably the plays of Wedekind.

In one respect, however, the tentatively adopted general rules encouraged dramatists to concentrate on purely verbal experimentalism, 'fine writing'. Dramatists often believed that by neat phrases, jokes and telling metaphors they could overcome the weaknesses of the conventional genres. This led, at an extreme, to the poetic dramas, but in many other plays, from those of N. C. Hunter to John Whiting, there were many individually telling lines, brilliant aphorisms and witticisms. Denis Cannon's *Captain Carvallo* (1950), with its preposterous Ruritanian story featuring a romantic hero (played by Laurence Olivier in London) with a girl in every soldierly billet, was redeemed by what was then described as its 'Shavian' wit.

John Whiting, however, was the exceptional dramatist of his time, in that he appreciated the advantages of the existing rules perceptively but did not lack the courage to break them. He was not influential. His reputation was not (fairly) firmly established until two years before his death in 1963, with the Royal Shakespeare Company production of *The Devils* (1961). His early play, *Saint's Day* (produced at the Arts Theatre Club in 1951), was chosen in an Arts Council competition but dismissed by *The Times* as 'having a badness that must be thought indescribable', while *Penny for a Song*, written after *Saint's Day* although produced before, in 1950, was a light-hearted poetic comedy, set in Dorset at the time of the Napoleonic war, and was generally considered to be 'promising', that most damning of adjectives for the ambitious writer.

Whiting started with several advantages over other contemporary writers. He believed in heroism, to begin with, and had the backing of his war experiences to add credibility to this belief. He was also an actor, fascinated by the allegorical possibilities of drama. He wanted his characters to be symbols of wider themes, but actable parts as well, not just the cartoons of moral or political polemic. He was a precise craftsman as a dramatist, who often gave his audiences the credit for more understanding of what he was saying than they actually seemed to possess. He shuffled around his symbolic characters, deliberately confusing the allegorical patterns in such a way that his scepticism came through, rather than his message. He was also an élitist in this sense that he did not strive for instant popularity, for democratic intimacy in the theatre and he was certainly prepared to upset prevailing beliefs. In a note on the trend towards intimacy in the theatre, which he dismissed as being merely cosy, Whiting stated: 'But, my God, there is power in the remote, isolated figure neither giving nor asking for understanding or love. Isn't it, perhaps, the power of the theatre, to which a return must be made sooner or later?' (*The Art of the Dramatist*, published posthumously, 1970).

Only Nigel Dennis among his contemporaries possessed quite the same vision of the stoical hero, standing out against the populist frenzies of the time, and Augustus in Dennis's *August for the People* (1961) was certainly a less telling figure either than Whiting's Rupert Forster in *Marching Song* (1954) or Grandier in *The Devils*.

Although Whiting was dissatisfied with *Marching Song*, it was perhaps the most accessible and competent of his early plays. Rupert Forster, a war hero and a disgraced general, is certainly a 'remote, isolated figure', bearing his fate with stoicism. His external fate is to be put on trial in his own defeated country, as a scapegoat whom politicians, such as the prime minister John Cadmus, can blame for losing the war; but his internal suffering is worse. Forster was a war criminal. He led his men into a mass slaughter of children in a village. The children were delaying his advance, and he felt that he had to be ruthless. Having slaughtered the innocents, he was shocked with his own brutality and simply could not give the necessary orders to capture a bridgehead. And so he lost the campaign and was placed in solitary confinement in a mountain cell. From this cell, he can only hear the calls of the mountain goatherds, which he interprets as hymns to the joy of life but discovers to be merely bawdy songs.

In *Marching Song*, Whiting was clearly determined to upset prevailing public assumptions. He was asking audiences of a victorious country, Britain, to recognise the political problems of a defeated country; and then asked the question as to whether they were very different. He was suggesting that a hero could also be a war criminal, whose crime could not even be justified by eventual victory, thus anticipating, say, Rolf Hochhuth's *Soldiers*. He also implied that the things which keep us going in times of trouble are not hymns but friendly obscenities. In the play, Forster is surrounded by semi-symbolic characters, a doctor, a priest, a brash and selfish movie-director, an ex-mistress and an innocent working-class girl. Their names are redolent of the period, Anselm (for the priest), Catherine de Troyes (for the ex-mistress) and Dido (for the working-class girl), all orientated in the 1950s fashion towards literature rather than the streets. Whiting also accepted totally the disciplines of a well-made play. *Marching Song* has a Hero, a decision taken at the Crisis which leads to Forster's suicide, a middle-class drawing-room set and is concerned with the last thirty-six hours of Forster's life. Whiting even deliberately exploits the limitations of the genre, by, say, pacing out a much smaller space in the centre of the drawing room and thus indicating that the so-called restrictions of the Unity of Place are not restrictive enough. A cell would be enough for the spiritual action with which he was concerned.

After the comparative failures of *Marching Song* and *The Gates of Summer* (1953), Whiting wrote nothing more for the theatre for five years, until he was commissioned by Peter Hall, who had long admired Whiting's work, to write *The Devils*, based upon Aldous Huxley's *The Devils of Loudun*, for the first Royal Shakespeare Company season at the Aldwych. The terms of the commission are interesting, for clearly Hall wanted to encourage writers to work outside the demands normally imposed by commercial theatres. He needed a play for his newly formed permanent company and one which broke away from conventional formulae, in the general direction of Epic Theatre. Whiting accepted the task with alacrity, but he retained (unlike other epic writers, including Brecht) two cardinal features of the well-made play: the Hero and the Crisis. Grandier, a priest in seventeenth-century France, is more superficially attractive than Forster, a warm, humane man whose capacity for love brings about his downfall. A young, deformed nun, Sister Jeanne, falls in love with him, although they have never met, and accuses him of haunting her dreams through the power of witchcraft. Grandier, who has enraged the Church and State authorities with his liberal views, is tortured and eventually murdered, having discovered through suffering his true vocation, which is to praise God through the beauty of nature.

In *The Devils*, Whiting dispensed with the Unities and became one of the first dramatists after the war to recognise the full potentiality of an open stage, with areas defined by props and the historical situation defined by language. At one point, the backstage area represents Paris, the midstage the town of Loudun and the forestage Grandier's room. He had benefited from watching Brecht's company in 1956 and learnt how to handle a theme which rambled over time and the body politic of France. He imitated the grim wit of British Jacobean drama to capture the French seventeenth-century atmosphere. Casual lines, such as those of the workmen beneath a scaffold who say of a hanged man that he has 'dripped through his heels all night', evoke Tourneur and tell us much about Whiting's capacity to visualise a scene and an age.

Too much must not be claimed for Whiting's originality, but his death at the age of forty-six was a great loss to British theatre. In *Marching Song*, he had shown his ability to work within the rules, effectively, even disturbingly, while in *The Devils* he proved that he could break those rules selectively, without losing control. Hall's commission also demonstrates that many of the literary inhibitions of the time were due to a lack of opportunity. Could writers be blamed for sticking unimaginatively to the formulae of well-made plays, if those alone helped to guarantee productions? Whiting himself stated in a *Time and Tide* interview,

> I could have written *The Devils* with one set and five
> characters and put it on in a smaller theatre...(but) I was

given everything I wanted. No compromise whatsoever
was made. How many English playwrights in the last three
hundred years have been given the kind of opportunity
that Peter Hall gave me? (9 March 1961)

The structure of plays (so the argument ran) reflected to a
large extent the nature of the theatre system, which in turn
mirrored the value placed upon drama by society in general.
The success of *The Devils* suggested that a new theatre system
reflecting different values was on its way. And yet even within the limits of the existing system of the 1950s a certain
timidity prevailed, an unwillingness to question. If we compare the well-made plays from France or the United States
with the more intellectually ambitious plays in Britain, we
notice a lack of radical enquiry even into that key element in
Western democratic thought, the nature of the individual
self.

Chapter 4

The search for self

In terms of theatre, Britain suffered from a bad balance-of-payments deficit after the war. We owed so much to movements which had been imported. We looked to Broadway for the best commercial theatre (the musicals), elsewhere in New York for the best acting school (the Method) and the most challenging naturalistic drama (the plays of Arthur Miller and Tennessee Williams). We looked to Paris for the most influential philosopher-dramatist (Jean-Paul Sartre), the best boulevard dramatist (Jean Anouilh), for the best mimes (such as Marcel Marceau), for the best religious dramatists (Paul Claudel, André Obey), for the most stimulating *avant-garde* drama (which at first meant Jean Cocteau's plays and then those of the Absurdists, such as Arthur Adamov and Eugène Ionesco) and the most prestigious example of a national theatre (the Comédie-Française) of a type we lacked.In addition, we looked to the Moscow Art Theatre for the best ensemble (naturalistic) acting and for the most recent 'classics' (the plays of Chekhov). Two names in this brief list are conspicuous by their absence: Antonin Artaud, who died in 1948, and Bertolt Brecht, who died in 1956. They were known to students of European theatre, but not, in the early 1950s, to the public at large.

In return for these riches, Britain could offer some great individual actors, some competent dramatists working in an old-fashioned style, some good but not outstanding directors and poetic drama. We were left with some debts which could have led to a cultural inferiority complex, exaggerated rather than offset by the remarks of politicians who would argue that we were to the Americans what the Greeks were to the Romans, a major cultural influence on the leading military and economic power of the day. We weren't, at least not on the level of the theatre; and to demonstrate this fact, Peter Daubeny from 1951 onwards would bring over troupes from abroad to the Cambridge, Stoll or Prince's theatres in an apparently never-ending flow of excellence. Daubeny introduced to London audiences the work of Jean-Louis Barrault and Madeleine Renaud, Edwige Feuillère, Roland Petit, Martha Graham, the Moscow Art Theatre, the Classical Theatre of China, Les Ballets Africains and Sacha Guitry; and in 1964, to celebrate the four hundredth anniversary of Shakespeare's birth, he launched the World Theatre Seasons with the Royal Shakespeare Company organisation at the Aldwych. In 1956, he also brought over Brecht's Berliner Ensemble for a season which proved more influential than its critical reception at the time seemed to imply.

If, from this welter of international influences, I were forced to pick (as, for reasons of space, I am) one area where British drama was shown to be palpably deficient, it would be in that pervasive theme, the Search for Self. This supermarket phrase contains many different sorts of goods. On a political level, a belief, however tentative, in individual judgments was the cornerstone of Western democracy. The Marxists might claim that individualism was a myth, for inevitably in their view our minds reflect our statuses in the largely mechanical cycles of production and exchange. The nineteenth-century arguments about whether heredity or environment was most responsible for the formation of minds still simmered on; but despite this scientism, the belief persisted that the individual in society could choose, that these choices represented worthwhile decisions and that the capacity to choose (even between limited alternatives) was a human right to be upheld and defended by the social system. Sometimes, this cause was defended more polemically, as Freedom, while at other times cautiously, as the right to say No, sometimes religiously (Free Will) and sometimes humanistically or existentially. But the general cause which linked those on the left (such as Jean-Paul Sartre) to those on the right (such as Henri de Montherlant) was the belief that individuals had choice, which could be exercised for good or ill. The questions raised from this premise were connected with the kinds of choice. To what extent could man be regarded as 'free'? What constituted the Selfness of the individual man?

Most European dramatists presented cautious, thoughtful

views: none blew the trumpet of individual freedom without trying to remember the rest of the orchestra. Albert Camus, for example, was a pessimist. If a man were given 'freedom', he would promptly try to test its limits, like Caligula, thus causing the suffering of those around (1944, *Caligula*). Those who followed the Italian dramatist, Luigi Pirandello (1867–1936), emphasised the unknowability of man's inner self, which was shrouded certainly from others and perhaps from the person concerned, behind layers of masks, acts and games. Pirandello was also fascinated by the subjective nature of our perceptions of the world, by the way in which people can live in fantasy pagodas of their own creation, and he involved a theory, based on his own experiences of coping with a half-mad wife, that these roles which we invent for ourselves protect us from pain and also act as stalking horses behind which we can plot our revenges. His *'Henry IV'* (1922), a brilliant and bizarre play, concerned a man apparently transfixed in the role which he played in a medieval pageant. But behind this fantasy to which all his friends and servants are forced to submit, there lurks a jealous, bitter and alert mind which seeks revenge against a former mistress and her lover.

Although Pirandello's plays were never popular in Britain, those of Jean Anouilh, whom he influenced, were. Anouilh's early career had been much encouraged by Georges and Ludmilla Pitoëff, two actor-directors in Paris in between the two world wars, who had also championed Pirandello. Anouilh, to judge by the number of West End productions, was the most successful dramatist of any country in London after the war. Laurence Olivier and Vivien Leigh appeared in his *Antigone* (1949, London), Dirk Bogarde and Mai Zetterling in *Point of Departure* (1950), Paul Scofield in Peter Brook's production of *Ring Round the Moon* (1950), Isabel Jeans and Ronald Squire in *Ardèle* (1951) and Margaret Rutherford in *Time Remembered* (1954). A caravan of successes followed, including *Invitation to the Castle*, *Waltz of the Toreadors*, *The Rehearsal*, *Becket* and *The Lark*, which were presented in London (usually by H. M. Tennent Ltd) in star-spangled productions.

Within the limits which he set himself, which were those of a man ambitious both for commercial success and critical esteem, Anouilh was—and is—a brilliant technician. He could take similar stories and treat them in totally different ways. The romantic young lovers of his early plays, whose pure emotions become corrupted by the world's artifices, could seem (as in his *Pièces noires*) either lambs cruelly led to the slaughter or adolescents regretfully maturing with age. The idyllic irony of his *Pièces roses* could become the terse epigrams of his *Pièces brillantes*. Devices such as the 'play within the play' or themes such as that of a young girl forced to act a role which then either conquers or succumbs to her 'real self' were made to seem either flippantly fantastical or forcefully bizarre. His skill lay in manipulating the tone of a play, achieving the right effect at the right time and not being seduced away from the overall atmosphere for the sake of a good joke or telling scene.

But in comparison with Pirandello's plays, Anouilh's often seemed superficial. Both dramatists were concerned with human role-playing. Their characters assume different disguises—or are they disguises?—to suit changing situations. But Pirandello gave a specifically emotional need to this activity, self-protection, whereas Anouilh often did not. Role-playing in Anouilh's plays is often a method of coping with boredom, or of seducing a girl whom the seducer doesn't want anyway, or of recreating a nostalgic past. It is rarely linked to a deep or precise feeling: it is more often a genteel pastime. In *Time Remembered*, for example, the doting mother of a rich young man reconstructs in the gardens of her country house the exact circumstances in which her son fell in love with a girl, Leocardia. Like '*Henry IV*', *Time Remembered* is concerned with a dream world, through which 'reality' breaks. But in *Time Remembered*, the young man is protecting no emotion, no sense of pain: he cannot remember what Leocardia looked like. That indeed is the point. Ennui swamps all.

Many other writers were concerned with the theme of role-playing. Some (like Luigi Chiarelli, who influenced Pirandello) took the half-moralistic, half-satirical line that man's capacity for self-deception was infinite, particularly in the corrupting circumstances of urban societies. Others expressed the view that life was a walking shadow in any case and thus linked role-playing with the assertion that the

whole world was a delusion, dimly perceived through erring
senses, misinterpreted by the mind and then further corrupted by emotionalism. Man was adrift in an absurd
universe, where nothing could be certainly known and
where communication was impossible. On this level, the idea
of role-playing merged towards the themes which dominated
Arthur Adamov's early plays, where all forms of action are
equally vain and where even the 'honest' man can be confronted with an image of himself totally at odds with his own
self-estimation and which nevertheless conquered his real
nature: just as Adamov's Dr Taranne, a respeeectable
professor, is forced to accept his public image as an academic
crook and sly sexual pervert. Jean Genet twisted the theme in
another direction. Role-playing was the be-all and end-all of
our lives. Essentially, men's lives are sordid and debased, but
they seek the chance to redeem themselves through quasi-
sexual, mainly sadistic rituals. Society is full of institutional
figureheads (judges, generals, police-chiefs, murderers)
which reflect the ritualistic transformations of the Self into
objects of static public contemplation. Just as we wish, in our
lives, 'to make a name for ourselves', so these 'names', these
'reputations', represent a flowering of the Self, after which
the person dies. Genet interpreted bourgeois society as a
massive projection of personal fantasies into public institutions and he was championed by left-wing writers, such as
Sartre, for doing so. But Genet admitted that he could not
imagine what a socialist society was like. The urge for
ritualistic transformation was innate in man.

Coupled with this interest in role-playing was its opposite
side, the quest for spiritual integrity. What was meant by
'honesty', 'truth to oneself', 'freedom and commitment' or by
dishonesty and 'bad faith'? Western writers generally agreed
that material wealth damaged the soul. The riches which corrupted young innocents in Anouilh's plays also turned ardent socialists into members of the decadent bourgeoisie in
Sartre's, crumbled in ashes in the hands of Lord Claverton
(in T. S. Eliot's *The Elder Statesman*), transformed a holy shrine
into a vulgar tourist trap in Ronald Duncan's *This Way to the
Tomb* and nearly lured away an ascetic knight from his
austere castle in Avila to plunder and colonise the Spanish-
American coast in Montherlant's *The Master of Santiago*. If

post-war drama in Paris and London seems unduly centred around the follies of the rich, it is worth remembering that these prime images of capitalism were nearly always presented unfavourably. True wealth lay in spiritual integrity.

But what did integrity mean? Paul Claudel and Sartre, from the standpoints of their different faiths, answered this question with most conviction. To Claudel, man through his Christian belief was drawn towards God. His obedience to his pre-ordained destiny defended him against worldly temptations. His great religious love-stories, *Partage de midi* (1906) and *Le Soulier de satin* (1928–9) received acclaimed productions in 1948 and 1943 respectively by the Barrault/Renaud company in Paris, the echoes of which could be felt throughout the 1950s and particularly in the columns of the *Sunday Times*, written by Harold Hobson. Integrity meant accepting the laws of God (as revealed through the Scriptures), not in the spirit of mere duty but with the fervency of a grand passion. Sartre, of course, would not have accepted that there were Laws of God to obey. He was an existentialist, which meant that in his view, *existence* (the primary life of a person) preceded *essence* (the pattern of behaviour to which the person aspires). Unlike the old absolutist moralities, among them Christianity, which assumed that God had a pattern (or essence) for man in his Mind before man himself was created, the existentialists assumed that living preceded the formulation of a pattern.

Two elements in Sartre's definition of integrity were contained in two words, *freedom* and *commitment*. Because no divine essence preceded the creation of man, the individual was brought into a world where there were no laws which he had to obey. Absolute morality was in any case thought to be an absolute impossibility, in that language itself was not capable of expressing absolute principles. The individual first had to recognise that there were no divine laws and that he was thus able to live 'freely': without stock reactions, bad habits and environmentally acquired prejudices. Having reached this state of 'freedom', he was then in a position to decide what sort of person he wished to become. Freedom preceded the formulation of moral judgments. Sartre believed that the free man would inevitably recognise the desirable logic of Marxism, and so become committed in a political sense. It has been suggested that Sartre's chief contribution to social philosophy has been the attempt to reconcile the Christian concept of free will with the Marxist idea of evolutionary socialism.

The plays of Sartre best-known in Britain were those, at first, connected with the war, allegories about the Nazi occupation of France (such as *Les Mouches*, 1943) or about the French resistance (*Morts sans sépultures*, 1946). Within this context, his views were readily accepted. But it was more disturbing to find the same logic in non-war situations, as in *Huis clos* (1945) where three people after death are imprisoned within the mutual hell of their own natures, trapped by their 'bad faith' in an arbitrary universe, or in *La Putain respectueuse* which was considered to be a crude tract against racism in the United States. Sartre was primarily concerned to redefine the nature of conscience and the relationship of this conscience to political action. 'Bad faith', the equivalent to original sin among existentialists, could mean social conditioning, or human weakness and illogic, or hypocrisy, or the failure to recognise the importance of Marxism. It was thus a broad and heavy cudgel of abuse which could be wielded by the supporters of Sartre against anyone they disliked, thus arousing the indignation of the opponents of Sartre. Sartre was disliked by Western politicians for taking the 'wrong' side in the Cold War, by philosophers for muddling the purity of philosophy with the tangles of politics and art, by Christians for denying that the laws of God existed, and by many humanists. The humanists argued that Sartre was supplying alternative dogmas to match those of the Church. Is it ever possible for man either to be 'free' or to know the pattern of life so completely that he can commit himself to certain courses of action in advance? Among the post-war French philosopher-dramatists, Sartre was perhaps the most optimistic. He believed in the human capacity for voluntary change, and his works revealed a tenacious enthusiasm to describe the various logical ways in which, first, free will could be accepted as an attribute of man, and, second, this will could be harnessed to positive, concerted action.

Claudel and Sartre, together with many other writers, both indicated ways in which, in their opinions, man could be true to himself. The fact that their outlooks were so totally opposite should not prevent us from recognising that at a certain level their searches were similar. They may have been alike in another respect as well, in that they were both well aware of the cultural and philosophical traditions to which they belonged. They were willing prisoners of these traditions, content (although that word may seem a strange one to use in the case of the continually questioning Sartre) not to stray too far beyond them. Henri de Montherlant regarded them both with sceptical, quizzical eyes. Montherlant, always unwilling to be drawn into any dogmatism, regarded a man's character as something which was determined by many forces, his birth, his rearing, his cultural environment, and that vital coherence which came from the interaction between personal will-power and these formative forces. The heroes of *The Master of Santiago* and *Malatesta*, two roles played by Sir Donald Wolfit in London in 1957, are almost exact opposites. One was a chivalric knight, Don Alvaro, maintaining the high ascetic ideals of sixteenth-century Spanish Christianity; the other, Malatesta, was a feudal tyrant in Renaissance Italy, a violent voluptuary in the age of the Borgias. Both obeyed the standards of the age which had formed their characters, and both struggled against the social changes surrounding them. Their individual characters lay in their energy, not in their moral opinions, such as they were. Montherlant carved his plays with exceptional care, so that their very form should represent the ages to which his heroes belonged. *The Master of Santiago* is a stately play, set in a wintry castle, grey and sombre, with one splash of brilliant colour (the capitulary mantle of the Order of Santiago) on one wall. The play proceeds classically, towards a decision at the crisis. The setting of *Malatesta* varies from Rimini to Rome, with short turbulent scenes, violent in action, ecstatic in language and with many unanticipated turns in the plot. Even Malatesta's death seems arbitrary, the result of a minor grudge.

And yet were not all these writers in a sense pontificating about the nature of Man—in their very efforts to explain what the Self was, how will-power worked and so on? Had they not forgotten that they too were men? Had not the time arrived when, as Alain Robbe-Grillet put it, a writer should cease to be God to his characters? Were they not losing a sense of what it feels like to be alive? One important trend in the search for Self movement was the desire to get beneath the role-playing, the commitments, the jargon about freedom and all the other accidents of heritage in order, quite simply, to capture the sensation of being.

Samuel Beckett, a Dublin Irishman, a former friend of James Joyce who lived in Paris, did not interpret the search for self as meaning simply the attempt to define one's character. Individual characteristics (personal moralities among them) were of less importance than the basic human awareness of living, the sense of growing or dwindling away, waiting for something to happen, the cycles of friendship or alienation. With single-minded dedication, he strove to develop a dramatic means through which these inner rhythms could be captured. He chose to write in French because it was not English or Irish-English. His native language had too many personal associations to be used with the objectivity suitable for his themes. He would sometimes write a script in French and then translate it back into English for British audiences, as he did with his first major play, *En attendant Godot* which he translated as *Waiting for Godot* (London, 1955).

In a similar way, he was careful not to betray too many signs of specific religious beliefs. *Waiting for Godot* has many references to Christianity, but any traces of religious belief are promptly contradicted by expressions of doubt. Christianity is used within the play as just one of those habits of fear or hope which keeps a person going through the endless process of waiting. Many critics tried to associate Godot, the mysterious being for whom the two tramps, Vladimir and Estragon, are without reason waiting, as God. Godot never appears, and Beckett in a rare comment, once stated that Godot was not God.

If Godot is not God, then what (many asked) does the play *mean*? All that happens in *Waiting for Godot* is that two tramps are waiting, by a tree, in some discomfort, for someone to turn up. He doesn't come, and their isolation is only disturbed by a fat tyrant, Pozzo, presumably representing capitalists as a whole, and his slave, Lucky, who spouts ridiculous gibberish at the flick of Pozzo's whip. At the end of the first act, a young boy arrives to tell the tramps that Godot will not come today. In the second act, the tramps are still waiting, Pozzo and Lucky reappear with their roles reversed, and the same young boy (though denying that he is) comes once more to say that Godot won't come on that day either. The play infuriated many critics, including Ivor Brown who said that he could 'find no satisfaction in the moanings of the mentally deficient'. Brecht saw *Waiting for Godot* as a justification of social inaction and also hated it.

These comments totally mistook the nature of *Waiting for Godot* and the literary tradition to which Beckett belonged, for while it is true to say that he wished to divest himself of links with the past, his background among the 'stream of consciousness' writers of the 1930s (such as Joyce) affected his approach both towards the writing of plays and of novels. Joyce wished to record all the thoughts and sensations which floated through the dreams of one Dublin man during a night (*Finnegans Wake*, 1939). He chose a private language, with an associative logic involving puns, word games and particular memories that melted into each other. Beckett also wished to present an inner flow of consciousness, but instead of choosing a language dense with private associations, he evolved a primary language which would convey the flow directly, instead of through the mist of confused memories. The contrast is illustrated by two of his novels: *Murphy* (1938), where the language is rich with local associations, and *Malone meurt* (1951, translated by Beckett as *Malone Dies*). *Malone Dies* is about the sensation of dwindling away into death, the situation is not local, nor is the language, which is bare, simple and direct.

Similarly, *Waiting for Godot* is basically about waiting for something to happen. Nothing happens, of course, for the simple reason that if it did, the play would no longer be about waiting, but about something happening. Beckett's problem was how to translate the waiting feeling into dramatic terms. He did so by carefully balancing one type of expectation against another, which on a literary level resulted in an almost hypnotic antiphonal prose-poetry, one short phrase counterpointed by another, and, on a social level, captured a mood of irresolute sceptical uncertainty, which was perhaps the familiar feeling of the 1950s when different optimistic ideologies of the 1930s and 1940s were proving false. *Waiting for Godot* is not a pessimistic or even nihilistic play exactly, unless waiting itself is a form of pessimism. Beckett balanced out pessimism and optimism, death and birth, leaves falling and growing:

Vladimir:
Astride of a grave and a difficult birth. Down in the hole, lingeringly, the grave-digger puts on the forceps.

One of the paradoxes about *Waiting for Godot* was that it was regarded by most critics and impresarios as theatrically intractable and extremely obscure, and yet it became a popular success. The tramps from *Godot* set up a fashion of their own in Britain, influencing Harold Pinter in his plays (such as *The Birthday Party*) and revue sketches (notably *The Black and White* from *One to Another*, 1959). They were imitated in television comedy programmes, such as *The Arthur Haynes Show*, while as Martin Esslin pointed out, *Waiting for Godot* was a great success in Sing Sing prison, before audiences who knew nothing about the theatre but everything about waiting.

Just as *Waiting for Godot* can be roughly summarised as being about waiting, so *Krapp's Last Tape* (1958) is about trying to recollect exactly what happened when one was young, *Breath* is about breathing, *Happy Days* is about feeling that life is ebbing away in deadening habits, among them the effort to remain cheerful, *Play* is about recurring sexual jealousies, *Endgame* is about the loss of the past and the death of the future, and *Not I* is about listening to oneself speaking and rejecting that strange, familiar voice. Beckett presented these underlying states of feeling in striking visual symbols, which (with his intense, precise language) was his most telling trademark as a dramatist: the parents in the dustbins in *Endgame*, the woman buried to her waist and then to her neck in sand, in *Happy Days*, the spotlit, chattering, disembodied Mouth in *Not I*.

Beckett's plays are sometimes considered to belong to that loose genre known as the Theatre of the Absurd; but this association can be misleading. He did not believe with the Dadaists in nonsense for its own sake, nor did he explore with the surrealists the illogic of dreams and nightmares. He was not exactly an allegorist, like Eugne Ionesco, whose first plays (such as *The Bald Prima Donna*, 1950) were also produced in London in 1955; nor did he even insist, with the relentlessness of the philosopher-dramatists such as Camus, that the universe was 'absurd'. His aims were more limited and more sharply defined; and his importance to post-war European theatre can scarcely be overestimated, despite the fact that, although he influenced other writers, none chose to follow him down the narrow path which he trod so carefully. His plays represented a certain extreme, a boundary, for nobody else has attempted to express the nature of human experience on so basic a level. Once you have dramatically expressed the sensation of breathing, how much further into the heart of human consciousness can you go? To that extent, therefore, Beckett blocked off the 'search for self' movement. From Beckett onwards, writers either had to move towards the *nouveau roman* approach, where they try to capture exactly each fleeting impression without superimposing any overall reasoning or shape, or away from such introversion altogether.

Beckett was also a radical writer, not in a political, but a technical sense. He re-thought the whole nature of play-writing in order to achieve his aims. None of the so-called rules of play-writing mattered to him at all; but he was exceptionally aware of his craft. Beckett is a singularly 'pure' dramatist, in that he achieves exactly what he sets out to do, neither more nor less, and it is impossible to imagine how any of his plays could have been written differently. He also exposed the pretentiousness of many dramatic styles around him; the Freudiana of Tennessee Williams, the poetic drama in Britain; even the philosophical pondering of Sartre in *Being and Nothingness* (1943) seemed just contorted beside the view of human consciousness presented by Beckett. Sartre once wrote: 'The Self is the Hole in Being, the Being through which Nothingness enters the World', meaning that the Self has no innate rules to obey, but has an infinite capacity to control the pattern of the Self-to-come. Beckett would have dismissed such thoughts as jargon and, from Beckett onwards, the theories of existentialism ceased to be so intellectually appealing. He therefore purified the dramatic language (and, some would add, rarified it as well) by getting rid of preoccupations which had dominated the theatre for too long and by expressing others so exactly that further statements were unnecessary. He provided a scale against which other writers could be measured. He was an authentic genius at a time when talented writers were ten a penny.

The European 'search for self' movement was distinguished by its high-seriousness (and occasionally pretentiousness) its radicalism and its diversity. The only genre in Britain which shared such high aims and was rewarded with a similar critical esteem was that of poetic drama; but as soon as we hint at such a comparison, the deficiencies of the home-brew become apparent. The moralising of the poetic plays tended to be pious rather than stimulating, its literary values derivative, and its social ones conservative. There was also a sense of strain which afflicted the dramatists of the genre, which they did their best to conceal either by adopting a flippant, good-humoured wit or by pretending that they weren't really writing *poetry*, only dramatically heightened prose.

The most notable poetic dramatists wereT. S. Eliot and Christopher Fry, although the genre also included such able writers as Ronald Duncan, Norman Nicholson and Dannie Abse. Eliot once defined his task as a dramatist like this: 'to take a form of entertainment and subject it to a process that would leave it a form of art.' It was a curious formula from so notable a critic. It sounds like alchemy, transmuting base metals into gold. It sounds as if Eliot were expecting the artist to limit himself to those themes, ideas and techniques which were in popular use and to rely on his ingenuity to produce something artistic from them. This was precisely the approach which many poetic dramatists took. They accepted the conventions of their time and tried to add 'art' to them, usually in the form of poetic dialogue, which might mean metrical verse or the rich, sensuous language of a Dylan Thomas.

What did Eliot mean by 'entertainment' and 'art'? His early play fragments, *Sweeny Agonistes* (1928) and *The Rock* (1934) were furthest from the demands of the theatre as he understood them. The choruses, though influenced by the Jazz Age, were modelled on Greek drama, not on West End plays; and a similar attachment to Greek tragedy shaped the form of his first major play, *Murder in the Cathedral* (1935), with its choruses, sacrificial hero (Thomas Becket) and dialogue-soliloquy-chorus pattern. It was written to be performed in Canterbury Cathedral, which in itself stressed Eliot's concern for the religious origins of drama; although it could also be argued that Eliot was trying to escape from the trap of proscenium arch theatres. Other dramatists followed his example in writing plays for churches: Fry's *A Sleep of Prisoners* (1951) was first performed in the University Church, Oxford.

But Eliot also wanted to write for conventional theatres, and so, from *The Family Reunion* (1939) to *The Elder Statesman* (1958), he accepted as a basis for his plays one familiar genre, Society Drama, but emphasised certain elements which would bring it closer to Greek models. As we have seen, Greek dramatic practice and 'well-made plays' had elements in common, among them the Hero, the Crisis and the Unities. Eliot's later plays were therefore 'well-made', 'natural' but not 'naturalistic', and set in elegant apartments among the fairly wealthy, reasonably leisured middle classes. His themes are also, if only superficially, related to Society Drama. *The Family Reunion* is apparently about whether Harry, Lord Monchensey, will take up residence as the Squire of Wishwood, the family estate. *The Cocktail Party* partly concerns the marital problems of Edward Chamberlayne, a barrister, and his society hostess wife, Lavinia. Much of the dialogue is concerned with the social nuances of taste. Should one take cocktails before dinner or was Charles Piper right when he asserted in *The Family Reunion* that,

> All that a civilised person needs
> Is a glass of dry sherry or two... ?

Here Eliot was mocking small talk but, like a true Society dramatist, he was capable of taking such habits seriously, not (of course) as serious alcoholic recommendations, but as signs of character. The Uninvited Guest in *The Cocktail Party* drinks gin with a little water on certain occasions (suggesting a warm austerity of character) but not on others, indicating that an analyst who is indirectly driving his patients should not drink at the same time.

Eliot, however, was not concerned with social 'good living' but with 'spiritual', particularly with man's relationship to God and his own inner destiny. Society at best was merely a metaphor for this spiritual process. He thus tried to transform Society Drama so that it could convey spiritual aspirations, as well as material ones. His problem was that Society Drama was usually defiantly contemporary, fixed within its ephemeral set of social values (reflected in the dresses and sets). He therefore tried to bring to the foreground not only the general Greek dramatic ideas which we have mentioned, but other devices which had become buried with time, such as the Blind Seer, the Furies and the Presence of the Gods. Art, for Eliot as for Christopher Fry and Ronald Duncan, implied the expression of fundamental values, timeless ones, and so, in the process of transforming Society Drama into Art, he sought the universal statement in the temporary phenomena and required a heightened language for this purpose.

The prime characteristic of Eliot's early heroes is their sense of destiny. Harry, Lord Monchensey, in *The Family Reunion* can scarcely avoid having one: the Furies are pursuing him. Not everyone has this clear pattern to life, and those that do, may not initially recognise their fates. In this sense, the Eliot Hero is 'better than average'. Harry is both privileged and tormented by the Furies. Lesser men, who had committed his crimes, would have had less bothersome consciences: they would have settled down into an awkward complicity with their guilts, being neither unhappy nor happy. But Harry is prepared to face the consequences of his actions, even to the point of abandoning Wishwood. There is a spiritual hierarchy in Eliot's plays with Harry near the top. Celia Coplestone in *The Cocktail Party* recognises that society life in London has nothing to offer her. Her failed love affair jolts her back to her spiritual destiny. Her vocation is to be a missionary among primitive tribes who eventually murder her, and the seer, Sir Harcourt Reilly (the Uninvited Guest), foresees her future in the shape of a mystical aura.

But Celia is not the heroine of *The Cocktail Party*, spiritually elevated though she is. The central character, Edward, has a lower destiny, which is to recognise his limitations, to love his wife in as much as he is capable of loving and not to fool himself with false hopes. He is thus a few rungs below Celia on the spiritual ladder, although above perhaps Peter Quilpe, whose destiny is merely Hollywood. *The Cocktail Party* therefore reveals a change of direction in Eliot's writing. Instead of the central character being a hero with outstanding spiritual qualities, Edward is closer to the norm of mankind. This indicates, first, that Eliot was no longer aspiring to reach the heights of tragedy but rather the foothills of ironic comedy, and second, that he had become dissatisfied with his previous attempts to introduce the classic spiritual struggles of Greek drama into the framework of Society Drama. In a similar way, he toned down the obvious poeticisms of his writing. Instead of the massive, metaphor-conscious choruses of his early work, with their thundering rhythms, he chose a very subtle type of verse, which often amounted to little more than a semi-regular beat beneath apparently naturalistic dialogue. As C. S. Lewis once dryly remarked 'Eliot's stage verse imitates prose, with remarkable success.'

Perhaps the most striking difference between Eliot's standards and our own is that he regarded drama as being primarily a verbal medium, an opinion which he shared with other writers. When in trouble, he tried to write his way out. Christopher Fry was a much more flamboyant phrasemaker. Eliot respected simple language and distrusted poeticisms. Fry, on the other hand, had too clear a picture of what poetry looked (and sounded) like. His verse was full of natural images, evocations of the Gods, classical quotations and rhetorical conceits. Fry was the Euphues of the 1950s. The Duke of Altair in *Venus Observed* greets Perpetua, the beautiful daughter of his agent, from his couch in his observatory like this:

And Endymion, when the moon had borne him
Fifty daughters, was rewarded with
An eternal siesta; his breast and belly rose
And fell like the sea; his breath played
All day with the motes of dust,
While all about him suffered, withered, and
Crumbled into the dust his breath played with....

And so on, a pretty speech, but a little slow and narcissistic for a contemporary seduction.

Eliot was more austere, carefully varying the length of lines to match the dramatic situation, eager not to sound poetic. Both Fry and Eliot were careless, however, about the non-verbal rhythms, so important in the structure of scees, the rhythms of movement and gesture, of exits and entrances, and the balance between characters. Fry would allow important characters, such as Thomas Mendip in *The Lady's not for Burning*, just to stand around the stage, with nothing much to do or say, nodding in from time to time. Eliot would forget about the important cross-currents of reaction and counter-reaction which can flow around the characters on stage, often preferring to group them all together, until a scene sounded and felt like a badly written piano concerto, where the pianist has a floridly written part while the orchestra is reduced to a vamp accompaniment. The trouble with their methods of introducing verse into drama was not that the metre itself sounded artificial but that too many other types of theatrical rhythm had to be ignored for it to work.

Even on a verbal level, however, Eliot's stage poetry lacked the concision of his normal verse, and this was partly because he believed that tense, neat verse could not be appreciated in the rougher medium of drama. Because the verse was to be spoken, not savoured through reading, it could not afford to be as precise and accurate as ordinary poetry. Subtle metrical patterns had to be replaced by a generalised, theatrical beat, best illustrated by the somewhat heavy choruses of *Murder in the Cathedral* and *The Family Reunion*: the stresses in his later plays were less obvious, but also somewhat hypnotic. Eliot too was self-conscious about the influence of the Jacobeans, particularly Shakespearian tragedy. He wanted to avoid the too familiar stresses of the iambic pentameter, and that sing-song delivery then associated with Shakespearian verse-speaking. He was thus hemmed in by inhibitions. He could not seek new, delicate, metrical forms, on the grounds that audiences would have no time to appreciate them: he could not pursue old and familiar forms of stage verse, for fear of falling under the Jacobean spell. He could not be 'poetic', except on certain specific occasions, for fear of breaking his links with Society Drama. He could not be too prosaic without failing to build up towards those ritualistic moments which he regarded as being of the utmost importance.

He was, in short, tongue-tied by too great a respect for religion and art, by his sense of history and by his uncertainty as to what would work on stage and what would not. He was in the worst, and not the best, sense a conservative, because he tried to assert the contemporary validity of old 'truths' without going through the trouble of re-thinking them and arguing them out in detail. If we compare Sartre's treatment of the Orestes story in *Les Mouches* with Eliot's in *The Family Reunion*, we must realise that Sartre, whether we agree with him or not, had at least troubled to think again about the meaning of the legend. The whole object of *Les Mouches* is to consider what the former concepts of guilt, justifiable retribution and atonement could mean in an occupied country for someone who does not believe in God. Eliot felt no such necessity. His version is basically Orestes in modern dress, set in a country house in Yorkshire, and adapted to Christianity. His task may have seemed simpler than Sartre's, but in some respects it was more difficult theatrically, for Eliot was not trying to say anything new. He had to achieve the dignity and profundity of the original story, without having much in the way of fresh insights to help him. This was where his poetry became his greatest temptation, for he could conceal his lack of inspiration beneath the pallid glow of a false Culture.

The comparative failure of Eliot's attempt to find a new form of stage poetry was, however, only one aspect of a much wider sense of strain which afflicted his efforts to transform the sow's ear of entertainment into the silk purse of Art. He also had to present his heroes and seers as elevated men, and he often did so in external ways. The opening scenes of *Murder in the Cathedral* are like the drum rolls before the star, Becket, arrives. The Women of Canterbury, representing normal mankind, fear the disruption which Becket's presence will cause, and yet they also dread the decaying peace. Within this peace, everything goes wrong, harvests ruined, floods, imminent starvation. Eliot seems to be expressing over-literally the ancient theme that the well-being of the State depends upon the sacrifice of its 'king', in this case a spiritual king. Ordinary folk suffer from the 'strain on the brain of the small folk who stand to the doom of the house'; but not Becket. Becket is too elevated for that. He shrinks away from the normal nastinesses of life (such as 'the raw nobility whose manners match their fingernails').

This air of superiority also characterises Eliot's seers, including Sir Harcourt Reilly, whose final remark to all his patients ('Work out your salvation with diligence') would be enough to make most sensible people ignore his bill as an analyst. This paternalism is particularly infuriating because neither the heroes nor the seers do anything, except submit to their destinies. Becket is offered four temptations: to become Lord Chancellor and reform the laws of England, to be a cheerful courtier, to lead the barons against the king and to seek his own martyrdom. Becket dismisses all these courses of action as vanity, but there is something quintessentially vain about equating law reformation and chatting up chamber-maids as being *equally* vain. There is the lofty dismissal of all meddling in worldly affairs. 'There is nothing quite conclusive in the art of temporal government,' states a Priest, 'but violence, duplicity and frequent malversation'; which means that there is no absolute difference between good government and bad. This may be true, if you take an absolute perspective in which the whole of human history may be summarised as an undistinguished ripple on an eternal sea. But there may be a great deal of difference if one happens to be suffering under a bad government.

During the late 1950s, there was a marked swing of taste away from Eliot's plays and from those of other dramatists in Britain who had either sat in his shadow or basked in his sun. It was a moral revulsion, rather than an aesthetic one, which had political and social roots and consequences. It became impossible any longer just to dismiss politics as the uncouth squabbling over power from which a sensitive man would shrink. Politics hung over our lives in the threatening shape of a mushroom cloud. Men were either going to have to solve their problems or cease to be men. Corruption did not mean the Bird sitting on the Broken Chimney, as in *The Family Reunion*: it meant Auschwitz and the Siberian labour camps. It was impossible to believe that the destinies of the tribe should be determined by the garb and habits of a hero-king, archbishop or prime minister. Bertolt Brecht in *Galileo* stated the conflict succinctly. 'Unhappy is the land which has no heroes.'—'No, unhappy is the land which has a need for heroes.' In the post-war world, heroes might come and go but, if there was not one on hand at the crucial hour, the red button could be pressed by a fool.

Chapter 5

Breaking out: the angry plays

Jimmy Porter in John Osborne's *Look Back in Anger* (1956) was the exact opposite of Eliot's Becket and Lord Monchensey, of Whiting's Forster and all those other heroes of the time who could afford to disdain political power from a stance of natural superiority. Jimmy hungers for power from the position of social inferiority, with the sick, back-of-the-throat taste of continual defeat. His education (at a redbrick university) has left him with a Hunger for Culture, but with an uncertainty about values. Only the safest classics are good enough for him. He is loaded down with longings and aspirations totally at odds with his circumstances in life. He lives with his wife, Alison, in an untidy attic flat. He earns his living minding a market stall in a drab Midland town. His ambitions, almost too vague to define, are thus thwarted on all sides. He does not know what he wants. 'There aren't any good brave causes left.' And if he did know, his social situation would have stopped him from attaining them. Failing any other outlet for his energy, Jimmy's frustrations turn into self-loathing and are then re-directed outwards, into aggression against Alison.

Alison, in some respects, is Jimmy's natural enemy, the product of a well-off army family, thus middle-class and socially secure in the way in which Jimmy is not. She is also a stoic, a private missionary perhaps and something of an uncomplaining masochist, who endures a verbal cannibalism in order to bring, not religion, but respectability into Jimmy's disordered life. She does not retort to Jimmy's taunts about her middle-class background. She does not even tell him when she is pregnant, for fear that he may feel obliged to look after her. She wills her own downfall. An actress friend, Helena, urges her to leave Jimmy, and Alison does so. Helena becomes Jimmy's mistress, but when Alison returns, having lost her baby, Jimmy tells Helena to go. For better or worse,

Jimmy and Alison are locked together. Alison fully accepts her 'debasement': 'I want to be a lost cause. I want to be corrupt and futile:Jimmfutile'. Jimmy, who has longed for 'a kind of burning virility of mind and spirit', settles down into a marriage of emotional cripples, making the best of defeat.

Jimmy was thus a black retort to Eliot's white statements. He does not want to 'work out his salvation with diligence'; he resents his lot as a young plebeian in a world dominated by unseen middle-aged patricians. From a certain distance, however, opposites can have the similar dissimilarities of twins. Reverse sides of a coin still belong to the same coin, and an outside observer might have concluded that the heroes and anti-heroes of British drama in the mid-1950s were both disguises to conceal a national uncertainty. One might pretend that he was doing nothing, because no action quite merited his spiritual attention; and the other, that he was doing nothing, because there were no causes left to fight for and he was a self-confessed layabout in any case. Jimmy and Harry, Lord Monchensey, are both unwilling to take part in normal, everyday action. They do not struggle to 'better' themselves, either in the sense of striving for better jobs and standards of living, or in the sense of taking social and political action for the general betterment of society. To that extent, they both opt out, and tend to deride others who do not opt out. They might have opted out for different reasons, one from a fear that society is biased against him, and the other from a disdain for the fleshly world; but they both make a virtue of non-commitment.

Was this general attitude, as the Sartreans and Brechtians might claim, symptomatic of decline, of a loss of national purpose which resulted in a decay of personal moral fibre? Perhaps so, and yet it could be argued that in the mid-1950s, the most positive political attitude which Britain could take was that of opting out. This was the period of de-colonialisation, of slowly re-building and re-directing British industry after the war, of a necessary *stasis*. The most futile gestures (such as the Suez campaign, which took place in 1956) partly derived from a failure to recognise this fact. It was psychologically hard to adjust from a wartime situation, when there were causes to fight for, to a peacetime one, when such causes could prove just quixotic or excuses for bullying. If nationally the best policy seemed to be a cultivation of one's own garden which had fallen into neglect, internationally we were surrounded with awful warnings. Those inclined to the left were faced by the spectacle of Russian tanks rolling into Hungary; those of the right watched in despair the fiasco of Suez. Jimmy's passive, twisting anguish reflected the anxieties of the age, and it broke up the death-mask of loftiness with which previous writers had attempted to disguise their emotions.

The dry and defeated theatre critic, Bernard Link in David Mercer's play *After Haggerty* (1970), began every lecture on Modern British Drama with a statutory reference to *Look Back in Anger*; while the 'real' theatre critic, John Russell Taylor, called his guide to contemporary plays and playwrights, *Anger and After*, thus regulating what went before to a pre-Osborne Dark Age. In many respects, however, *Look Back in Anger* is just a conventional, wordy and rather clumsy play, and twenty years after, we might well wonder what was so significant about it. It has been both over- and under-estimated. 1956 was a year of theatrical changes, as well as of political disillusion. *Waiting for Godot* transferred to the West End, the Berliner Ensemble visited London for the first time, and while regional theatres were closing around the country in the face of commercial television, there were three hopeful signs for the theatrical future. Coventry, rebuilding its own town centre after the war, announced plans to include a new repertory theatre, the Belgrade, as part of the scheme: it was to be the first completely new theatre to be built for thirty years. Joan Littlewood's Theatre Workshop at Stratford-atte-Bowe had survived its years of make-do-and-mend, to become a lively, exciting ensemble with a particular gift for attracting writers, dedicated actors and, finally, critics and audiences. Brendan Behan's *The Quare Fellow* opened at Littlewood's Stratford in the same month, May, that *Look Back in Anger* was premièred at the Royal Court. Lastly, there was the new presence of the English Stage Company itself, formed to encourage new writers and to combat the decline of the vital theatre clubs. *Look Back in Anger* was the first major success of the English Stage Company at the Royal Court. The rest of the season contained Arthur Miller's *The Crucible*, Ronald Duncan's *Don Juan* and

The Death of Satan, and two plays by writers who were primarily novelists, Angus Wilson's *The Mulberry Bush* (a leisured and literary play, set in a university) and Nigel Dennis's *Cards of Identity*. A worthy season, without surprises, except for Osborne's play, the sole manuscript of note to have arrived through the normal channels of the post.

In a year of changes, *Look Back in Anger* came to symbolise the urgent demand for change, and if we require a useful illustration as to what we were changing from, the leading H. M. Tennent production of the year was Enid Bagnold's *The Chalk Garden* at the Haymarket, with Peggy Ashcroft, Edith Evans and Felix Aylmer, which concerned a widow living with an old retainer in a country house on the South Downs. It was a comedy with sinister undertones whose dialogue (according to Kenneth Tynan) provided speech of 'exquisite candour, building ornamental bridges of metaphor, tiptoeing across frail causeways of simile, and vaulting over gorges impassable to the rational soul'. The key word, indeed, was exquisite.

The Chalk Garden was the high point in a West End season dominated (as before) by middle-brow, middle-class, middle-aged tastes. Terence Rattigan's invention, 'Aunt Edna', represented the audiences for whom he was supposed to write; genteel, tea-sipping matinée fodder. She would have hated *Look Back in Anger*, just as the young audiences who supposedly liked Osborne's play would have hated to be associated with Aunt Edna. Kenneth Tynan wrote in the *Observer*: 'I agree that *Look Back in Anger* is a minority taste. What matters, however, is the size of the minority. I estimate it at roughly 6,733,000, which is the number of people in this country between twenty and thirty.' Did *Look Back in Anger* represent a class and age rebellion? Was that its true significance?

Perhaps so, but on this level it is easy to exaggerate its claims. Class may have been a barrier to widespread appreciation of the theatre, particularly in the West End, but *Look Back in Anger* was scarcely the chief battering ram against it. Jimmy is snobbish in his tastes, more of an Aunt Edna than Alison. The only character who emerges with his solid good sense intact is Alison's father, the Colonel. Nor was Jimmy a typical proletarian example: he was a minor spiv. Nor could Osborne claim to be a 'working-class writer', like Arnold Wesker or Bernard Kops. *Look Back in Anger* expressed, above all, middle-class discontent, and its class significance (if we want to consider the play in such terms) was not that it was a proletarian play but that it presented such a gloomy picture of a dispossessed ex-graduate that the truly working-class plays at the Theatre Workshop seemed cheerful by comparison.

Was it then a play of Oedipal rebellion? Osborne quickly became associated with a group of writers, including Colin Wilson and John Braine, who were known as angry young men. Osborne, through Jimmy Porter, was voicing the natural uncertainties of the young, their frustrations at being denied power, their eventual expectations of power and their fears of abusing it, either in running a country or a family. The familiar features of Oedipalism are there, staring through Jimmy's malignant-innocent eyes, his desire to shock, his loquaciousness, his sexual longings and his dread of responsibility, his curious ambivalence towards the Colonel, who is both noble and an *éminence grise*. Did this play acquire its prestige because it was staged in an 'old' country, with firm traditions, relentlessly upheld? Was Jimmy a youth knocking at the door of a stately country mansion, threatening to knock it down if it is not opened. In a sense, it is opened to him, through his marriage to Alison. He has one foot in the mansion's hall, and this is what confuses him. He has wandered into a world which looks more impressive from without than within. He has lost his main enemy, but not the habit of fighting.

There has been a strong tradition of Oedipal drama in Britain. Christopher Marlowe was an angry young man, and so once was Noël Coward. If we wish to search for other Jimmy Porters in British theatrical history, we can find them, disguised as malcontents in Jacobean tragedy or as rakes and dandies, ever-shocking the bourgeoisie. If we extend the field to include Irish and German writers, we can drag into this category the whole Romantic movement of doomed and cursed heroes, the Fausts and Manfreds, Brecht's Baal and even the Shavian heroes whose rebelliousness swaggered with the Dandies and thrust with the Marxists. The Romantic movement was based upon angry young men, Blake, the young Wordsworth, Shelley and Byron. If we bear this in mind, we may feel inclined to reverse the normal pattern of explanation: Jimmy Porter was acceptable *because* he was an angry young man, not *despite* his anger.

But the Oedipal argument also has its flaws, for the effect of *Look Back in Anger* was not to glorify the young rebel, but rather the reverse. Although there were many films and plays in the late 1950s which presented the angry young man as a hero, uncertain or otherwise, they came from different territories, from the United States (with James Dean and Marlon Brando) and from British universities, with their satirical revues. Jimmy was neither an *East of Eden* rebel, nor a *Beyond the Fringe* one. Osborne made no attempt to glamorise the anger. Jimmy was not just the critic of his society, he was also the object for criticism. He was the chief example of the social malaise which he was attacking. Through Jimmy Porter, Osborne had opened up a much wider subject than rebelliousness or youthful anger, that of social alienation, the feeling of being trapped in a world of meaningless codes and customs. Osborne's ambivalence towards Jimmy is apparent even from his descriptions of him in the script: Jimmy is 'a disconcerting mixture of sincerity and cheerful malice, of tenderness and freebooting cruelty'. The significance of these divided feelings was that it represented as well the tension between the longing for security and the desire for change: alienation, in short, in action, where we feel dissatisfied whatever we do.

The theme of social alienation came to dominate the drama of the subsequent years, much as the 'Search for Self' movement dominated French drama after the war. The theme emerged through the wry comedies of Mortimer, Cooper and Orton, in the sense of 'losing roots' (a subject tackled by Mercer and Storey), in the fear-ridden world of Pinter, in the Marxist interpretations of 'alienation' expressed by Arden, Bond, Brenton and Griffiths: in many disguises and forms, but with the same underlying urgency:

The World is out of joint; oh cursèd spite
That ever I was born to set it right.

In his subsequent plays, Osborne also developed two themes

expressed in *Look Back in Anger*, the rottenness of the State (usually, but not invariably, Britain) and the problems of being an alienated man. This is not to suggest that his plays do not have a wide range, of historical situations and techniques, but rather that, at some point and particularly in his early plays, this variety combs and folds around these central preoccupations.

These themes also suggest the limits of his work, for at worst Osborne can become a confused and predictable writer. He can hit out clumsily at easy targets, as in his satire on royal weddings in *The Blood of the Bambergs* (1963), and diffuse his 'State of the Nation' attacks until they include everyone and everything, as in *A Sense of Detachment* (1972). He botched up an adaptation of a difficult play, *A Bond Honoured* (from Lope de Vega's *La Fianza Satisfecha*), by not appreciating the difference between an existentialist rebel, living in a world where 'good and evil are men's opinions of themselves', with the God-defying hero of de Vega's play, whose sacrilege is the reverse side of his god-centredness and who experiences a miraculous conversion.

At best, however, Osborne managed to combine these themes within precise and direct statements. His capacity to write strong central characters and vivid, passionate dialogue fired the imagination of other writers, who without his rhetorical gifts caught something of his inner urgency. In *The Entertainer* (1957), Osborne considered the decline of Britain through the dead eyes of a stand-up comic, Archie Rice, who works within the tatty variety shows (with nudes), the remaining fragments of a once-great music-hall tradition. Laurence Olivier played Archie and the Blues song was a *tour de force* both for the actor and for the writer, for it had to represent the kind of genuine feeling for which Archie had craved, without knowing why. The loss of ordinary dignity, in private and in public life, leads to a personal despair. In *Luther* (1961), Osborne was concerned with a man who is frightened of his own rebelliousness. It is partly a historical account of Martin Luther's life, although the second act, which condenses history, is less successful than the first, where Luther grapples with the conflicts caused by his intellectual belief in the justice of his cause, his doubts that his rebelliousness may derive from more personal, less honourable reasons and where he finally forces himself to defy the Papacy at the Diet of Worms: 'Here I stand. God help me, I can do no more.'

With such characters as Jimmy Porter, Archie Rice and Martin Luther, Osborne proved his capacity to write magnificent single roles, a talent which no actor or manager could ignore. Osborne revitalised the star system, and the old stars (such as Olivier) and the new ones (Kenneth Haigh and Albert Finney, who first played Jimmy and Luther respectively) were quick to seize the opportunities. *Inadmissible Evidence* gave an equally good chance to another young actor, Nicol Williamson. It was a play about a guilty, middle-aged solicitor, Maitland, whose sexual fantasies merged into (and derived from) the realities of his daily life, his different relationships with his wife, mistresses and daughter. In *Inadmissible Evidence*, Osborne extended his attacks on society to include the way in which social codes can deform the sexual instinct, a theme which was also part of *Under Plain Cover* (1963) and *A Patriot for Me* (1966). In *Under Plain Cover*, a quiet young couple, brother and sister, play sexual games together, mainly sado-masochistic, until their secrets are exposed to the world of a meddling reporter; while in *A Patriot for Me*, based on the career of the master spy Redl in the Austro-Hungarian Empire before the First World War, he showed how a prevailing social atmosphere, encouraging homosexuality, might still not prevent, may indeed assist, the blackmail of a homosexual—with international, as well as personal, repercussions.

The year 1966 appears to have been a turning point in Osborne's career. He had formed a particularly close association with the Royal Court Theatre whose artistic director, George Devine, discovered *Look Back in Anger* and appeared briefly in *A Patriot for Me*. Devine had the insight to encourage Osborne and the authority to give him advice: but in 1966, he died, which was a great personal loss to Osborne. The impact of this loss can perhaps be seen in *A Bond Honoured*, written at Kenneth Tynan's instigation for the National Theatre: the conversion episodes at the end of this play give the impression of being absent-mindedly written, very clumsy and brief. But after 1966, there was also a change in direction in Osborne's plays: they were no longer so heavily dependent on strong central characters. In the quiet *Hotel in Amsterdam* (1968), despite an acidly ironic part for Paul Scofield, the main character is off-stage, the domineering father-figure of a film crew for whose instructions the others wait. *Hotel in Amsterdam*, like *West of Suez* (1971) and *A Sense of Detachment* (1972), is an 'ensemble' play. *Time Present* (1968) was a return to the theme expressed in *The Entertainer* in that a dead Edwardian actor-manager is remembered as having belonged to a golden age of Britain (and the theatre): the nostalgia attached to the music hall in *The Entertainer* now spreads to the whole Edwardian period, and it was this mixture of nostalgia and self-loathing which characterised *West of Suez*, about the decaying colonial heritage of Britain. Osborne's later plays, however, lack that telling ambivalence towards the alienated man, so notable a feature of his early plays. The attacks against society are all-out slaughter; the nostalgia becomes sentimental. Sometimes both emotions are present, cheek by jowl, in the same play. In *The End of Me Old Cigar*, a slaughterous first act is followed by a sentimental second: and its production in 1974 at the Greenwich Theatre (as part of an Osborne season) had a poor critical reception, not an unusual fate for Osborne's plays, for many had received 'mixed' reviews, except that this time critical impatience seemed to give way before plain boredom.

Osborne's contribution to the theatre cannot be seen simply in terms of his plays. His influence particularly during the late 1950s and early 1960s was pervasive, but largely indirect. Few dramatists tried to mimic the Osborne style in the way in which Pinter was imitated. The success of *Look Back in Anger*, however, destroyed several inhibiting myths about plays: that the theatre had to be genteel, that heroes were stoical and lofty creatures, that audiences needed nice people with whom to identify. Even the recognised clumsiness of Osborne's plays were indirectly encouraging to other dramatists, for it seemed to prove that passion and dramatic substance mattered more than obedience to the rules. Other writers of the time were not likely to be so overawed by the complexity of writing plays, nor, with the example of Osborne's success, were they so likely to be deterred by the hopeless impracticability of finding managements to produce their works. Osborne also demonstrated that it was possible to write vivid and powerful speeches without making them sound verbally narcissistic. His background as an actor gave him an instinctive knowledge as to what lines would work in the theatre and which would not. He had also given the first telling expression in modern British theatre to the theme of social alienation.

Osborne's success also helped the theatre in one highly practical way. At the end of its first season, the English Stage Company was in dire financial straits. Brecht's *The Good Woman of Setzuan* had been a box-office disaster, partly because it coincided with the Russian invasion of Hungary which provoked more anti-communist feelings in Britain. Wycherley's *The Country Wife* (with Laurence Harvey and Joan Plowright) restored their bank balance to a proper equilibrium, but only at the expense of drawing the Royal Court away from its policy of encouraging new British writers. Without *Look Back in Anger*, the English Stage Company might never have been in the position which it acquired of being able to attract new writers: it would not have had the prestige, nor indeed the money, for *Look Back in Anger*, after a moderate beginning, became a box-office success, and was brought back to the theatre in the second season. The off-shoot income from *Look Back in Anger* (including the film) kept the English Stage Company solvent over the following years, enabling George Devine to tackle ever more ambitious programmes. Over the next seventeen years, from 1956 to 1973, the English Stage Company presented 273 productions, of which 221 were by contemporary writers, 178 by British ones. It acquired an international reputation. Among the authors it assisted were John Arden, Ann Jellicoe, N. F. Simpson, Arnold Wesker, Edward Bond and David Storey: its directors included Tony Richardson, John Dexter and William Gaskill, who took over from George Devine when he retired in 1965. The revival of post-war British theatre was substantially due to the group of writers and directors who gathered around George Devine; while the springboard from which the English Stage Company dived into the cold and treacherous waters of sponsoring new plays was *Look Back in Anger*.

In retrospect, the development of British theatres after 1956 seems astonishingly rapid: at the time, however, as the

Arts Council reports for the period indicate, it seemed desperately slow. The surface of the theatre during the late 1950s still seemed parched, but gradually the arid top-soil was scraped away to reveal not rocks, but springs. In 1957, the West End was still providing the familiar diet of light middle-class comedies (*Roar Like a Dove* and *Dear Delinquent*), farces from the French (*The Egg*), gentle revues (*At the Drop of a Hat*, *Share My Lettuce*) and comfortable musicals (*The Bells Are Ringing*). The temporary enthusiasm from Brecht during 1955–6 seemed to have died away, after Hungary, and such writers as Ionesco, Beckett and Adamov were still only cult enthusiasms. It would have taken a perceptive man to guess that so much energy and talent would emerge from the theatre during the next few years, from these surroundings, from that (almost) dead calm.

And yet the signs of a revival were there. In 1957, *The Entertainer* transferred from the Royal Court to the Palace Theatre, and the first play by another writer, less angry and more systematic than Osborne, Robert Bolt's *Flowering Cherry*, came to London from the Oxford Playhouse. Some financial burden on impresarios was raised in 1957, when Entertainments Tax was also abolished, the first sign (other than the slowly growing strength of the Arts Council) that the government was recognising the impoverished state of the theatre. In Coventry, the Belgrade Theatre was nearing completion and Bryan Bailey (like George Devine) announced his intention to encourage new playwrights. In London, a younger group of commercial impresarios was emerging, headed by Michael Codron and Donald Albery. There were also signs that the two honourable homes of Shakespeare-orientated theatre, the Old Vic and the Shakespeare Memorial Theatre at Stratford-upon-Avon, were enjoying new leases of life. John Gielgud struck up a powerful friendship and collaboration with the most inventive of the younger directors, Peter Brook, a partnership between the old theatrical world and the new which resulted in the Stratford production of *The Tempest*. At the Old Vic, John Neville was playing Hamlet, Derek Godfrey Titus Andronicus, Keith Michell Antony. Younger actors, in short, were testing themselves with fair success against the great classic roles. At the other Stratford (-atte-Bowe), Littlewood was experiencing the first traumas of success.

By 1958, it was not necessary to pore over these embryonic stirrings of life to wonder how many would hatch. It was a year when, quite suddenly, we seemed to have a number of new dramatists, working in different styles and genres, but each making interesting contributions. There was John Mortimer, with his two short ironic comedies, *The Dock Brief* and *What Shall We Tell Caroline?*; and N. F. Simpson, whose nonsense plays, *A Resounding Tinkle* and *The Hole*, were premièred at the Royal Court. Peter Shaffer's *Five Finger Exercise* achieved a sensible, first play run in the West End; luckier than Harold Pinter, whose first major play, *The Birthday Party*, received a rough and short welcome at Hammersmith, damned by most critics including Kenneth Tynan, but perceptively praised by Harold Hobson and afterwards earning a cult reputation. Arnold Wesker's *Chicken Soup with Barley* opened at the new Belgrade, Coventry, the first play in a trilogy about working-class social changes, starting in the Depression and ending with the mid-1950s. Shelagh Delaney's *A Taste of Honey* opened at Stratford-atte-Bowe, transferring to the West End, a startling enough achievement from a nineteen-year-old girl from Salford, which reflected the merits of this careful, sensitive study of a girl eager for life and resolutely enduring the troubles of mere existence. Joan Littlewood had now established the style for which as a director she became noted: the use of songs in *A Taste of Honey*, the jazz trio ramming home the new atmosphere of pop, the direct playing towards the audience, particularly well exploited by Avis Bunnage, one of the several remarkable new members of her casts. Littlewood began to stimulate a new tradition of British musicals, far removed from the Ruritanian splendours of Ivor Novello and the university charms of Sandy Wilson and Julian Slade. Her musicals were based upon rock and pop, on working-class scripts and librettos, written by Wolf Mankowitz (*Expresso Bongo*, 1958, and *Make Me an Offer*, 1959) or Frank Norman (*Fings Aint Wot They Used T'Be*, 1962), with music by, say, Lionel Bart.

The year 1959 was also a playwrights' year and another new theatre opened, the Mermaid, in London. The Mermaid was inspired, organised and almost physically built by its remarkable founder-director, Sir Bernard Miles, a much loved character actor. The Mermaid was lucky enough to start with that rarest of British phenomena, a hit musical, *Lock up your Daughters*, based upon Fielding's *Rape upon Rape*. The Royal Court presented two winning entries from an extraordinary New Plays competition, run by the *Observer* newspaper, Errol John's *Moon on a Rainbow Shawl* and John Arden's *Sergeant Musgrave's Dance*. Two intelligent dramatists of apparently stock 'naturalistic' plays emerged, with plays about the war: Beverley Cross's *One More River* and Willis Hall's *The Long, the Short and the Tall*, whose central character reminded many critics of Jimmy Porter. Hall later teamed up with the novelist Keith Waterhouse to become a highly successful partnership, with such plays as *Billy Liar* (1960), which ran the whole gauntlet of commercial achievement, becoming a film, the basis of a television series and a musical; *Celebration* (1961); and *Say Who You Are* (1965). Hall also adapted Billetdoux' telling comedy *Chin Chin* (1960) and (with Waterhouse) de Filippo's *Saturday, Sunday, Monday* (1973) for the National Theatre. There were new plays from recently recognised dramatists. Brendan Behan's *The Hostage* transferred to the West End from Stratford-atte-Bowe. If Osborne's *The World of Paul Slickey*, a musical about the sordid world of the press, was a disappointment at the Royal Court, N. F. Simpson's *One Way Pendulum* became an unexpected hit, the first British play of the Absurd to do so.

The trend continued for the next five years or so. In 1960, Robert Bolt and Harold Pinter had their first undoubted successes, *A Man for all Seasons* and *The Caretaker*. Lionel Bart produced a hit musical, *Oliver*. In 1961, four new theatres opened in the regions, at Guildford, Croydon, Nottingham and Chichester, while the Prince Charles Theatre (later to become a cinema) opened in London. Apart from two notable new plays from John Whiting and John Osborne, *The Devils* and *Luther*, there was an idiosyncratic comedy from J. P. Donleavy, *Fairy Tales of New York*, a novelist whose previous play *The Ginger Man* (1959) had failed to show the same rich command of dialogue and fantasy. Antony Newley's musical, *Stop the World, I Want to Get Off*, showed a welcome attempt to break away from the format of other musicals, particularly in its central character, played by Newley himself, who was a clown, a fall guy for modern industrial Britain. *Beyond the*

Fringe arrived in London from Oxbridge via Edinburgh, its satirical edge and free-association wit instantly making other intimate revues seem old-fashioned. In 1962, three new dramatists of serious comedies emerged, Giles Cooper (*Everything in the Garden*, 1962), Charles Dyer (*The Rattle of a Simple Man*) and David Turner (*Semi-Detached*). Edward Bond's first play, *The Pope's Wedding*, was staged for a single Sunday performance at the Royal Court.

If we added to this already lengthy list, the names of dramatists whose first London successes were achieved during the following three years (Bill Naughton, Frank Marcus, David Mercer, David Storey, Henry Livings, Joe Orton, James Saunders, Ann Jellicoe, Barry Reckord, Athol Fugard) or consider a selection of the outstanding productions during these years (*O, What a Lovely War!*, *Entertaining Mr Sloane*, *The Royal Hunt of the Sun*, *The Marat/Sade*, *The Homecoming*, *The Killing of Sister George*, *Armstrong's Last Goodnight*, *Inadmissible Evidence*), we can begin to realise the extraordinary transformation of British theatre within the eight or nine years from *Look Back in Anger*. Nor can we measure this change simply in terms of new writers, although it was perhaps a revolution led by dramatists. Two new 'national' companies had been formed. Peter Hall was appointed the artistic director of the Shakespeare Memorial Theatre in 1960 and immediately set about creating a company which could rival the heavily subsidised national companies abroad. He opened a London branch at the Aldwych Theatre, established a 'permanent' ensemble with a team of resident directors (including Peter Brook, John Barton and Michel Saint Denis) and caused the name of the company to be changed, to the Royal Shakespeare Company. A National Theatre company was also formed, under the leadership of Sir Laurence Olivier, which began its life at the Chichester Festival Theatre and took up a London residence in the transformed Old Vic while waiting for a new National Theatre to be built.

Public tastes too were changing. In 1960, the editor of the *Stage Year Book* pointed out with some surprise that Enid Bagnold's *The Last Joke* with Sir John Gielgud had been a disaster while Noël Coward's *Waiting in the Wings* could scarcely have been regarded as a success; while *The Caretaker* was a hit. Michael Codron, who presented *The Caretaker* commented that public tastes were surprisingly volatile. If Pinter's play had been presented a couple of months earlier, it would probably have been a complete failure. There was a sudden coming-together of fairly firm cultural traditions and a new desire for change and experiment. The mixture of old and new characterised the period. It partly explains why dramatists led the revival. After all, the theatre was still considered to be primarily a literary medium. Playwrights handed over their scripts to directors, who would then cast the plays accordingly. Later on, in the mid-1960s, this demarcation of duty started to be regarded as old-fashioned. There were attempts to alter it, by improvising plays, by experiments in group writing, by laying the emphasis not upon the written text but upon group work and sometimes by asserting that the true value of the theatre lay in its ability to present 'social' subjects, where the role of the writer was that of a reporter. In the early 1960s, the dramatist was still the first cause of a production: he was the architect, the actors and even the directors were the builders.

The situation of dramatists during this fertile period differed also from that in the years immediately after the war. In the early 1950s, there had been a marked division between the 'professional' dramatists, such as Rattigan and Coward, who possessed highly trained instincts for what was practical in the theatre, who knew how to phrase lines of dialogue and to organise the development of scenes, and those literary dramatists, such as Eliot and Ronald Duncan, who were intellectually more ambitious than their professional rivals but had derived their stagecraft at second and sometimes third hand. The dramatists of the late 1950s often seemed to combine good theatrical knowledge with intellectual ambitiousness. There were many actors among the writers, Osborne, Pinter, Charles Dyer, Henry Livings, Stephen Lewis (who wrote *Sparrers Can't Sing* for Joan Littlewood) and Alan Ayckbourn (whose first play, *Mr Whatnot*, was produced in 1964). None of them wished to lumber his fellow professionals with unspeakable lines. They knew the difference between good exits and bad ones. But they were also quick to absorb new ideas and a few could even distinguish between the trivial cult and the more profound movement. Other dramatists, lacking their practical stage experience, had the

opportunity through the Royal Court or the growing repertory movement to try out ideas without the old risk of costly
failure. 'New plays' seasons had replaced the old theatre
clubs. Most impresarios ran them, from Michael Codron and
Donald Albery at the Arts Theatre Club, to the nationals and
the few reps with studio theatres, to amateur companies,
such as Questors in Ealing, who had also built themselves a
new theatre which opened in 1964. Dramatists who were
neither actors nor products of new plays seasons, had probably received some dramatic experience in other media, for at
this time writers turned towards the stage from radio, films
and television. This range of practical experience and the
diversity of background led to a remarkable variety of ways
in which plays were written or conceived; which in turn provided a cross-fertilisation of interests among the writers
themselves in that they were prepared to borrow ideas
(sometimes technical ones, sometimes of themes and stories)
to see whether they could handle them equally well. Tradition and experiment, flexibility and richness: four attributes
of an epoch which was suddenly and surprisingly rich in
theatre. The leading dramatists of the day possessed them
and they nearly transformed British theatre.

Chapter 6

How the West End was (nearly) won: the playwrights of the early 1960s

The West End has traditionally provided two very valuable guides as to the merits of new plays, the tests of 'pleasure-popularity' and of 'exposure'. It is scarcely necessary nowadays to point out that these are not the only tests. Good plays are not invariably popular. For much of the nineteenth century, Shakespeare was regarded as the first nail in the bankrupt manager's coffin, and it was the reckless devotion of certain actors, coupled with the eloquence of some critics, which helped the public eventually to respond more favourably. But if Shakespeare's plays had not possessed emotional warmth, richness, variety, humour and sheer dramatic strength, no proselytising from enthusiasts could have persuaded audiences to come, year after year; and to that extent popularity not only indicates a deep human response to primary feelings but also acts as a useful check to the fervours of those who would like the public at large to think as they do. Enthusiastic reviews, as all press officers know, are helpful to the success of productions, but they do not guarantee hits; if, however, satisfied audiences tell their friends and a word-of-mouth enthusiasm spreads, then hits happen. The commercial value of good reviews is that they can provide that initial boost to productions which can carry them through the awkward first weeks before the swell of popular opinion gathers strength.

The West End, the heart of British commercial theatre, depends upon box-office successes, hence upon strong public responses to productions. All British theatres, even in the age of subsidies, require box-office support, but the difference between the subsidised theatres and West End ones in this respect is one of degree. The costs of launching a West End production in the late 1950s and early 1960s had continued to escalate; and so quick box-office returns were vital. Subsidised theatres can also plan regular changes of programme, perhaps on the repertory principle, with the result that managements are not so dependent upon the success of single productions. The total commercial reliance upon the box-office led, as we have seen, to many inhibitions, timidity in choice of plays, reliance upon stars, an unwillingness to challenge popular prejudices, an attachment to old genres such as mystery plays and the habit of prolonging hits endlessly. Agatha Christie's *The Mousetrap*, an average thriller with an astonishing capacity for survival, opened in 1952 and is still running in 1976. But, with all these faults accepted and taken for granted, the West End still provided the dramatists of the post-war theatre revival with two acid tests. Would their plays prove 'popular', away from the confines of the comparatively small-scale and assisted theatres which gave them their first airings? And would they survive that constant exposure, the chatting and tit-bits of conversation, which usually attended West End productions? Would the anger-and-after playwrights have any influence on the main body of British theatre at all?

The answer must be a qualified 'Yes'. There were three main areas of change, which I am calling the 'comedies of middle-class decline', 'Epics and documentaries' and 'nonsense plays'. Categories are always misleading, unless they are recognised to be just rough and ready ways of sorting out complicated subjects. Good dramatists, to begin with, resist categorising, in that their work can often be convincingly considered from different angles. Changes were also taking place in British theatre which made only a marginal impact on West End theatre: local documentaries and perhaps 'working-class' drama, a category which I have resisted because, first, the West End has never been so solidly against working-class plays as its popular image would lead one to suspect (*Love on the Dole* 1935 and *Hobson's Choice* 1915 are examples) and therefore the presence of similar examples in the 1960s was a change in degree but not of kind, and, second, the so-called 'kitchen-sink' dramatists who might be regarded as belonging to a working-class genre were more often associated with such writers as Harold Pinter and Samuel Beckett. One particular area of change, Brecht's influence, will be left to another chapter, but his ghostly presence must be temporarily assumed to drift from shoulder to shoulder, from study to rehearsal room, in this haunted theatrical house.

1   Comedies of middle-class decline

Many comedies after the war had shown middle-class families in difficulties, either financial ones (as in Langley's *Little Lambs Eat Ivy*), marital ones or generation squabbles (as in Vernon Sylvaine's *As Long as They're Happy*). These problems, however, could be solved (and usually were) and they did not challenge the basis of middle-class life. The comedies of middle-class decline were not radical in the sense that they attacked the bourgeoisie from the standpoint (say) of a Brechtian Marxist, but they did present a picture of seedy snobbery, of sexual hypocrisy and of social failure unredeemed by idealism. In the introduction to his 1970 collection, *Five Plays*, John Mortimer wrote about his comedies, written in the late 1950s and early 1960s:

> The Macmillan era was a time for low comedy in high
> places. Pre-war attitudes lingered. The middle-aged
> formed hopeless and isolated pockets of resistance, in law-
> courts and seaside hotels, and private schools.... So I have
> attempted in these comedies to chart the tottering course
> of the British middle-classes in decline....

This genre began gently, but acquired an increasing toughness and ability to cut to the quick as the years went by. Its origins can perhaps be traced to the light satire of the mid-1950s, particularly on radio. The BBC had run two remarkably successful series which were, in appearance, 'documentaries' and, at heart, comedies of manners: the *How To...* series, with Stephen Potter and Joyce Grenfell, and the *Hilda Tablet* programmes, written by Henry Reed and directed by Douglas Cleverdon. These programmes were funny, very observant and affectionate even towards the objects of their civilised malice; but in the theatre, the affection of such programmes came to be replaced by a restrained bitterness. John Mortimer, a barrister by professional training, and Giles Cooper won their reputations on radio: their work

for the theatre retained the intimacy, verbal irony and conversational quality of that medium. They also shared the
technical problems caused by changing from one medium to
another. Having started by writing half-hour plays for radio,
with the occasional sketch for *Monday Night at Eight*, they had
to extend the scale of their writing to suit the stage.

Mortimer's *Dock Brief* (produced on radio in 1957) formed
one half of a stage double-bill with a short play for the
theatre, *What Shall We Tell Caroline?* Both plays were good-
humoured studies of middle-class failures. The most defeated of all barristers in *Dock Brief*, who has never had a case
in his life, was selected at random to defend a self-confessed
murderer. He makes elaborate plans for the defence, hoping
to win an Indian Summer reputation, but he dries up in
court, tongue-tied before the Majesty of the Law. His client
secures an unexpected acquittal on the grounds of inadequ-
ate representation. *What Shall We Tell Caroline?* was set in a
prep school, in a pretend *ménage à trois* situation, where the
wife of a headmaster spends so much time flirting with an
assistant master without going to bed with him that she fails
to notice that her daughter, Caroline, has grown up.
Caroline no longer requires the false security of a preserved
marriage, the basis on which all the other sexual games depend.

When Mortimer tried to extend the limits of his one-act
plays, to tackle full-length plays with wider moral themes
and greater diversity of characters, he ran into difficulties.
His characters needed to 'grow' in size and complexity: the
neat vignettes of half-hour plays weren't suitable. This meant
that he could not treat them simply as stock types, adopting a
satirist's casual arrogance towards them: he needed to understand them and perhaps to feel with them as much as
against them. In *The Wrong Side of the Park*, 1960, he again
tackles an enclosed family situation, where fantasies abound:
the wife remembers her first husband with a false sexual
nostalgia, while her second husband buries himself in work,
and the general atmosphere of disillusion causes them all to
sink still further beneath the rising cost of living. *Two Stars for
Comfort* (1962) is set in a riverside pub, where the landlord is
so keen to cheer everyone up that he womanises all the
female waifs and nearly kills his barman by urging him to

forestall age and a dicky heart by taking too much exercise. Mortimer, whose dialogue, witty, literate and knowledgeable, was always regarded as an asset, seemed in these plays to be trying to extend the scale of his work simply by writing more words: the speeches are longer, the jokes within them a little more contorted, with the result that the characters lose the sharp definition of the earlier plays without gaining in emotional warmth. His study of judicial sadistry, *The Judge* (1967), was a rather predictable analysis; and, like his other plays, it seemed to sacrifice emotional force and moral insight to a pat sketching of sinister foibles. It was as if the cartoonist had taken to painting in oils without rethinking his craft. The exception to this rough rule was his personal account of his youth, *A Voyage Round My Father* (written for radio in 1963, subsequently staged in 1970), where his portrait of a blind barrister, his father, who refuses to admit his blindness is written with a gently stressed and deeply felt emotion.

Giles Cooper possessed a wit more acid than Mortimer's, was more moralistic and terser in his blanket condemnations. In *Everything in the Garden* (1962), he described how a respectable wife of a husband who earns just too little to maintain his family in a true suburban style, takes to prostitution to raise the household income, only to discover that her neighbours have joined the same profession. *Everything in the Garden* suffered from having no clear ending. Two were tried out before the production transferred from the Arts Theatre Club to the West End. In a sense, Cooper's vision of mankind was too bleak to achieve surprise, happy or even definite endings. Once his theme had been stated, that greed makes prostitutes of us all or that (as in *Happy Family*, 1966) childhood games can be prolonged endlessly into adult life, there seemed to be no possible change or progression. Matters can only go from bad to worse.

Cooper helped to focus the general attack upon the declining middle classes upon one specific theme, the sexual hypocrisies. This became a familiar topic with dramatists, who either shared Cooper's rather grim puritanism or else seized on the contrast between surface respectability and inner lechery with a wild delight. Frank Marcus was the most sophisticated of these writers, carrying into his skills a wide technical knowledge of European drama, of Molnar's plays and Schnitzler's, of the Viennese and Paris schools of inter-war bourgeois/sexual drama. Marcus's *The Formation Dancers* (1964), about the changing relationships between two men and two women, has the formal delight of Schnitzler's *Reigen* (which Marcus once directed), while *Cleo* (1965, Bristol) about a footloose, innocent (though not celibate) young girl, is structurally similar to Schnitzler's *Anatol*. Marcus was also not so hypnotised by sexual hypocrisy that he could not see the wider social implications. The two lesbians in *The Killing of Sister George* (1965) are made vulnerable by their relation-ship. June Buckridge, an actress on a long-lasting BBC serial, is sacked from her job as 'Sister George' because her lesbian habits (such as attacking two nuns outside Broadcasting House) are bringing the institution into disrepute. The ten-sion between respectability and sexual longings produces unlikely sacrificial lambs.

Marcus rarely attempts to shock in his comedies: it would destroy the balance of his writing. Joe Orton, on the other hand, retained a child-like enjoyment in 'shocks', which is perhaps best illustrated by his sketch in *Oh! Calcutta!* (1969) about the sexual behaviour of a tea-bound family in the Home Counties: 'I couldn't come, Eliza, so I pee-ed up your yoni.' Such lines in the early 1960s would have been banned by the Lord Chamberlain, but Orton under the grip of cen-sorship was still capable of shocking, outraging but also il-luminating grey areas of inhibition in a manner unmatched by his contemporaries.

He was a writer of exuberant sexual farces. His characters are like McGill cartoons, in bright primary colours, with bulging fantasies and spouting gags which seem almost to be surrounded by bubbles. His first play in London, *Entertaining Mr Sloane* (1964), was somewhat in Cooper's vein, but less moralistic and more comically hard-hearted. A brother and sister look after a young ruffian, Mr Sloane, apparently out of the goodness of their hearts and because they want to let a room; but they both fancy him and their sexual interests en-courage them to overlook his occasional crimes, such as beating up and killing their father. His criminal activities in fact help them to gain power over him, so that they arrange to share him on a monthly basis.

Entertaining Mr Sloane was regarded as a 'black' comedy, although its farcical elements (particularly in the dialogue) are obviously present. There were other writers of black comedies, catching on to this combination of sexual 'daring' (defying taboos and so on) and implying violence behind locked doors. Johnny Speight was one, with his play *The Knackers Yard* (1962) about a cane fetishist and a landlady, James Broom Lynne, another, with his study of a middle-aged Boy Scout (in *The Trigon*, 1962) and Bill McIlwraith, a third, whose *The Anniversary* dealt with the desperate attempts of a family of young men to escape from the domination of their mother. None of these writers, however, followed Orton into a love of preposterously wild and complicated stories, which succeeded both in sending up dramatic genres (detective stories in *Loot*, Feydeau farces in *What the Butler Saw*) and in being high comedies whose superficial absurdity concealed telling observations of reality.

As a genre, however, the comedies of middle-class decline had both the merits and defects of some Restoration comedies of manners. The characters were often rigidly conceived, often as sexual stock-types: they were lesbians, poofs, sadists, masochists, knicker-lovers or pederasts, with the result that there was little capacity for internal change and the fun (and drama) eventually derived from the surface wit. The stories were often one-dimensional. Marcus must be exonerated from this general criticism, for his plays were rarely limited to sexual horseplay, and so must Orton, who used caricature like a card-sharp, tossing the pasteboard figures from hand to hand, in an extraordinary display of farcical skill. The genre produced some very skilful, popular but also somewhat contrived comedies of sexual manners, such as two based upon Iris Murdoch novels, *A Severed Head* (1963) and *The Italian Girl* (1968); together with David Turner's farce about Midlands greed, *Semi-Detached* (1962).

These comedies cut away the cant and cosinesses which surrounded the middle-class comedies of the early 1950s. They were puritanically thorough in scouring away the cosmetics which disguised the horrors of family life, and, like many puritans, they went too far until the mere mention of Boy Scouts or punishment evoked an immediate chuckle of sexual recognition. They also loosened the bonds of gentility which had constricted the West End, so that, say, Charles Dyer's two sensitive comedies, *The Rattle of a Simple Man* (1962) and *Staircase* (1967) are clear and not prim studies of two evolving relationships, between a timid man in London for the Cup Final and the whore he visits having *lost* a bet, and between two homosexual barbers. The degree of sympathy which Dyer brought to his characters only served to highlight the scathing rigidity with which middle-class deviants were generally treated, thus indicating certain limitations in the way in which dramatists considered the 'middle classes'.

Mortimer meant by 'middle class' the isolated pockets of resistance to change, the shabby genteel, the boarding houses and tatty private schools. Others meant prim families perching precariously on their frustrations. It could be argued, however, that, first, the dramatists had failed to identify the new middle classes (such as the growing band of property developers), had second, failed to ask what role if any the middle classes could play in society, were suffering from double standards in that rich sexual deviations were treated scathingly and poor ones defended, and had lastly forgotten to enquire whether the blanket phrase, middle classes, could any longer be used to cover (and damn) so many different kinds of people and life styles. The targets for comedy were too easy, the questions raised too blurred and the results were sometimes as mechanical as the pro-middle-class comedies which they replaced.

2   Epics and documentaries

The 'well-made play' formulae helped rather than hindered the writers associated with comedies of middle-class decline. A single drawing-room set, for example, could become a cartoon of what they were trying to satirise. The Unities, from Scribe onwards, have always had the effect of cramming action and information into small spaces, physical and in time, which helps the organised confusions of farce writers. Sometimes, these writers seemed to draw the constrictions still tighter around them for comfort, preferring the concentration provided by the well-made play to the risks of diffusion presented by other dramatic approaches. It was also easier to encourage impresarios to present single-set, small-cast, proscenium-arch plays in the West End, and so the comedies of middle-class decline, often tried out at the Arts Theatre Club before transfer, made an immediate impact on the commercial theatre.

Other writers, however, sought a more expansive approach and so deliberately broke the the well-made play rules. During this period, they did so with some sophistication, assisted by the example of Brecht but without any slavish attachment to his methods. Both Robert Bolt and Peter Shaffer started by writing well-made plays, dramas not comedies. Bolt's *Flowering Cherry* (1957) obeys the Unities, has a central character, Jim Cherry, who dies at the Crisis, and is naturalistic in the sense that its six characters are believable, if rather 'stock', creations, talking in the language of everyday life. Peter Shaffer's first West End success, *Five Finger Exercise* (1958), concerned the arrival of a German tutor into an English middle-class family: he provides, despite his attempts at detachment, a catalyst for the various emotional tensions in the household. Both writers were thus capable of writing successful plays, according to the standards of the mid-1950s.

But neither was satisfied with these standards. Bolt, a teacher and a historian, wished to tackle historical themes, often in a vein of moral (perhaps moralistic) seriousness: he was also attracted to allegory. In *A Man for All Seasons* (written for radio in 1954, staged in 1960), he took as subject the life of Sir Thomas More, whose discreet, saintly idealism contrasts with the casual, good-humoured but eventually cruel pragmatism of the Common Man. The Common Man (as Narrator) quotes from twentieth-century texts to illustrate the sixteenth-century story and takes part in the action, upon which he is commenting. He is More's Executioner. By using the Common Man in this way, Bolt dispensed with the Unities of Time and Place; and also prevented too close an identification with More, who was played in London by that most gently commanding of actors, Paul Scofield. The result is almost a shock to the audience's feelings, for structurally they are encouraged to watch the story through the eyes of the Common Man (their ally), whom they must finally morally reject as More's Murderer, the agent of a regal decree.

Peter Shaffer also broke away from the well-made play to tackle a historical subject on an epic scale. *The Royal Hunt of the Sun* (1964), an account of the conquest of the Inca Empire in Peru by a handful of Spanish mercenaries, has a linking narrator, an old man recalling the past. This technique, almost a development of the old 'flashbacks', provided a focal point against which the details of the campaign could be assessed, and it could also be used to bridge awkward gaps in the story which would otherwise have needed scenes to fill. But Shaffer, writing for the new National Theatre Company and the new Chichester Festival Theatre with its large thrust stage, was determined to tackle his subject in a more ambitious style than Bolt had chosen in *A Man for All Seasons*. Shaffer was also working with John Dexter, a director who ranks with Peter Brook in his awareness of the possible visual impact of a production. Shaffer and Dexter aimed for 'a kind of total theatre, involving not only words but rites, mimes, masks and magics'. 'The text cries for illustration. It is a director's piece, a pantomimist's piece, a musician's piece, a designer's piece and, of course, an actor's piece, almost as much as it is an author's' (Peter Shaffer, preface, *The Royal Hunt of the Sun*). The National Theatre Company revelled in the play, not only the principals (such as Robert Stephens's athletic god-king Atahualpa and Colin Blakely's dour, grim and spiritually destroyed Pizarro), but also lesser members of a larger cast. *The Royal Hunt of the Sun* gave the opportunity for a fresh flamboyance, in, say, the mime scenes of the Great Ascent of the Andes and in its use of the glowing central image, the Inca Sun which shrivelled and grew black as the gold from the empire piled up in Pizarro's small room.

In such plays, Bolt and Shaffer showed their ability to absorb some Brechtian techniques, and some from Antonin Artaud who had demanded a theatre of mime, ritual and inarticulate cries. Both writers preserved features of the well-made plays, a definite crisis, and strong conflicts between two characters who (like Pentheus and Dionysus in Euripides' *The Bacchae*) represent opposing forces, sometimes moral, sometimes super-moral in the sense that they were beyond normal ethics but represented almost principles of life. Such conflicts were represented (in Bolt's plays) by More and the Common

Man or between the principals in *The Tiger and the Horse* (1960) whose title illustrates the opposition, deriving from Blake's maxim, 'The tigers of wrath are wiser than the horses of instruction.' In Shaffer's plays, the opposing sides might be Atahualpa and Pizarro, or Mark and Gideon in *The Battle of Shrivings* (1970), or Martin Dysart and Alan Strang in *Equus* (1973).

Bolt and Shaffer maintained a fair and careful balance between the opposing sides, as it was necessary for them technically to do, for the crisis would probably represent the conquest of one side over the other and a crisis must not be anticipated without giving away the story. But it might be fair to add perhaps that in these conflicts 'romantic' attitudes usually prevailed, at least on an emotional level. Atahualpa might be killed, but Pizarro the cynic suffered the more prolonged and terrible fate. John Bowen, the dramatist, once pointed out after a production of *Disorderly Women* (his version of *The Bacchae*) that the rivalry between Pentheus, the 'rational' man, and Dionysus, the god of intoxication and wine, was central to modern drama and that, among the members of his cast, most were pro-Dionysus and anti-Pentheus. Rational, cold, 'civilised' and 'pragmatic' men were proved to be more deluded than the idealistic, passionate, instinctive or sometimes just intoxicated ones. The passionate, confused adolescent in *Equus* has more vitality and strength than the analyst Dysart whose very methods seek to destroy the irrational. Civilisation meant concrete and sterile calm: primitive emotions were life-giving, god-centred and joyful, even in acts of cruelty.

Bolt and Shaffer were also verbally precise and restrained writers, not enjoying the literary conceits of Fry and others. John Arden, however, who also tackled epic subjects and themes, delighted in the power of language and was more influenced than the others, by Brecht. He chose once more broad conflicts as a method of welding diverse material into a play, but he brought to the genre an enthusiasm for ballads, dialects, little poems and ancient maxims, which were partly intended to particularise historical situations. *Sergeant Musgrave's Dance* (1959), his first play to attract much attention, was a parable against war. Four deserters from an army return to a snowbound colliery town, where they intend to execute leading citizens for bourgeois war crimes. Their revenge fails because the deserters quarrel amongst themselves. Arden used black humour, ballads, Brechtian analysis and scenes almost constructed on Jacobean models to establish a boisterously bitter mood, which has characterised at least one side of his subsequently prolific writing career.

His ambitious use of language is perhaps best demonstrated by *Armstrong's Last Goodnight* (1964), set in sixteenth-century Scotland, where King James in Edinburgh was trying to establish his authority over the border barons, notably the Armstrongs of Gilnockie. Arden demonstrated that language was part of this battle. He 'invented' a dialect of medieval Scots (based on the poems of Dunbar and Henrysson) so broad that it risked being incomprehensible to modern audiences: and then went still further, by inventing a dialect of this dialect, to contrast Armstrong's language (in the wild regions) with that of Lindsay, the King's representative. It was an astonishing feat and perhaps the most surprising part of it was not that audiences found the language difficult to follow but that it was less formidable to comprehend in the theatre than the text would suggest. The superb balancing performances (at the National Theatre's production) of Albert Finney as Armstrong and Robert Stephens as Lindsay helped to make the language comprehensible, but the rapid development of the story also sustained the dramatic flow, covering the awkward passages. Arden saw the story as an account of the difficult process of centralising a society under one government, a theme appropriate both to the emerging countries of Africa (such as Zaire), which inspired Arden, and to Britain, which was politically facing growing demands for the devolution of power.

Armstrong's Last Goodnight also illustrated (with Whiting's *The Devils*, *The Royal Hunt of the Sun* and Peter Brook's production of Peter Weiss's *The Marat/Sade*) the growing freedom with which dramatists were using stage areas. In *Armstrong's Last Goodnight*, the 'up left' section of the stage represented King James's court in Edinburgh, the 'up right' area was Armstrong's border castle, while the space between represented an immense physical and cultural gap. By such use of the stage, language, linking ballads and narratives, Arden was able to encompass themes (even the growth of Arthurian Britain in *The Island of the Mighty*) which previous dramatists would have regarded as intractable. But such plays required companies trained in group mime, movement, singing and dancing, as well as the more conventional skills of acting; and in the early 1950s such troupes were rare indeed. The growth of 'permanent' companies in Britain, although they were never permanent in the sense that some East European teams were permanent, began most noticeably in the late 1950s, after the visit of the Berliner Ensemble in 1956, and Shaffer and Arden benefited from the new National Theatre Company, just as Whiting was commissioned to write *The Devils* for the Royal Shakespeare Company.

The first director after the war (apart from Sir Barry Jackson) to insist upon permanent companies as the necessary pre-requisite for epic and documentary plays was Joan Littlewood, who established the Theatre Workshop company in 1945, with the poet-dramatist, Ewan MacColl. They started with a small, impoverished touring company, travelling around small towns in the North of England. MacColl wrote documentary plays (with ballads) about such subjects as nuclear warfare (*Uranium 235*, 1952), while Littlewood's influence was particularly felt with her versions of 'classic' plays and novels: *Arden of Faversham* (1954) and *The Good Soldier Schweik* (1954)—the first Theatre Workshop production to transfer to the West End. In 1953, Littlewood and MacColl took over a run-down music hall, the Theatre Royal, Stratford-atte-Bowe, in the East End of London. Her company was a 'collective', though run by a benevolent dictator, the first of many to emerge in the next twenty years. Actors, stage-hands, writers, directors and musicians shared and shared alike, splitting up packets of cigarettes when times were bad and dodging the council inspectors who insisted that the Theatre Workshop was evading by-laws. This company of equals produced an astonishing range of new actors (among them Harry H. Corbett, Roy Kinnear, Murray Melvin, Barbara Ferris, Victor Spinetti, Brian Murphy and Avis Bunnage), but they also expressed a team comradeship which came over to the audience with a boisterous friendliness (sometimes intimidatingly so).

This comradeship enabled Joan Littlewood to tackle cer-

tain themes, particularly naturalistic studies of whole communities, which required immaculate ensemble playing.
Alun Owen's *Progress to the Park* (1958) was one such play,
based on his knowledge of Liverpool; *Sparrers Can't Sing* by
Stephen Lewis, an actor in her company, was another, set in
Stepney. Littlewood's use of neighbourhood backgrounds
(assisted by the designer John Bury) was an attractive feature
of the Cockney musicals (*Make Me an Offer* and *Fings Aint Wot
They Used T'Be*), while an excessive jollity took some of the
tension away from Behan's *The Hostage*. Littlewood's productions usually had a basis in naturalism, which was particularly evident in the way in which she stressed the relationships between the characters on stage, a constant commentary on the development of community lives. When, say, Barbara Ferris came on stage in *Sparrers Can't Sing*, the audience
was able to guess that she was the sister of so-and-so, the
daughter, grand-daughter, girlfriend and rival of others. The
actors conveyed the working patterns of lives, and Littlewood supplied in her programmes factual information
about areas, such as the ethnic distribution of population in
Liverpool. If the basis of her productions was this kind of
documentary realism, it did not prevent her from tackling
certain subjects in a non-naturalistic way. A documentary
musical about the First World War, *O, What a Lovely War!*
(1963), using period songs and anecdotes compiled by
Charles Chilton, was set within the framework of a pierrot
show, the grim statistics of war contrasting with the pom-
pom costumes and jingoistic lyrics; while, on a lighter level,
Mrs Wilson's Diary (1967) was a musical satire, based on a
series in the satirical magazine *Private Eye*, treating the private
life of the Prime Minister, Harold Wilson, and members of
the government, with a cartoon disrespect.

Littlewood's company faced two main problems. Its very
success, coupled with West End transfers, caused the original
group and its successors to break up. Joan Littlewood left
Stratford-atte-Bowe in despair in 1961, fearing that a permanent company in Britain was almost an impossibility, for her
casts were always being lured away to the richer pastures of
the West End and films. The second problem was that when
the company did stabilise temporarily, an inbred bonhomie
seemed to reign, spilling over from the stage into the foyer

and the surrounding bars. Littlewood was an exceptionally tough but kind nurse of talent: only George Devine at the Royal Court had a similar record for discovering and nurturing new writers, actors and even composers of musicals. Alun Owen, Shelagh Delaney, Brendan Behan, Frank Norman and Thomas Murphy were among the writers, Lionel Bart one composer; but very often, away from the atmosphere of her Theatre Workshop, they seemed to be hankering back to their home at Stratford, a phenomenon which, though touching in its way, may have prevented their growth as artists.

The example at Stratford encouraged the growth of local 'documentaries' in Britain. Littlewood's own essays in this field (such as *O, What a Lovely War!*) provided a useful half-way house between ordinary plays and dramatised documentaries (such as those of Piscator and of the Living Newspaper in the United States during the 1930s). For the growing regional repertory theatre movement in the 1960s, the local documentaries provided a means of establishing a theatre's identity as part of a town or region, without losing its function as a theatre. At Stoke-on-Trent, Stephen Joseph and Peter Cheeseman began a small 'theatre-in-the-round' in 1962, within the shell of a disused cinema. Cheeseman, who eventually took over from Joseph, was particularly concerned to ensure that his theatre would reflect life in Stoke. He incorporated writers on to his staff, such as Peter Terson, and encouraged the whole company to research into the behaviour of the town where they were resident. The first result of the local documentary movement was to draw in a range of working-class themes which had previously been untapped. If we compare the plays of Arnold Wesker and Bernard Kops, 'working-class' dramatists of the late 1950s, with the plays of Peter Terson and Alan Plater, from the 1960s, the impression is strongly that the first two writers are writing from personal views and experiences whereas the second two are taking a deliberately more 'objective' stance. Wesker wrote plays with strong central characters whose individual problems represented those of the community. Such characters were Ronnie Kahn in *Chicken Soup with Barley* or Beatie in *Roots* or even Pip, the middle-class recruit who organises a revolt in the ranks in *Chips with Everything* (1962) and then rats on his new followers. This method was successful up to a point but it meant that the diversity of life had to be channelled through one man's apprehension of it. Because Terson worked with two main companies, Cheeseman's at Stoke and the National Youth Theatre, he was able to write for a group of people, whose identities he often knew, providing many parts, and was not tempted to limit himself to one or two. In plays such as *Zigger Zagger* (1967) and *The Apprentices* (1968), Terson tackled themes of football enthusiasm and local factory life which involved large casts, many detailed portraits of individual characters and a sense for the rhythm of working lives.

Peter Cheeseman, with or without the help of Terson, concentrated on subjects connected with Stoke. His yearly programmes included adaptations from novels by Arnold Bennett and other writers associated with Stoke and the pottery towns, dramatisations of such subjects as the building of the North Staffordshire railway (*The Knotty*, 1969), the local reorganisation of six towns into one city (*Six into One*, 1970) and a local industrial dispute (*The Fight for Shelton Bar*, 1974). His example was imitated in local theatres around the country, at the Hull Arts Centre, at Bolton and Bristol, and at Newcastle, where Alan Plater staged a coalmining documentary, *Close the Coalhouse Door*, which transferred briefly to the West End. The techniques of these documentaries, short naturalistic scenes, company teamwork, and avoidance of central 'heroes', ballads, songs and music derived (often at second and third hand) from the plays staged at Joan Littlewood's Theatre Workshop, particularly in the years from 1955 to 1961. This genre, which became particularly popular in the late 1960s, remains Littlewood's great contribution to British theatre.

3 Nonsense plays

Both the comedies of middle-class decline and the epic and documentary movements were, by and large, rationally conceived and developed. Even when writing plays about sensible men who misunderstand the force of irrationality, dramatists in Britain tended to write sensible, logical plays like

Equus. On the continent, however, there had been since the early years of the century a movement which attacked rationality itself, order in art and society, scientism and logic. In 1896, W. B. Yeats saw Alfred Jarry's *Ubu Roi* and trembled at the impact which such a 'barbaric' play could have upon Western civilisation. 'After us…' he wrote, 'the Dark Gods!' *Ubu Roi* was a clown play, with a monstrous central character, Ubu, who represented greed and the love of power, and kept his conscience in a suitcase. Jarry's main targets included industrialisation, science, falsely logical thinking, the Church and most forms of established authority. He once wrote a mock-scientific article, *How To Construct a Time Machine*, which was taken seriously by some; and founded the mock academy of Pataphysics. After the First World War, the followers of Jarry developed Dadaism, an attack on all forms of rational thinking. The world itself, according to the Dadaists, was the result of random happenings, with no order or pattern: they therefore constructed deliberately 'random' works.

This general approach split into two directions in the inter-war years, and re-emerged after the Second World War. The first trend was towards 'chance' art, represented at the beginning by (say) Tristan Tzara cutting up a Shakespeare sonnet, tossing the individual words into a hat and drawing them out at random. In the 1950s, chance acquired mystical connotations. American composers such as John Cage and Christian Wolff tried deliberately to get rid of the organising influence of their minds and training as composers, so that they could hear what random sounds might provide. Various methods were tried for achieving randomness, from dice-throwing to photographing the stars and placing notes on a sheet of paper where the stars appeared. The second trend emerged from this movement, for it was discovered that apparently random associations, say, between two images, might nevertheless contain a strong emotional force. Thus, surrealism was born. The Theatre of the Absurd (as Martin Esslin termed it) derived from surrealism in main, although it had other facets. The word, Absurd, could mean the serious argument that the universe itself was 'absurd', since God did not exist and thus the universe lacked an ordering principle. Or it could mean a theatrical attempt to capture the non-

1950s (British) Musical

...ad Days by Dorothy Reynolds and Julian Slade: June 1954. Produced by
...nis Carey, with Alan Dobie (The Tramp), Eleanor Drew (Jane) and John
...rner (Timothy), at the Bristol Old Vic.

2 · *1950s (British) Revolt*

Look Back in Anger by John Osborne: May 1956. Directed by Tony Richardso
with Kenneth Haigh, Alan Bates and Mary Ure.

3 *Theatre Design in the early 1960s*

The interior of the Chichester Festival Theatre, which opened in 1962. It was the first major 'open-stage' theatre in Britain, and its design was influenced by the Festival Theatre at Stratford, Ontario.

4   *The RSC in the early 1960s*

Troilus and Cressida, directed by Peter Hall, with Michael Hordern (Ulysses
Peter McEnery (Patroclus) and Patrick Allen (Achilles) at the Shakespear
Memorial Theatre, Stratford-upon-Avon.

sense of dreams. Or it could mean something like the Theatre of Cruelty, proposed by Antonin Artaud, 'where violent physical images pulverise, mesmerise the audience's sensibilities, caught in the drama as if in a vortex of higher forces', these forces being partly those of man's unconscious, with its nightmarish aspirations.

Britain was a late developer in the Theatre of the Absurd. W. H. Auden and Christopher Isherwood's *The Ascent of F6* (1937) borrowed some ideas from the Absurdist movement, but was mainly a rational allegory, with scenes constructed in styles from Shakespeare to Coward. Nor, even in Paris, did a wide range of writers emerge in this genre until after the Second World War, despite the earlier attempts of Picasso and Cocteau. In the 1950s, however, there were many Absurdist writers in Paris, among them Eugène Ionesco, Arthur Adamov and Armand Salacrou. In Britain, the first Absurdist plays emerged during the late 1950s and they were strongly influenced by radio comedy shows, particularly the Goons. The cheerful nonsense tradition was thus stronger in Britain than the strictly Absurdist plays, which had philosophical and psychological over- and under-tones. This difference is illustrated by the contrast between Ionesco and N. F. Simpson. Ionesco's *Rhinoceros* and *Amédée* are moral allegories, which use dreamlike nonsensical situations to establish moral points which are also insights into human nature. *Rhinoceros* (performed at the Royal Court in 1960 with Sir Laurence Olivier in the main part of Berenger) concerns an ordinary man living in a country where other men are gradually turning into rhinoceroses. On a literal plane, the story is absurd, but as an allegory it could be applied to those countries where violent militants take over. *Amédée* is about a growing sense of guilt, represented by an expanding corpse in a bedroom.

Ionesco's plays are thus often parables. But N. F. Simpson simply enjoyed nonsensical ideas. He delighted in *non sequiturs*, in false paradoxes, in taking metaphors seriously and showing how they could be literally achieved. The principal characters in *A Resounding Tinkle* (1957) are called the Paradockses, an eccentric suburban couple who keep an elephant as a pet, but want to exchange it for something smaller, such as a snake. In *One Way Pendulum* (1959), he again kept to a suburban situation, where the contrast between the living-room set and what went on in it (the construction of the Old Bailey) was bizarre enough to provide the necessary comic tension between normality and the fantastic possibilities of hobbies run wild. *The Cresta Run* (1965) was less successful in that the initial situation (a spy story) was extraordinary in itself: therefore, the tension did not exist.

Other writers followed Simpson into the genre of nonsense plays, among them Spike Milligan (a member of the original Goon team), John Antrobus and (later) John Grillo. Milligan's first plays, *Oblomov*, *Son of Oblomov* and *The Bed-Sitting-Room* in which he also starred were very successful in the West End in 1964 and 1965. A more serious, Ionesco-like version of Absurdist drama was shown by Barry Bermange, whose first main play, *No Quarter* (1964) concerns a fat man and a quiet man seeking shelter in a collapsing hotel: in some respects, the sense of cosmic anxiety in Bermange's plays is closer to the European models (not only Ionesco, but also Boris Vian and Max Frisch) than any other British playwright. James Saunders provided his own form of serious 'absurdity' in such plays as *Next Time I'll Sing to You* (1963), which is preoccupied with the lack of contact and understanding between men: similar to the themes of Pirandello and Adamov. By 1965, the cheerful nonsense of Simpson had become somewhat old fashioned. The Happenings movement had started, introducing the chance element into British drama, while the Theatre of Cruelty season had been staged at the LAMDA theatre club, an experimental event which proved to have great consequences for subsequent trends in the theatre. The good-humour had gone and in its place, a new ambitiousness, a pretentiousness perhaps, had taken over.

These three groups each provided West End successes and the impresarios who were preceptive enough to recognise the changes which were taking place began to prosper from them. Michael Codron and Donald Albery are examples. Within the ferment of change, however, it is scarcely surprising that many of the dramatists mentioned seemed not to be quite in control of their crafts. They aimed high and, more often than not, missed the targets. One dramatist, however, succeeded both in being (within strict limits) 'experimental' and in refining the techniques thus discovered into a highly controlled art form.

Harold Pinter, like Osborne, was originally a professional actor, working under the name David Baron. In the early 1950s, he went to the Central School of Speech and Drama, and afterwards toured with two great barnstorming actors, Sir Donald Wolfit and his Irish equivalent, Anew McMaster. He also appeared at reps and on television. On his actor's sensitivity and training, many of his writing techniques depend. On one level, his plays are conventional. They normally take place in box sets, have not only curtains after acts but also curtain lines, and many scenes reveal the shadowy outlines of stock 'mystery' plays from the early 1950s. The interrogation scenes from detective stories are transformed in Pinter's hands to the friendly-menacing baitings of (say) Stanley by Goldberg and McCann in *The Birthday Party* (1958) or of Davies by Mick in *The Caretaker* (1960). The soliloquy confessions of drawing-room dramas become such speeches as the hesitant reminiscences of Aston in *The Caretaker* where he describes (at the end of Act Two, the traditional place for curtain confessions) that he has undergone shock treatment at a mental hospital. The crisis decisions of well-made plays are changed into the final rejection of Davies at the end of *The Caretaker* or the surprising choice of Ruth, in *The Homecoming* (1965) not to return with her husband to the United States but to stay with a clutch of men wishing to use her as a family whore. Pinter's plays reveal careful evolution from old familiar forms to new ones, and to appreciate the different elements in the metamorphosis, it is necessary to realise the significance both of his personal background (as a Jew in the East End) and of the influence of other writers, notably Samuel Beckett and Franz Kafka.

Pinter was born in Hackney, East London, in 1930, the son of a Jewish tailor. He suffered under the barely concealed prejudice against Jews, which during the 1930s and 1940s often erupted into open hostility:

...I went to a Jewish club, by a railway arch, and there

were quite a lot of people often waiting with broken
bottles—*we* didn't have any milk bottles. The best way was
to talk to them, you know, sort of, 'Are you all right?' 'Yes,
I'm all right.' 'Well, that's all right then, isn't it?' And all
the time keep walking towards the lights of the main road
(Harold Pinter, interview in *Theatre at Work*, 1967).

Pinter's early plays were called sometimes 'comedies of
menace', but the roots of this menace lay not with an
unspecified or cosmic fear of disaster, but with the real
threat of physical violence. His characters, like Stanley the
lodger in *The Birthday Party*, sometimes try to talk their way
out of trouble, a mock belligerence concealing their terror.
Stanley almost bullies Meg, his landlady, who mothers and
flirts with him. Davies, in *The Caretaker*, is both a highly defen-
sive man and an aggressive one. But behind this aggression is
the terror that they will not reach the lights of the main road.
Stanley's retreats are cut off by Goldberg and McCann, two
smartly dressed invaders of his territory, who play games
with him and eventually drag him away, dumb with fright, to
God knows what destination. Davies, having been rescued by
Aston from one beating, is eventually cast out of his refuge
to suffer in presumably other brawls.

We rarely see open violence in Pinter's plays: the gun in
The Dumb Waiter (1959) is pointed, but the curtain falls before
it is fired. The lack of bloodshed, however, never persuades
us to believe that blood cannot or will not be spilt: the
violence may take place off-stage, but we do not doubt its existence. But the menace is not just physical. As in Kafka's *The
Trial*, the world contains a variety of threats of being lost or
excluded, of losing one's way or finding death unexpectedly.
Because the outside world is so frightening or too complicated, Pinter's characters often cling on with ferocious
tenacity to their few belongings, particularly their rooms. In
The Room (1957), a married couple, Rose and Bert, live in a
small bed-sitter, which represents their security. But are they
'secure'? Is their landlord really the owner? Will their flat be
rented to another young couple, Mr and Mrs Sands, who
have heard that the place is for let? Or is the blind Negro in
the basement threatening to take over their world? Behind
the loss of personal belongings, or the threatened loss, is the

fear of an emotional abandonment. In *A Slight Ache* (1961), an apparently solid and wealthy couple sit in a sunny garden room, having breakfast. But the husband, a writer of 'theological and philosophical essays', has a slight headache, which may or may not have anything to do with the mysterious presence of a tramp at their garden gate. The wife is fascinated by the tramp, the husband is apprehensive about him; and eventually the tramp takes over from the husband who is handed the beggar's tray of matches to sell.

The menace in Pinter's plays therefore operates on three levels, of physical violence, of the labyrinthine problems set by the outside world and of the dreaded loss of emotional security. Pinter took the now familiar theme of social aliena-tion and presented it in emotional terms which both trans-cended and explained the other, more limited explanations. He knew what it felt like to be a real outcast in society, not just someone who was suffering from 'divine discontent' or an Oedipal rebel. His plays, however, are rarely grim, although they can be frightening. His dialogue provides a ripple of constant pleasure, which partly derives from the ac-tual jokes and partly from the sheer accuracy with which the underlying emotions are conveyed. His language is mainly naturalistic: Bamber Gascoigne has termed it 'distilled naturalism', in that much ordinary explanation has been omitted and that the strong sub-text has to be grasped or felt through fragmentary lines. When, for example, Ruth in *The Homecoming* (1965) meets the sexual aggression of one of her husband's brothers, Lenny, the conflict between them which Ruth wins is expressed casually but intensely through a dis-agreement over a glass of water:

Lenny: Just give me the glass.
Ruth: No.
(Pause)
Lenny: I'll take it then.
Ruth: If you take the glass...I'll take you.
(Pause)
Lenny: How about me taking the glass without you taking me?
Ruth: Why don't I just take you?

The Homecoming can be regarded as a transition play in Pinter's development in that it is the most complete statement of one constant theme, the search for emotional security, but also suffers from the trend towards ellipsis which sometimes becomes a Pinter mannerism. The title, *The Homecoming*, has several meanings. Teddy, a college professor in the United States, returns after a six-year absence to the house in North London where he was reared: his wife, Ruth, also from North London, comes with him. But Teddy's mother, Jessie, is dead, and the house (now scarcely a home) is run by his father, Max, his uncle Sam and his two brothers. Ruth's arrival in this all-male ménage is greeted with a mixture of hostility (from Max) and sexual longing. Her presence means the restoration of a mother-wife to the family, hence in another sense the coming of home. Ruth accepts these male emotions with an unexpected calm, as if she too had come into her own as a woman. The final irony is that Teddy, whose homecoming it should have been, returns suddenly to the United States, leaving Ruth behind. Teddy is someone who has lost his roots, both by being educated in a manner which has lost him an accent and a strange, rough sub-culture and by becoming too 'rational': he distrusts and fears the instinctive emotions which surround him.

The Homecoming suffers from Pinter's desire to work out his theme on many levels, all at once. The few critical moments at the end of the play reveal an intense consciousness which scarcely leaves room for any single event to work with a full dramatic impact: not Sam's death, not Max's dethronement as head of the house, not Ruth's enthronement as Queen Bee. The abruptness affects the tone of the play, as well as the plausibility of the plot, and for once Pinter's instincts in assessing the theatrically practicable effects seems to desert him. His later plays, *Landscape* and *Silence* (1969) and *Old Times* (1971), on the other hand, reveal a remarkable constancy of tone which sometimes takes precedence over his undoubted talent for controlled shock. In these plays, Pinter does not push around his characters to make them fit his themes, and a controlled allusiveness of language extended the limits of his 'distilled naturalism', bringing the sensitivity towards verbal rhythms and images closer to that of Beckett. The humour, delicacy and seriousness of Pinter's plays cast a spell over many of his contemporaries. The word, Pinteresque, was coined to cover those many half-humorous, inconsequential, elliptical strips of dialogue which cropped up in plays by many writers, from Johnny Speight to Joe Orton. But this was surface mimicry. Unlike Osborne, Pinter uncovered no ideas which writers other than he could explore in greater depth, and his best plays, notably *The Caretaker* and *Old Times*, are complete statements of situations requiring neither commentary nor appendices. Those commentators who argued that the sudden and rich growth of dramatists in Britain during the late 1950s and early 1960s was more apparent than real, that the colourful blossoms did not imply deep roots, were nevertheless often prepared to concede profundity to Pinter. He was the first major dramatist to have been produced by the change in theatrical climate.

Chapter 7

Brecht: cool ambiguity

Before taking over as the first artistic director of the English Stage Company at the Royal Court, George Devine visited the Theater am Schiffbauerdamm in East Berlin, where the Berliner Ensemble, under the guidance of Bertolt Brecht, had been in residence since 1949. Devine described his impression in *Encore*, April 1956:

> (The theatre) is situated...in a city divided against itself; and there it manages to thrive. To get to it, you must cross from the ghastly glitter of the Western sector...into the vast sadness of East Berlin. Under its red neon sign, the atmosphere of the theatre is quiet and informal. The group appears to function in a natural and unneurotic manner, and by West End standards, the kind of theatre they believe in seems carefree and dedicated, but without polish.
>
> To watch a Brecht production is to stumble upon the agreeable chaos of an artist's studio, to have the artist turn up a picture and tell you, 'This—is more-or-less finished.' Such an ability to work in a truly artistic manner is unique in the theatre of the world, and most enviable. But underlying the informality, there is something vital and real. The audience makes this a people's theatre...Brecht's dedicated public gave the production an air of religious ritual. That is the best kind of theatre atmosphere. Although the actors seemed to be like children playing, they gave the impression that they worked because they liked and believed in what they had to portray. Such devotion changes everything that comes off the stage. There was none of that affected clichéd acting which is current in our theatre.
>
> The Ensemble is clearly sustained by a strong artistic conception. Behind the simplicity, and the beauty of décor

and costumes, every aspect of the production had been studied and worked on until it was absolutely polished...In *The Caucasian Chalk Circle*, there is a scene in which twenty peasants are gradually convulsed with laughter. The detail of observation and execution of this scene was entirely remarkable and it must have been achieved with much care: one peasant in the front started laughing, the mirth rippled gradually then and overcame all twenty of them. In British theatre, either repertory or West End, I imagine a producer taking the same scene: 'Right, okay. Off we go. Yes, it starts with you and it goes right through. No, no. You weren't very good, and I didn't believe in your laughter, try it again. Good...we open on Monday.'

Brecht's influence on British theatre is a curious one. Although his best plays (a nucleus of perhaps six) are acknowledged to be masterpieces, they have not acquired a widespread popularity in Britain. They have received few West End runs (for various reasons) and even an immediately attractive work, like *The Threepenny Opera* (1928) which was produced before the war in Paris and New York, and even made into a film, had to wait until 1955 before its first London production. There were isolated productions of his plays in the 1930s, such as *Señora Carrar's Rifles* at the Unity in 1938, while in 1955 Joan Littlewood played Mother Courage in a Theatre Workshop production. The arrival of the Berliner Ensemble at the Palace Theatre in 1956, under the auspices of Peter Daubeny, attracted much attention but not general acclaim; which may or may not have been due to the fact that their three productions (*Mother Courage*, *Trumpets and Drums*—a version of Farquhar's *The Recruiting Officer*, and *The Caucasian Chalk Circle*) were played in German. London audiences had responded very favourably to the Moscow Art Theatre and the Comédie-Française, which suggests that a foreign language was not necessarily a barrier to a warm welcome, although Brecht's German had its own idiosyncratic flavour which was hard to appreciate and his plays were not as familiar then as they are now, nor of course as widely known as those of Chekhov and Molière.

Brecht was also known as a dramatic theorist, although the

translations of his writings in the early 1950s were complicated and cumbersome: Sir John Gielgud dismissed his views
as 'pointless and humourless', an extraordinary assessment
apparently which becomes more understandable when one
reads the English texts on which it was based. Brecht's
reputation fluctuated wildly even in Europe: Sartre admired
him beyond any other writer or director in the world,
whereas Ionesco dismissed him as a postman, because he was
always delivering messages. Marxists often admired Brecht
for his politics rather than his art, whereas others objected to
his art because of his politics. George Devine's admiration, as
the above extract indicates, was based upon something other
than Brecht's plays, theories or politics, although it could be
argued to encompass all three: it was the *style* of the Berliner
Ensemble, its informality (Devine was charmed, rather than
irritated, by the fact that the curtain was delayed twenty
minutes to allow for his arrival), its workmanlike atmosphere, the austerity of presentation, the company relaxation, the proletarian audience, and even perhaps the size of
its government grants.

This informal style was understandably hard to achieve at
the Palace, before an audience who may well have been
members of the proletariat but certainly didn't look like
them, dressed in their West End best, sitting in plush seats
before an ornate proscenium-arch stage. But the style was
not a matter of fashionable or unfashionable incidentals: it
derived from the roots of Brecht's art. The Berliner Ensemble seemed 'workmanlike', partly because Brecht used to insist that no bourgeois trappings should disguise how theatrical effects were achieved. At one time, he wanted to keep the
house lights half on, so that members of the audience could
see one another and not get too carried away by the drama.
He often encouraged smoking in the theatre, because
'nobody can be fooled while smoking'. He believed that an
audience of workers would appreciate watching other people work, operating the lights, moving the props and casually
preparing themselves for their entries on stage. This
emphasis upon stage-craft was intended to take away the
false mystery from the theatre, its illusory glamour, thus
allowing a truer concentration upon the dramatic arguments.

If the surroundings at the Palace were unsuitable for such honest austerity, there would soon be built many theatres in Britain which were suitable for little else; and perhaps the first major lesson which British directors learnt from Brecht was the effectiveness of the 'anti-illusion' approach. It was not necessary to pretend that the audience actually were watching a living room somewhere: a table and chair would do, if they were the 'right' table and chair. You did not have to disguise set changes or have a convincing moon. If you must have a moon, Brecht argued, dangle it down on a piece of string. In the 1960s, theatres were built where the old sort of stage illusions were almost impossible to achieve. The Octagon Theatre, Bolton (completed in 1967), had an open stage, whose shape depended upon adjustable patterns of seating. Pulling out the seating platforms became a job for the young enthusiasts around the theatre. Peter Cheeseman, working 'in the round', positively welcomed the austerity of his converted cinema at Stoke, where ordinary illusions were impossible and behind the acting area was always a row of faces. Plays which apparently depended upon naturalistic illusion, such as those of Chekhov and Ibsen, were staged with simple effectiveness without built sets; while Shakespeare's plays often seemed to benefit from doing without scenery, which is scarcely surprising for Elizabethan playhouses usually did so.

It was easy to do without theatrical pomp and ceremony and to pretend that the production was Brechtian. It was much harder to capture the other side to Brecht's stagecraft, his use of astonishing visual effects and the sheer care with which he chose his props. One aspect of Brecht's work was quite impossible to imitate, his use of language. Brecht was recognised first of all in Germany as a poet. During the 1920s, he used to sing his lyrics in beer-houses, becoming almost the Bob Dylan of his day. He wrote his own tunes, before collaborating with the composer, Kurt Weill. His poetic style was partly a reaction against High German (for which there is no exact British equivalent, not even Oxford English) but one which also avoided the regionalisms of Low German. Ernest Bornemann has described the verbal problems which faced Brecht:

In the public mind…poetry remained rhymed thought,
and prose remained narrated thought. There was no
precedent (a) for colloquial poetry; (b) for plain
storytelling. There was no German equivalent to writers
like Kipling, Mark Twain or Hemingway.

The language itself militated against it: you either wrote
Hochdeutsch or you wrote dialect. And if you wrote dialect,
like Anzengruber, Rosegger and Reuter, you remained a
parochial figure….

Brecht was the first writer of his generation who broke
out of this vice of language and made up a tongue of his
own, based upon a juxtaposition of four utterly alien
worlds: (1) South German colloquialisms; (2) an anti-
metaphorical poetry of colours, textures and other
concrete images; (3) officialese; (4) anglicisms and other
exoticisms (Ernest Bornemann, *Encore*, July 1958).

In the case of Brecht, the normal problems of translation
were unnaturally exaggerated. Deliberately stilted Brech-
tianisms sounded merely quaint in English. One simple example is provided by the language of *The Threepenny Opera*,
set in Soho, which Brecht had never visited. Brecht, however,
did not want *the* Soho, the district of London. He wanted a
totally re-constructed 'bad man's' language, using the jargon
from Westerns, Chicago-style movies and occasional anglicisms: something which sounded stilted, strange and violent.
Similarly, in *The Caucasian Chalk Circle*, he required a simple,
formal language for the parting between Simon the soldier
and Grusha the serving maid. They exchange tokens and say
goodbye like this:

> Simon: Now I must harness the horses. The young lady
> will understand that. It would be better for the young lady
> to go into the third courtyard (Act 1, Scene 2, *The Caucasian
> Chalk Circle*, translated by J. and T. Stern, with W. H.
> Auden).

In English, we can sense Brecht's intentions. It is indeed similar to British 'restraint'. Brecht did not want to write a florid
parting, nor did he wish to give his lovers regional accents,
with the implied condescension of a bourgeois writer who

knows that the working classes don't speak properly. Instead he concocted a simple, restrained language ('the young lady' instead of 'you') which conveyed a dignified, but not over-gracious, politeness.

The suppleness with which Brecht used his new proletarian language, with its prim exactness, its slang, deliberate roughnèss and officialese, fascinated his disciples and caught on with his public in Germany. But it also caused problems in Britain with one important aspect of Brechtian dramatic theory, the *Verfremdungseffekte* (or the 'estrange-ment' effect). The nature of Brecht's verbal style helped ac-tors to achieve the estrangement effect without falling into a dull, documentary flatness. Lacking Brecht's language, Bri-tish actors had to work towards 'estrangement' by other means, often contorted and unnecessary ones.

Brecht summarised 'estrangement' in one quick example. Let us suppose that the dramatic event is a traffic accident. In 'normal' (or as Brecht would have termed it, Aristotelian) theatre, the dramatist would encourage the audience to 'identify', say, with the driver, who would be the Hero of the play. But this, according to Brecht, was far too personal an approach. It laid emphasis on one man's role in a situation which might involve many others. It could also be falsely emotional: 'catharsis' for Brecht was a dirty word. Why should we wish to purge our emotions through drama? They were required for action in daily life. His type of theatre (which he called 'epic') was like the reconstruction of this accident within a court. Various witnesses would be called who would act out their versions of what had hap-pened. Their acting illustrates their views and experiences, within an atmosphere of detached concern. Brecht sought to encourage among his actors, and through them his au-diences, calm assessments of the historical situations which he presented on stage; and he assumed that such rationality would eventually lead to Marxist commitment.

This sounds as if Brecht wanted to run contrasting views of the same event, side by side, in the style of the Japanese film, *Rashamon*. Occasionally Brecht attempted something like this, as in *Der Jasager* and *Der Neinsager*, where from the same situation different moral conclusions are drawn. But usually 'estrangement' led to an organic rather than structural approach, not two separate scenes but one scene where two or more views were expressed with conviction, neither being exactly 'correct'. Audiences were, however, encouraged to look for the underlying causes behind the dramatic situation. In 'Aristotelian' theatre, Brecht argued, the dramatic emphasis is upon what is going to happen. In 'Epic' theatre, the stress is upon why the event has happened, what caused it and how it can be prevented from happening again. To stop the audience bothering about the mere plot development, he sometimes told the story in advance, by means of placards, story-tellers and songs; but Brecht was a deceptively pragmatic dramatist and he would often conceal vital details of the plot if he thought that he could gain some telling surprise.

In Britain, 'estranged' acting was at first held to be the exact opposite of 'Method' acting. With the Method, the actor was encouraged to identify closely and single-mindedly with his role. Under Brecht's system, actors were encouraged to stand aside from their roles, even to the point, in rehearsals, of not acting, but simply of describing what their characters were supposed to be doing and why. Reason and objective description appeared to replace 'identification' as the key to the formation of a stage character. In fact, this oppostion was more in theory than in practice. Brecht was, to begin with, a keen observer of naturalistic effects. The wagon in *Mother Courage* had to be an exact replica of those used in the Thirty Years' War: Mother Courage's knife had to be shaped in a particular way and to be handled with an instinctive ease. He was also an admirer of professional acting skill, wherever he saw it. He advised the members of the Berliner Ensemble to watch John Gielgud's acting in Coward's *Nude with Violin* (1956). It proved to be one of his last company instructions, for he died before their London visit.

Where Brecht most differed both from the Method enthusiasts and many subsequent Brechtians was in his flexibility of approach. He was influenced by three great German directors of the 1920s, Erwin Piscator, famous for his documentary plays staged at the Volksbühne in Berlin, with whom Brecht collaborated in a version of *The Good Soldier Schweik* (1927), Leopold Jessner, a classicist who would stage plays with the minimum of scenery and the maximum concentration on theme and debate, and Max Reinhardt, with his great flamboyance and love of spectacle. All these influences are illustrated in the extraordinary first scene from *Mahagonny* (1927), where a lorry rolls on to an empty stage. One side of the lorry flaps up—and out tumbles a shanty town: a single stage image, but stunningly effective—as flamboyant as Reinhardt, as concentrated as Jessner and as concerned with topical realities as Piscator. It has been argued (by the critic, Peter Ansorge, for example) that Brecht's influence on British directors was to recall them to an austerity of staging and argument, a sort of Marxist puritan revolution; and indeed some directors, such as William Gaskill, were inclined to interpret Brechtian methods along these lines. But Brecht was no Brechtian, and this emphasis upon austerity ignores Brecht's blood-and-thunder imagery, his sensuous delight in tattiness as well as his love for a cold Chinese order, his appeal to romantic symbols and his deliberate vulgarities. In *Mother Courage*, the mute daughter of Mother Courage climbs on to the roof of a cottage, carrying a drum which she beats to warn the soldiers sleeping in a nearby town of an imminent attack: she represents all those helpless sufferers from war and her gesture, culminating in her death by being shot, is a rallying call for the weak against the strong. Peter Brook was surely right when he argued (in his preface to the play-text of *The Marat/Sade*) that there was little essentially incompatible between Brecht's theories of estrangement and the shock tactics of Artaud.

If Brecht was continually flexible in his technical ideas, he was also far less rigid than is commonly supposed in his political views. He remained a Marxist to his death, and his ideological flexibility was within those limits. If he said little or nothing which flatly went against Marxism, he explored the doubts and ambiguities in communism, balanced one sort of good against another, both in his plays and in his private life. He kept a bank account in Austria, lest the East German régime should collapse. He was a survivor, and one source of his appeal to British directors was that he was someone who had lived through the turmoil of European politics during the twentieth century, had apparently coped psychologically with traumatic experiences and had emerged with his good humour and sanity relatively intact.

He was born in 1898, the son of an industrialist, though he preferred to talk about his peasant origins, on his mother's side. During the First World War, he was a student and a pacifist, escaping imprisonment only through the intervention of his headmaster and by becoming a medical orderly in the war. This experience transfixed his mind with the cruelty of battle. His father was ruined in the massive inflation in Germany during the 1920s, leaving Brecht with an affectionate contempt for the bourgeoisie, regarding them as crooks and parasites (like Mr Peachum in *The Threepenny Opera*), but also (like Mother Courage) as victims of a class system whose innate violence they supported but could not control. He witnessed the rise of fascism, opposed it vigorously, was thus on the Nazis' elimination list and endured the banning of his plays from public theatres. In 1933, he was forced to escape from Germany with his wife, Helene Weigel, the actress, taking refuge in Denmark where he edited an anti-Nazi paper. After the outbreak of the Second World War, he fled to the United States, where, as an unhappy refugee, he wrote his four best-known plays (*Mother Courage*, *Galileo*, *The Good Woman of Setzuan* and *The Caucasian Chalk Circle*) which he later revised. He fell foul of Joe McCarthy's Committee of Un-American Activities in 1947 and escaped again, this time to Switzerland, where, after a production of *Mother Courage* in Zurich, he attracted the attention of the East German régime, who invited him to establish the Berliner Ensemble. Even there, among those who were apparently sympathetic to his Marxist views, his battles were not over. He had to wheedle and fight against bureaucracy in the East as well as the West, but, almost miraculously, managed to survive and develop his work.

Brecht himself was thus almost a symbol of how to survive in a hostile world, and his reputation had the sort of international political aura which was once attached (though in a dissimilar way) to Byron. He developed a method of coping with intractable régimes, based upon the character Schweik in Hasek's novel. Brecht told a Schweikian story about a bandit who came down from the hills to invade a farm. Gun in hand, he ordered the farmer, 'Obey me—or else!' The farmer, without a word, prepared the richest dishes, brought the most intoxicating wines until, after a time, the bandit

The first Director of the National Theatre Company

ord Olivier as James Tyrone in *A Long Day's Journey into Night* by Eugene
'Neill, directed by Michael Blakemore: December 1971.

6 *Alternative Antigone*
The Freehold Company in their version of *Antigone*: November 1969.

The RSC at the Aldwych

avesties by Tom Stoppard, directed by Peter Wood, with John Wood (Henry
rr), Beth Morris (Cecily); 1974.

8 '*Another Happy Day*'

Happy Days by Samuel Beckett, directed by Peter Hall, with Alan Webb as Willie, Peggy Ashcroft as Winnie. This production by the National Theatre was originally staged at the Old Vic, but was chosen to start the previews at the new Lyttelton Theatre in the National Theatre on the South Bank. At the opening performance at the Lyttelton, Willie was played by Harry Lomax.

died from various surfeits. The farmer tipped the bandit's body out of the window and answered briefly, 'No'. The good soldier Schweik always managed to get his own way by apparently collaborating with the authorities. Brecht's interview with Joe McCarthy's investigation team was a triumph of Schweikian evasion. He was even thanked for his help.

The sly stance of a Schweik may have been the proper, if not a complete, response to fascist régimes: Brecht wrote *Schweik in the Second World War* to prove that effective rebels were not just those who blew up munitions factories. But was this an adequate attitude to adopt in revolutionary or post-revolutionary situations? Here Brecht's parables were more naïvely written. In the first scene of *The Caucasian Chalk Circle*, he showed how a pastoral commune should work, with democratic discussions all round, worker solidarity guided by an area organiser and a peaceful rest at the end of the day while the peasants watch an improving (if also amusing) play. In *St Joan of the Stockyards*, Brecht demonstrated how an important strike (which, if successful, would have prevented the workers in the Chicago meat-markets from sinking into the direst poverty) was broken, because a vital message was not delivered from one group of workers to another. The culprit was an ardent social worker, 'St Joan', and this single act could have achieved more than all her charity and soup kitchens. Because she failed politically, Joan, a private do-gooder became an unwilling conspirator with the capitalistic bosses.

Previously, the stock emphasis in British theatre on most political matters was that political theory mattered less than the conscientiousness and general honesty of politicians. Brecht reversed this argument and helped to bring about a change, though perhaps only a marginal one, in British attitudes. Private virtue, according to Brecht, mattered less than the 'correct' political decisions, and he wrote *The Seven Deadly Virtues* to prove that conventional virtues could be crudely manipulated to suit the greed of the individual. Brecht wanted to raise the level of political consciousness among his audiences, not to touch their moral nerves. Brecht's views were both very attractive to a morally confused age (in Britain, as elsewhere) and also, to my mind, highly unconvincing, for most political decisions are at root

moral ones and no system in the world can withstand the im-
perfections of a humanity wishing to mess it up. Brecht presented two opposite responses—the Schweikian one, suitable
for a capitalistic society, where all morality could be forgotten beyond the plain need to survive, and the communist
one, where private morality didn't matter very much because
the system would take over. His own views were complicated
perhaps, but regrettably they were often simplified to this
Janus twinheadedness. By the early 1970s, a young director
like Keith Hack would delight in Brechtian sleaziness, all
amorality, roguery and greedy degradation, as his strange
early-Brecht version of Shakespeare's *Measure for Measure* at
Stratford-upon-Avon in 1974 indicated; whereas William
Gaskill's production of David Hare's *Fanshen* was so cool and
austere that it could have been an agnostic Sunday School
run by the Webbs.

The root problem was perhaps that the 'estrangement' approach sometimes had the effect, in Brecht but much more
so in the work of his disciples, of cauterising human feelings.
In Brecht's plays this was sometimes shown by his cartoon
exaggeration: his images of capitalism, derived from his experiences of wars, collapsing economies, bankruptcies and
the displays of excessive wealth, led to a delight in detailing
atrocities, which contrasted sharply with the decorums of
British theatre. In his lesser plays, Brecht relies very heavily
upon the assumption that the economic motive is the sole
one which links people together, and as if to demonstrate
that this is so, he chooses social extremes: extreme poverty
where hunger and the need to preserve the means of life rub
over all other thoughts, and extreme wealth where the enjoyment and preservation of privilege similarly cuts across
other considerations. From this stance, he could assume that
the logic of social living derived solely from economic factors, an argument which has to be developed very carefully
indeed if it is not to seem banal, palpably misguided and
doctrinaire.

Brecht's Epic drama particularly affected the social documentaries in Britain. Very often the style which was termed
Brechtian meant little more than a sequence of quasi-
naturalistic scenes, linked by a vaguely political theme
('Down with property developers', 'Bosses exploit workers')

and dotted with ballad songs. The externals of the style were immediately imitated: stories were told in advance by placards, as in *O, What a Lovely War!* where the details of the war were flashed on a screen behind the pierrot players. Internally, however, the scenes were not written with Brecht's literary skill. If we compare the writing of individual scenes from (say) Alan Plater's *Close the Coalhouse Door* or *The Tigers Are Coming, O.K.?* with any scene from one of Brecht's major plays, the sheer difference in thought, human understanding and dramatic calculation is immediately noticeable; and of course Brecht's verbal style haunted German audiences in a manner unmatched in Britain.

Brecht influenced many British dramatists of the 1960s: Plater, John Arden and Peter Barnes among them. But his direct influence was also great, in that Epic Theatre provided a constructive alternative to the well-made play. Peter Shaffer, Robert Bolt and John Whiting, none of them Brechtian, learnt from him the way to overcome the old Unities of Time and Place. He also changed methods in this country in two respects; first, by stressing that acting could be undertaken in an illustrative manner, and second, by demonstrating the importance of permanent ensembles. Before the example of the Berliner Ensemble, permanent companies, particularly national ones, were usually devoted to a particular style of acting, naturalism in the case of the Moscow Art Theatre, stylised classicism in the case of the Comédie-Française. These styles were greatly admired in Britain but they were also felt to be somewhat limiting. The Berliner Ensemble, however, demonstrated that a permanent ensemble could provide a process of continuing enquiry into the nature of drama, not just a set technique. The company discussions mattered, the slow evolution of points of view, of methods and of personal relationships within the company. A company, in short, could be a living entity, not just a factory for producing plays. Brecht's theoretical works, such as *The Messingkauf Dialogues* (published in Britain in 1963), illustrated the importance of general debate. This view of a permanent company, strongly proclaimed by critics such as Kenneth Tynan, who was to become the literary manager of the National Theatre, and also held by Peter Hall, the first artistic director of the Royal Shakespeare Company, changed the methods through which productions were developed. At one extreme it led to directors becoming company chairmen, with the basic decisions taken by the actors, and then brought together by the man whose duty it was to reconcile different points of view. At the opposite extreme, Brechtian directors would be philosopher-statesmen to their groups, imposing political-visionary outlooks on scripts which might not have been suitable for that purpose. If, as has sometimes been claimed, British theatre in the 1960s was to become a directors' theatre, the ultimate responsibility lies with the persuasiveness of Brecht.

Nor was it an indirect influence, for Britain produced at least three world-class directors in the early 1960s, Peter Brook, John Dexter and William Gaskill, all of whom were (at different times) under the spell of Brecht and never lost their affectionate respect for him. One practical consequence of this devotion was shown in the Shakespeare productions at Stratford-upon-Avon. Brecht was an admirer of Shakespeare, although he often couldn't resist fiddling with his messages. His version of *Coriolanus* formed part of the Berliner Ensemble's repertoire during their second visit to Britain in 1965, while in 1971, two East German directors, Manfred Wekwerth and Joachim Tenschert, directed an English 'Brechtian' version of the same play for the National Theatre. Understandably, Brecht would play down the heroic elements of Shakespeare's plots and emphasise the political, economic sides to them. Thus, Coriolanus was not a hero whose pride and bad temper alienates the fickle masses, but a tyrant: the working soldiers, not Coriolanus, won the war, he merely took the credit. This view somewhat alters Shakespeare's story.

At Stratford, under the guidance of John Barton, Peter Brook and Peter Hall, the stories were rarely altered to this extent, but, coupled with Jan Kott's influential book, *Shakespeare Our Contemporary*, there was a marked swing away from heroic acting and towards historical explanations of events. One example would be the Barton adaptation of the three *Henry VI* plays, under the title of *The Wars of the Roses*, directed with great success by Peter Hall in 1964. Another example, this time at the Royal Court in 1966 during William Gaskill's reign, was an 'estranged' *Macbeth*, staged deliberately against a light-coloured, sandy background, with full stage lighting, to avoid Gothic effects. In the sleep-walking scene, Lady Macbeth (Simone Signoret) washed her hands in daylight. It was like watching a rigged seance in a television studio: the ectoplasm was immediately identifiable as cotton-wool. The ghosts, the witchcraft, the delusions of Macbeth were all to be watched with clinical detachment; but unfortunately Shakespeare, for better or worse, did not write the play like that. He actually asked for ghosts.

Despite these (and other) lapses, Brecht's influence on British theatre had at least five important consequences, which taken together made him the most dominant single personality to affect drama since the decline of Shaw. He encouraged dramatists and directors once more to turn their attention towards politics as a profitable subject for drama, after more than a decade of post-war theatre in which politics was regarded as being vaguely anti-art. His methods helped to extend the technical range of writers beyond the confines of the well-made play and in the general direction of Epic drama. The example of the Berliner Ensemble set standards towards which the new 'permanent' companies in Britain aspired and also changed the tone within theatre buildings and auditoria away from the formal and ornate, and towards the informal, functional and austere. One important result from this change in tone was an avoidance of both heavily stylised acting and highly emotional acting, and thus a preference for plain and simple statements. Directors and dramatists in Britain could not really avoid the influence of Brecht in the 1960s, for even when they chose not to follow his example, to ignore his work, this in itself had to be a definite rejection—which in turn forced them to indicate why Brecht had no appeal for them. This resulted in genuine and far-ranging discussions about the nature of the theatre, which was perhaps the most important consequence of all.

Chapter 8
The Arts Council and its influence

Although one direction towards which the ghost of Brecht guided British theatre was that of austerity, this did not mean that Brechtian productions were cheap. On the contrary, they required permanent companies (which were expensive), long rehearsal periods, resident writers, musicians and designers, and, at the end, there was no settled product which could play for years in the West End. Within the existing 'commercial' system in Britain, a 'Brechtian' company could scarcely be formed, and even by the standards of other national companies (of a type which Britain in the late 1950s still lacked), teams such as the Berliner Ensemble were rare indeed and could only survive with large subsidies. The days of private patronage on this scale were over: in Europe as in Britain. Thus, directors with Brechtian ambitions (and even those without them) looked towards governments for support.

When Peter Hall took over the Shakespeare Memorial Theatre at Stratford, he issued a policy statement to the press (January 1960) in which he announced his intention to form a permanent company at Stratford, which would operate both there and in a second theatre in London (which was to be the Aldwych). At Stratford, the policy was to be centred upon the plays of Shakespeare and his contemporaries, while in London, the second theatre would show selected Stratford productions together with some modern plays. Actors would thus have the chance of being seen in the metropolitan shopwindow as well as working in its regional factory; and to prevent actors from drifting away from the company into films and television, singularly flexible contracts were devised. Such a policy was a daring attempt to transform the Shakespeare Memorial into a new national company, the Royal Shakespeare Company, and of course, it required money. Here there was a curious snag, in that the

Shakespeare Memorial Theatre had money, the proceeds from tours abroad during the 1950s, but not enough. Hall calculated that while his company had £100,000 in the bank, the chances of gaining substantial government subsidies were slight. Unlike other theatres in the country, the Shakespeare Memorial Theatre had been too successful from a box-office point of view to expect subsidies, and Hall gambled upon getting rid of the excess money in an attempt to establish a company of such merit that the State would be forced to support it lavishly in future.

The agency through which Hall hoped for government help was the Arts Council of Great Britain, and his great expectations (which were proved justified) were in themselves a sign of the growing importance of this body. There are perhaps three main phases in the Arts Council's development. The first ten years (from its inception in August 1946) was a period when its grants from the Exchequer were small (£235,000 in 1946, rising to £820,000 in 1955–6), tied to specific projects, and when the role of the Arts Council was primarily seen to be a marginal effort on the fringes of the main commercial theatre system. Most people in the theatre then, if they were not 'commercial' managements, looked towards other sources for financial help. They retained good will towards the Arts Council, however, particularly because the Council was active politically in getting rid of some of the restrictions on the theatre, notably Entertainments Tax (abolished in 1957). It was generally assumed that major increases in public patronage would come not from the Arts Council but from the local authorities who were allowed (under the 1948 Local Government Act) to spend up to a 6d. rate on arts subsidies. Few authorities took advantage of this power, but if we simply look at the possible sums involved (not those which were actually raised) the appeal of local, rather than centrally raised, money is obvious. The product of a 6d. rate in England and Wales would have produced about £8 million in 1948, while, by 1962, the sum would have been nearer to £50 million. This sort of money would have been impossible for the government to have given to the Arts, at a time of national austerity, without causing severe political problems. Local authorities also of course faced political problems, with the result that there was a massive gap between what could be raised through the rates and what was. According to *A Survey of Municipal Entertainment* (1964) the net expenditure of all local authorities in England and Wales on all forms of entertainment amounted to £2½ million during 1961–2.

During the second phase of the Arts Council's career, from 1956 to 1964, the grants from the government rose steadily, under a predominantly Conservative administration: from £820,000 to £3,205,000 in 1964–5. This period was particularly fruitful and optimistic, although it began in a mood of dire pessimism: it saw the inauguration of two national companies, the building of new repertory theatres (at, say, Coventry, Nottingham and Chichester), the arrival of the new dramatists—many of whom were helped by Arts Council grants, and the formulation of detailed policies (such as the *Housing the Arts* surveys and recommendations) about the 'revival' of British theatre. Much of this chapter will be devoted to the achievements of this period, but before assessing them, it is worth considering briefly the third phase, which began very optimistically and ended in pessimism, if it has ended.

When the Labour Party came to power in 1964, the Prime Minister, Harold Wilson, appointed a Minister for the Arts, Jennie Lee, whose declared purpose was to extend the role of arts in society. The sums given to the Arts Council accordingly increased dramatically in the following years: £5,700,000 (1966–7), £7,750,000 (1968–9), £9,300,000 (1970–1), £13,725,000 (1972–3) until, by 1974, the Arts Council were requesting an increase in their Treasury grant for 1975–6 in the region of between £5 million and £6 million, bringing the total amount for that year to about £25 million. That figure was considered by the chairman of its drama panel, J. W. Lambert, to be about half the amount required to keep the theatre system going in the new style to which it had become quickly accustomed. While the Arts Council was not a Grand Provider in 1956, and had not become one by 1964, it certainly gave the appearance of being one by 1974. The Arts Council was then helping fringe companies, community arts programmes, commercial touring companies, and the building (and running) of the new National Theatre, together with those companies which it had supported during the second phase, such as the repertory theatres, the English Stage Company, the Mermaid Theatre and the Royal Shakespeare Company.

The theatrical profession naturally welcomed this startling increase. Certain members objected about the increased government stake in the theatre, but they were in a minority. In comparison with other countries, British subsidies to the theatre were still low in the late 1960s. Furthermore, the Arts Council had become a victim of its own success. The expectations of all arts activities had greatly increased and having created this demand, it was up to the Arts Council (as best they could) to meet it. This was particularly true in the case of new repertory theatres, which were being built throughout the 1960s, usually through a collaboration between the local authorities concerned and the Arts Council. Having built a new theatre, it was necessary to find the money to run it, at a time of steeply rising inflation, when Equity, the actors' union, was understandably pressing for national wage increases. The combination of inflation, the Value Added Tax on the theatre introduced in 1972, the new Equity Agreements and costs of running elaborate new theatres meant that, despite the increased sums to the Arts Council, very many companies in Britain during the early 1970s were on the verge of bankruptcy. Among the theatres represented by CORT (the Council of Regional Theatres) it was estimated in 1974 that six (out of twenty-six) were chasing immediate bankruptcy, and they were all facing serious cutbacks in their programmes, which usually meant shutting the studio theatres and cutting off aid to the theatre-in-education teams. Even the Royal Court in 1975 was faced by the prospect of needing £100,000 more subsidy than it was given by the Arts Council, thus forcing it to face various, equally unwelcome choices: closing the theatre for stretches of the year, closing its studio theatre or deciding not to try out new plays but to rely upon trusted revivals. The whole purpose of the English Stage Company at the Royal Court Theatre was to give opportunities to new writers.

The increase in government subsidies had therefore not exorcised the spectre of financial uncertainty. It may also have caused undesirable side effects. There was, to begin with, a centralisation of patronage, which led to the charge that the drama panel of the Arts Council (which advised the drama officers in the disposition of grants) was almost as much of an élite as the old commercial élite connected with The Group. Charles Marowitz of the Open Space theatre was one of those who led the attack, arguing that the drama panel was composed (at least in part) of those directors who most benefited from subsidies. These charges may have been unfair, for many directors were careful not to contribute to discussions where their own claims were being debated; but it pointed to an inherent weakness in all patronage—in that there is simply no way in which one can say, in advance, that this theatre next year will be worthy of a £100,000 grant whereas that one deserves only £50,000. To meet the charges of preferential treatment, the drama panel increased in size, with the result that their discussions became very democratic but also very long and rambling. Immediately after the war, the motto of the Arts Council (coined by Sir Ernest Pooley) had been 'State support for the Arts, without State control'. It had always been a doubtful maxim, but now it had lost all credibility. By establishing its list of priorities, the Arts Council was inevitably controlling the pattern of arts activity in the country. The Council, of course, did not do so dictatorially: it was usually responding to pressures rather than initiating them. But by responding to some pressures and not to others, by (say) setting aside nearly £2 million for the annual upkeep of the new National Theatre, at a time when the fringe theatres were complaining that they lacked the few thousand pounds necessary for their survival, the Arts Council was inevitably furthering one species of theatre at the expense of another.

There seems to me nothing particularly wrong about such preferences: choosing one type of theatre rather than another is an important function of patronage. In a sense, however, the Arts Council, for historical reasons, wished to avoid this image of *choosing* rather than just *helping*. A certain pretence was maintained that it was still trying pragmatically to help all those who seemed to need and deserve help, rather like a National Patronage Service along the lines of a National Health Service. In view of its limited resources, however, it might have been better advised to concentrate on few ventures and hope that others would supplement alternative schemes. It might have been possible, say, to finance the regional repertory theatres through the Regional Arts Association, leaving the Arts Council free to concentrate on the national companies and national touring. As it was, the stillborn schemes, the starving babies, the screaming adolescents and shabby bankrupts all sooner or later landed up with the respectable arts managers on the doorstep of 105, Piccadilly, the Home of the Grand Provider, the Arts Council.

This situation was particularly frustrating because during the second phase of the Arts Council's development most of these problems had been carefully considered. Between 1956 and 1964, the treasury grants to the Arts Council were, as we have seen, comparatively small, which provided a firm financial boundary within which the Arts Council worked. During these years, the policy of the Arts Council was to make the existing system work better, a mixed economy of mainly commercial theatres with the occasional civic theatre and the few ventures which relied upon private patronage. It supported, say, the English Stage Company during its first crucial five years to the tune of £30,000, which though helpful was not enough to ensure its survival. The English Stage Company needed unexpected hits, such as *Look Back in Anger* from which royalties of £50,000 were obtained.

Because its resources were so limited, the Arts Council devoted its attention to giving marginal help where it was most needed and on being an influence rather than a major patron. One aspect of this non-financial power which the Arts Council acquired was the way in which it defined the needs of the theatre. It was extremely worried during the late 1950s lest regional theatre should virtually die out altogether, following a withdrawal of support from the big financial-theatrical companies, such as those represented by The Group. In its annual reports, drafted by its admirable Secretary-General, Sir William Emrys Williams, it would point out with increasing astringency that fine theatres were being sold for redevelopment and that existing legislation to protect such places was ineffective. It described how local theatres were falling into decay, praised and drew attention to those councils who were prepared to take advantage of the provisions in the 1948 Local Government Act either by taking over existing theatres or by deciding to build new ones. In 1958, it compiled a major survey of theatres and arts centres in Britain which resulted in an advisory document, *Housing the Arts in Great Britain* (published in 1959 and 1961), which had a decisive influence in shaping the future development of British theatre for the next fifteen years.

This report provided a blueprint for the building and renovation of theatres throughout the country. It was primarily concerned with the development of locally based companies, not touring ones. During the late 1950s and the early 1960s, the touring theatres rapidly declined (from about 120 in the mid-1950s to about 30 in the early 1970s) whereas the repertory companies grew in number, from about 20 companies to over a hundred. The report also led, in February 1965, to the establishment of a Capital Fund from the Treasury, of £250,000, whose specific purpose was to assist towns in building or renovating theatres. The Council was wary of detracting from the local initiatives which might bring such theatres into existence. Therefore, it formulated guidelines along which capital grants were to be given. The Arts Council would finance up to 50 per cent, but not exceeding this percentage, of the cost of building new theatres. The Council would match local councils 'pound for pound'.

If we compare the effect of this report with the projects outlined in *The Theatre Today* (published in 1971) which were either slow to develop (such as the Theatre Investment Fund) or scarcely developed at all (such as the Touring Grid Proposals), we can recognise in retrospect the influence of the Arts Council during this middle phase. The recommendations were not followed slavishly, but gradually during the 1960s there was an almost astonishing spate of theatre-building. Thirty new theatres were built in ten years, and even the much-delayed new National Theatre was started in 1969, after at least eight years of preparation and nearly 140 years of intermittent argument. The Arts Council was assisted by a buoyant climate of optimism in the theatre, which slowly petered away during the early 1970s. It had partly contributed to this optimism by its own efforts. Its work from 1956 onwards had shown a great concentration on the practical details of arts management. The theatre was a small enough institution and poor enough, for this meticulous care to reap rich dividends. By solving small problems with increasing success, a certain impetus was developed and sustained, which enabled the Council to win more support and to tackle bigger projects.

It may have been optimistic and prepared to nag councils and governments to get its own way, but under Sir William Emrys Williams's leadership it was also cautious. It formulated, for example, a theory for patronage. This theory started with certain assumptions, one being that 'nothing could be more undesirable than a unilateral system of public patronage in which a single body, such as the Arts Council, was the sole distributor of subsidies' (*A New Pattern for Patronage*, 1957–8). Several reasons were given for this dislike of centralised patronage. It did not include the old argument against State-controlled culture, but an equally telling one in favour of personal hunches, of gambling on ideas which may or may not come off, the 'caprices' which government institutions had to avoid.

> Patronage...works best when it has many centres of initiative, when its government is divided among several bodies rather than consolidated in one. A plea which fails in one quarter may succeed in another; the conservative habit of one distributing body may be offset by the adventurous outlook of a different tribunal. In its heyday the patronage of the Popes and Grand Dukes was often strongly flavoured with an element of sheer caprice which sometimes brought off miracles of art. Caprice is a luxury which an Arts Council must deny itself....The private body can gamble on long shots; a government agency is liable to public criticism if it does so.

Inevitably, the argument ran, the Arts Council would be forced to support institutions rather than people, and even when it did directly try to help people, as in its New Drama grants or bursaries to writers, it would have to institutionalise this assistance by (say) putting a guideline maximum and minimum. Personal hunches had to be avoided. This situation, as Sir William Emrys Williams realised, could lead to a de-personalising of patronage, and perhaps a de-grading of money. Because Arts Council money came from the tax-payer, hence from everybody but nobody in particular, the funds ceased to represent a personal commitment, except to the general principle that Arts were Good for Society. The National Library of Wales, as Professor Brinley Thomas of University College Cardiff pointed out, 'was instituted by the tireless efforts of dedicated men and women of all classes....' 'The miners of South Wales accepted a levy on their wages of 1s a man as their contribution, at a time when the average wage of a collier was 45s a week' (Arts Council Annual Report, 1960–1). Such a levy represented a clear personal commitment from the miners, which led to a considerable pride in their achievements. Similar local prides were raised by the building of local theatres at Chichester, Guildford, Leatherhead, Bolton and elsewhere. No amount of direct government aid could have replaced this ordinary pride in self-help, as the Arts Council was fully aware.

The role of the Arts Council was thus regarded in those days as assisting the growth of a general theatre system, with-in which other sources of patronage could operate, where necessary. Instead of demanding a greatly increased govern-ment grant for the Arts Council, the Council called for tax concessions for those firms and industries who were pre-pared to support the Arts. In 1957, about £50,000 a year was being given by industry to various arts activities, but this sum could have been increased 'ten-fold' if such donations were made tax-deductible. These concessions were not forthcom-ing, but, even so, industrial patronage was an important feature of arts development over the following years. The Little Theatre in Middlesbrough was built through industrial patronage, Pilkingtons the glass firm maintained its local theatre at St Helens, Vickers-Armstrong supported its local repertory theatre at Barrow-in-Furness, while industrial grants and city donations enabled the Mermaid Theatre in London to open in 1959. There were donations from televi-sion companies to the Theatre Royal, Windsor, and to pro-vide theatre training for directors.

Industry was one possible source of patronage. The local councils were another. If the £2½ million which they gave to the arts and entertainments in 1961–2 was only a fraction of the £50 million which they could have given, it was still more than the £13 millions which at that time was the total Arts Council subsidy to the Arts. When the Arts Council talked about a 'balance of patronage', there was during the early 1960s a time when this 'balance' existed—between the local authorities and the Arts Council. In the *Survey of Municipal Entertainment* (1964), already mentioned, it was shown that local council patronage was rarely in the form of outright gifts or subsidies, but was regarded as 'priming the pump', and financial repayment was usually expected at some stage. The Nottingham Playhouse was built from a lump sum received by the council when gas was nationalised; it also received an annual council grant, which it paid back with interest in rents and rates. Bournemouth, which subsidised a leading Symphony Orchestra, actually made a profit on its entertainments account in 1961–2: it spent £309,000 and received £315,000. Indeed, of the £2½ million spent by local councils, about £2 million was recovered. Thus, it could be argued (and was) that local councils exercised greater caution in the spending of public money and were determined to receive proper benefits, sometimes tangible ones like money, sometimes less tangible ones like an increase in the tourist trade, and sometimes social ones, such as those obtained by dovetailing the work of the education authorities in with the services provided by reps and arts centres. Theatres themselves, however, preferred their grants to come from the Arts Council, since they feared interference from local councils and arbitrary parsimony.

There were two other possible sources of patronage, private and trade union. Private patronage was mainly considered to come not from a few rich individuals (although they occasionally donated large sums, as Thomas Markland did at Bolton) but from supporters' clubs. Large sums could be raised, with work and efficient fund-raisers, through private patronage, particularly in the comparatively wealthy southern areas of England. Chichester Festival Theatre was largely built through private patronage, and also maintained this way, for its supporters' club (8,000 strong in 1969) contributed over £4,000 annually. In poorer areas of Britain, no such sums could be raised. Union patronage was always disappointingly small. Arnold Wesker tried to raise money from the unions for his Centre 42 project, which tooks its name from Clause 42 in the Trades Union Congress agenda for 1960. This clause began: 'Congress recognises the importance of arts in the life of the community, especially now when many unions are securing a shorter working week and greater leisure for their members.' But Centre 42 never received the consistent support which it required. In 1960, ten unions contributed a total of £335 to the Theatre Workshop, Stratford, a ridiculously small sum.

Nevertheless, there were hopes that union patronage would eventually develop into another element in the subsidy system. In its middle phase, therefore, the Arts Council was aiming towards a 'balanced pattern for patronage', which consisted of subsidies coming from five main sources: the government (via the Arts Council), the local authorities, industry, private sources and the trade unions. For various reasons, this pattern was never achieved. The complexities and (some would add) injustices of the rating system meant that local authorities were always unwilling to add further financial burdens on an already overstrained system: the tax concessions to industry were never granted, while inflation year by year ate away at those sums of money which private patrons might have been prepared to give. Union contributions dwindled to virtually nothing. And so gradually the Arts Council found itself seeking the money from the government which it had hoped would come from other sources. Its major partner in patronage remained the local authorities, but the balance between the sources changed. Whereas, in 1964, the Arts Council and the local authorities were giving similar amounts (though in different ways), by 1974 the Arts Council was giving three times as much as the local authorities.

Thus, the centralisation of patronage occurred which the Arts Council itself had wished to avoid, and perhaps such a centralisation was inevitable, given the current political and social climate. In a society such as Britain in the 1970s where the government controls 55 per cent of gross national product, a balanced pattern for patronage is perhaps an impossible ideal. The Arts Council, however, mitigated the effects of centralised patronage by being exceptionally detailed and careful in its procedures. This was also noticeable from the middle phase. The Drama section in 1957–8 received only £69,692 0s 7d from the total Arts Council subsidies, as compared to £650,318 11s 10d spent on music, opera and ballet, of which £302,000 (four times the drama subsidy) was spent upon the Royal Opera House, Covent Garden, alone. The Opera House was considered to be a special case, and the money given from the Treasury was for that purpose alone and could not be switched to other fields. The policy of the Drama panel was different: it handed out small sums of money to more than thirty-six projects, the largest amount being to the Old Vic (£12,000) and the smallest being £47 18s to research the possibilities of a touring grid.

Most of these amounts went to support individual, local repertory theatres outside the main commercial system. The Birmingham Rep received £5,000, the Belgrade, Coventry (which was being built) £5,686, Bristol Old Vic £2,000 and other theatres received subsidies ranging from £500 to £1,500. Although these sums were small the Arts Council was prepared to give them annually and local theatres learnt to rely on them. The Drama panel left some money aside to tackle particular problems, the most urgent being the shortage of new plays. Companies were given larger subsidies to tackle new plays (the English Stage Company, the Meadow Players), while direct bursaries were given to selected playwrights, many of whom (Wesker and Bond among them) are now well known. The panel was worried by the low standards of reps, partly caused by sheer pressure of work: it therefore encouraged and helped theatres to change from weekly to fortnightly (then to three-weekly) production runs, and sometimes helped individual companies to extend their rehearsal periods, without an equivalent extension of run. The detailed, sensible work of the Arts Council won them a reputation for reliable sensitivity, which can be a more valuable asset than mere generosity. During its middle phase, when the theatre relied (as it still does, though to a lesser extent) on box-office receipts rather than grants, the Arts Council gave invaluable support, small in terms of money, large in influence. The foundations of the current British theatre system were laid during this middle phase. What started out by being a rescue operation turned into a major reconstruction, and the consequences of Arts Council policy during this period are now visible throughout the country.

Despite the care with which it was undertaken, the reorganisation had consequences which may or may not be considered desirable and certainly were not fully realised at the outset. If we consider simply the main feature of the changes, the sudden rise of the reps and the decline of the touring theatres, the results were significant—but not necessarily significantly helpful. The local reps represented an ideal of theatre in society, an expression of regional talent and enthusiasms, which overflowed from the main auditoria into theatre-in-education programmes, local documentaries and studio theatres. An excellent ideal, shot through with humanistic values, which were expressed even in the homeliness of the buildings themselves, with their 'open' stages, coffee bars and meeting places. The reps also supplied the West End during the late 1960s with some of their most successful productions, such as Peter Barnes's *The Ruling Class* and Alan Ayckbourn's plays, which were originally always tried out at Scarborough. Nevertheless, the repertory system itself could be challenged. Reps may or may not have permanent companies, but they essentially pursue a policy of short runs, short production periods and usually of 'mixed' programmes, catering to different tastes in their communities. Touring companies, which supply productions to touring theatres, on the other hand essentially specialise. They look for 'hit' productions, which will attract audiences wherever they go and can therefore be held together for longer periods of time. A six-month tour provides the dramatist with a decent income from royalties: a three-week repertory run doesn't. Under 'normal' conditions, a 'touring' production should be better than a 'rep' one, because more money, time and planning has been spent on it.

If this is so, why did the touring theatres fail to compete with the reps? Because, some would argue, subsidies have systematically distorted the theatrical economy in favour of the reps. During the 1950s, the reps suffered most in competition with television, while the touring theatres seemed in a difficult situation but, with the backing of big commercial companies behind them, still fundamentally sound. Having given State aid to the reps initially, the Arts Council continued to do so, with the result that subsidies now build theatres, pay actors, provide workshops and publicity, and keep seat prices artificially low. 'We have blundered into a situation', one commercial manager told me, 'which encourages inbred, parochial repertory theatres at the expense of the touring theatres and the companies who supply them.'

The Arts Council recognised this problem and supported some touring companies through the Dramatic and Lyric Theatre Association (DALTA). This system has had some successes, notably in supporting several fine, non-commercial touring companies such as Prospect and the Actors Company. But it also caused problems. Tours are arranged through what is known as the guarantee system, whereby touring theatres agree to pay weekly guaranteed sums of money to the companies which visit them. These guarantees ranged in 1973 from £500 to £4,000. By subsidising certain touring companies, the Arts Council enabled them to accept far lower guarantees than would normally be considered viable. The Arts Council is able only to give grants directly to non-profit-distributing companies, such as Prospect, although commercial companies supplied most of the productions to the touring theatres. When subsidies were first handed out through DALTA, the commercial companies thus faced not only competition from the reps, but also cut-price rivals on their own touring territory. But the DALTA companies were never expected to supply more than a small proportion of the productions which the touring theatres need. By aiding a minority of companies, the Arts Council kept down the general level of guarantees, thus making it increasingly hard for commercial companies to keep going except on the routine level of low-cost comedies.

Without in any way wishing to hurt or damage the commercial system, without trying to impair the touring circuits, the Arts Council nevertheless succeeded (though perhaps only marginally, for there were other factors) in doing both. The incidental side effects of subsidies can be as important as the main ones. There is, for example, little point in handing out subsidies to writers if you are also indirectly damaging their royalties from tours. It would be possible to imagine several methods of de-centralising patronage, even today. The Arts Council, for example, could concentrate on national projects, such as the two national theatres with the

Royal Court. The Regional Arts Associations could subsidise the major reps, with perhaps direct government help as well as local authority aid and help from industry; while the local councils could look after community arts projects. The Arts Council has always tried to support the Regional Arts Associations, seeing in them alternative sources for patronage. Unfortunately, the first steps in devolution are always hard to take. The Arts Council itself has established the precedent whereby local reps look to the Arts Council for their annual subsidies, rather than to the Regional Arts Associations, with the result that the Arts Associations lack the authority to use patronage effectively. Perhaps the greatest lesson which the Arts Council has still failed to learn is actually to enjoy saying 'No' to requests for help. It has not discovered how to leave vacuums in the theatre system to allow other sources of aid to grow.

Chapter 9

Fringe alternatives

A few months before the government-backed Capital Fund was established to finance the building of new theatres, a movement began which included among its many aims that of doing without 'theatres' altogether. Exactly when the Fringe began depends on the definition of 'fringe'. Some would argue that the fringe companies which emerged during the 1960s were a logical development from the little theatres before and after the war. The word 'fringe' was in use before 1963 in connection with the theatre, but it had different associations. The revue, *Beyond the Fringe* (1960), drew its title from the many small companies which assembled at the Edinburgh Festival outside the main events. The small companies were the fringe and the revue was beyond them. Some 'fringe' companies at Edinburgh were professional, most were amateur or student companies; and they were all self-supporting. The concept of an 'all-the-year-round' fringe or of fringe theatre as an alternative to mainstream theatre was not then current. Later on in the 1960s, 'fringe' theatre became associated with the 'alternative' society, which might mean either an expression of political revolt (most noticeable in 1968, when the *évènements de mai* in Paris and the opposition to the Vietnam war in the United States provided a general Western momentum for political change, if not revolution) or the formulation of different life styles (communes rather than nuclear families) and cultures (pop-art, psychedelic experiences).

I have chosen two events from the years 1963–64, the establishment of the Traverse Theatre in Edinburgh and the Theatre of Cruelty seasons at LAMDA, as the ones which inaugurated the modern fringe. Both were important occasions in themselves from which much else derived, and both heralded the 'arrival' of two key personalities who were to influence many others. Jim Haynes and Charles Marowitz were both Americans, one who had settled in Edinburgh and the other in London. Haynes was not primarily a theatre director. He ran a bookshop in Edinburgh during the early 1960s, and then in 1963 took over a disused brothel to start the Traverse Theatre Club. The former brothel was a fascinating building, suitably sleazy, with many small rooms, linked by rickety staircases. The Edinburgh Authorities were suspicious of this venture, believing that Haynes might be using the brothel for even more immoral purposes. The tone of this building is significant: it reflected the under-ground—even vaguely illegal—origins of the movement. But within six and a half years, the reputation of the Traverse had grown to the extent that it received substantial local and State grants, found new premises, which were neatly con-verted, and had received warm tributes from such establish-ment figures as Jennie Lee and Lord Snowdon. Haynes at the old building launched into ambitious programmes of new, experimental and rare plays, staged very simply, within the confines of a bare room with lights. They included the first British performance of works by Adamov and Arrabal, the re-discovery of plays by D. H. Lawrence, the first plays by David Storey, Stanley Eveling, C. P. Taylor and Heathcote Williams. Haynes brought the La Mama company from New York to Edinburgh in 1967 and Grotowski's 13-rows Theatre in 1968, the first time that either company had visited Britain.

It is significant though that the more 'established' the Tra-verse became, the more ill-at-ease Haynes felt about its role. He left before the new theatre opened, and established the Arts Laboratory in Drury Lane, London, which became the centre for London's underground culture, just a few rooms where, surrounded by an exhibition of paintings and props for the next show, hippies could sleep for the night. Haynes was more than an entrepreneur for the *avant-garde*, whose willingness to say 'Yes' to everything which interested him more than made up for his lack of financial resources. He was also a prophet of the alternative society. The easy-going, chaotic and (Haynes would have argued) necessary tolerance caused problems with the authorities, who were particularly concerned about the prevalence of drugs and drug addicts at the Arts Lab. Although the Arts Lab nurtured several groups (among them Portable Theatre), it faced financial crises and, unlike the situation in Edinburgh, Haynes could not persuade the authorities (including the Arts Council) to help. Although the Arts Lab closed in 1969, its 'freedom' and 'tolerance' were not forgetten: somewhat of the same atmosphere was caught at the Oval House, South London, under the guidance of Peter Oliver.

Marowitz, however, was primarily a theatre director and a critic whose writing contains many brilliant passages of near-polemic. He ran workshop classes in London during the late 1950s, for actors who wanted to know about the Method; and as a teacher, he became associated with the newly-formed Royal Shakespeare Company and met Peter Brook. Brook was fascinated by the theories of Antonin Artaud, the French director, actor and writer, who died in 1948. With Brook and members of the Royal Shakespeare Company, Marowitz ran an open workshop session in the LAMDA drama school theatre, under the general title of The Theatre of Cruelty. This season in 1964 provided a representative mixture of various *avant-garde* genres. It included snatches of improvisation, an anti-fascist sketch by John Arden, a powerful short play linking Jackie Kennedy to Christine Keeler as two women suffering from the salacious curiousity of the press, a snatch from a Genet play and the first performance in Britain of Artaud's *A Spurt of Blood*. Many of the themes and outlooks which came to dominate fringe theatre were expressed in this season: but its title and main inspiration came from Artaud's manifestos, *Theatre of Cruelty 1 and 2*.

Artaud used the word 'cruelty' in an unusual way, not to mean necessarily sadism or the infliction of pain, but to indicate a superhuman inexorability which disdains the petty concerns of man. The theatre existed primarily to remind mankind of the non-human forces which control its destiny. 'We are not free and the sky can still fall on our heads' (*No More Masterpieces*). What sort of forces? Artaud was vague on this point, though he gave many illustrations. The forces were almost beyond definition: they were not necessarily volcanic or a new Ice Age, but more the primeval impulses towards destruction and creation, which belonged to the natural world and to the dark unconscious of the human mind. 'All great myths are dark....One cannot imagine all the great Fables aside from a mood of slaughter, torture and bloodshed, telling the masses about the original division of the sexes and the slaughter that came with creation' (*Theatre and the Plague*).

Some awareness of these dark forces come in human dreams and nightmares, according to Artaud, and so he urged directors and actors to call upon their memories of dreams. In this, Artaud had much in common with the Surrealists, whom he admired: 'The theatre will never find itself again...except by furnishing the spectator with the truthful precipitates of dreams, in which his taste for crime, his erotic obsessions, his savagery, his chimeras, his utopian sense of life and matter, even his cannibalism, pour out on a level not counterfeit and illusory, but interior.' The actor's task was to trigger off these interior emotions, something which could not be achieved by the conventional means of Western theatre. Naturalism or boulevard drama merely imitated the surfaces of life. Artaud wanted actors to grope beneath the surface, scratching the nerves under the skin. He wanted a theatre of violent physical images, of 'ritual' and 'shock', of mime and non-verbal cries. The closest likeness to his theatre he found in Balinese dance drama and the quasi-religious rituals of Mexico, which took place in the streets or the bullfighting arenas. 'Nobody in Europe.', he commented wryly, 'knows how to scream.' 'The actor is a heart athlete....We can indicate far fewer pressure points on which to base the soul's athleticism. The secret is to imitate those pressure points as if the muscles were flayed. The rest is achieved by the screams.'

There was some screaming in the Theatre of Cruelty season, but Brook and Marowitz sought to shock by other means. 'Shock' was considered important: on one level, it jolted actors and audiences alike out of their conventional responses, and on another, pricked the reflex action, the umpremeditated thought and gesture. 'Shock', of course, is a relative experience. Something which shocks us when we first encounter it may not shock us the second time; and the very atmosphere of an experimental theatre, where we are prepared to meet the unfamiliar, conditions us to receive 'shock' with calm. One sort of shock in the Theatre of Cruelty season was that of physical nakedness: Glenda Jackson stripped as Kennedy/Keeler in a bath. Nakedness was familiar in strip clubs but almost unknown in 'serious' theatre in this country, which was still under the laws of censorship. The LAMDA theatre club avoided prosecution by being a club. In 1963, Marowitz had staged a 'Happening' at a theatre seminar in Edinburgh, which involved a naked girl and caused a furore. By the late 1960s, nudity had become fairly usual both in fringe theatres and mainstream ones; but in 1963, it was still regarded as 'shocking'.

A cousin to the shock of nakedness was the assault on bourgeois modesties. In one scene, Keeler whipped a client, while in another, based upon an extract from Genet's *The Screens*, the actors squatted and mimed defecation. A second cousin was the assault on literature, neo-Dadaist in appearance, Artaudesque in effect. Marowitz's collage based on *Hamlet* reduced the play to a twenty-minute random synthesis of Oedipalism. A third cousin was the general attack on 'literary' plays, carefully planned as a military campaign, but with every appearance of spontaneity. On one level, members of the audience were asked to suggest words to the actors on which they could then improvise. This suggested that actors could do without formal scripts and that the relationship between the actor and his audience could be as free-flowing and supple (or as conditioned and rigid) as that of life itself. On another level, there was an attempt to replace conscious, verbal thought and argument with startling images. The chief example here was Artaud's own play, where a prostitute lifted her skirts to reveal a nest of writhing scorpions and a Man bites the Arm of God to fill the stage with A Spurt of Blood. Above all, there was an attempt to free the actor from his dependence on spoken dialogue, with all those other related pressures of imitation and character development, so that he could develop his expressiveness by other means—athleticism, mime, contacts with audience.

The Theatre of Cruelty season was a seminal event. It may have been anarchic, tatty, confused and often pretentious; but it was also full of ideas and vitality, and grasped at visions which it couldn't quite reach and couldn't even be quite sure existed. Its consequences were far-reaching. It trained the Royal Shakespeare Company actors for the shock tactics afterwards employed in Peter Brook's production of Peter Weiss's *The Persecution and Assassination of Marat as per-*

formed by the Inmates of the Asylum of Charenton under the Dir-
ection of the Marquis de Sade (1964), hereafter called
The Marat/Sade, with its mad scenes, eruptions of frenzy
stilled by momentary lethargies and reflective moments. Between 1964 and 1968, this production won no less than seven
major awards from British and American critics, gaining for
the Royal Shakespeare Company an unrivalled reputation
for excellence and daring. Less successfully, it also led to the
shock moments in Brook's *US*, a group-written play about
Vietnam, which culminated in a scene where live butterflies
were released into the auditorium. One was apparently
caught and burnt alive, a terrible image which symbolised
both the helplessness of Vietnam and the Buddhist monks
who burnt themselves in protest against the outrages. The
house styles of British acting changed. Once British acting in
general had been considered prim, upper-class and inhibited;
then, in the late 1950s, it was gruff, tough and virile; then,
from the mid-1960s, it was known for mime, style and
athleticism, with such productions as *The Royal Hunt of the Sun*
and Brook's *A Midsummer Night's Dream* (1970) with its trapezes and juggling.

If 'mainstream' theatre was influenced by the season,
'fringe' theatres were transformed by it. Apart from all other
considerations the season at LAMDA proved, with the example of the Traverse, that exciting new theatrical ideas could
be performed in rudimentary surroundings. In London,
many small theatres sprang up, some in pubs (King's Head,
Islington, in 1971, The Bush, Shepherds Bush, 1972), some in
converted cellars (including Charles Marowitz's Open Space
Theatre, 1968, and the Soho-Poly, 1970) and some in community centres (Oval House, 1966). But the Theatre of
Cruelty season also opened up lines of development which
fringe companies could follow. Non-verbal sounds and
noises, including screaming, were elaborated into impressive
tribal chants by the Roy Hart Theatre (started in 1967). Improvisational drama took a strange, Dadaist shape in the
hands of The People Show (1965). Artaudesque shock imagery influenced many companies, while others recognised the
potential of mime and sound together, exploited 'environmentally'. Ironically, under the wings of the most
'established' (though newly so) permanent company in the

country, several eggs hatched, which became chicks and fluttered their several ways without returning to the nest.

There are perhaps four distinct lines of fringe development which followed the Theatre of Cruelty season: the 'environmental' companies, the agit-prop ones, the multi-media groups and the neo-Dadaists. They each drew inspiration from sources other than the season, and need to be considered separately; but without the season, the impetus and the general recognition of what could be done by the fringe theatre might well not have been present. If we wish, however, to indicate the general importance of the fringe to British theatre, we need perhaps only to consider statistics from one year and from one section of their work, the production of new plays in fringe theatres. In 1971–2, 480 new plays were produced in Britain, a figure which was remarkably close to the average number of new plays produced in the early years of the century, when roughly 450–500 new plays annually were submitted to the censor. Of these new plays, 300 were staged in fringe theatres, and London fringe theatres alone staged 238 premières. More than half of the total output of new plays was produced in London fringe theatres; and while their quality varied sharply from the most careless and amateur show to productions which were of a quality to transfer to 'mainstream' rep and West End theatres, the importance of these 'new-play' productions cannot be ignored or brushed aside. Without the hard, ill-paid and enthusiastic work of the fringe companies, the vitality of British theatre (as gauged by the number of premières) would have seemed on the wane indeed, despite subsidies, the reps and the nationals.

1 Environmental companies

British 'environmental' companies were influenced by two key foreign movements. One came from Opole in Poland, where Jerzy Grotowski established his Theatre Laboratory in 1959; while the second came from the United States, from theatre communes, such as the Living Theatre, and Grotowski-inspired experimental companies, such as Richard Schechner's The Performing Garage (established in 1967).

The distinguishing feature of all these groups was the discovery of new actor-audience relationships which in turn led to the exploration of spaces within rooms and the attempt to develop various methods of surrounding or isolating acting and public 'areas'.

Grotowski regarded the relationship between the actor and his audience as fundamental to all forms of theatre; and was particularly concerned to remove the 'obstacles' which prevented this relationship from 'developing'. One obstacle was the proscenium arch, which kept actors and audiences in 'separate rooms', linked by a curtain, and reduced the public to the situation of 'voyeurs'. Another was the sheer size of the audience: he preferred a handful of spectators, not more than fifty, to a large house because with small audiences it was possible to establish personal dialogues. Make-up, costume and disguise could also be barriers, unless they were used for specific effects, but the greatest obstacle of all was the false 'performance mentality'—the attempts of the actor to show off, delude, seduce or conquer. Grotowski's training technique was thus designed to strip the actor of his normal protective masks, among them clothes; and he developed various physical training methods (linked to 'spiritual' ones, such as exercises in mental concentration) so that the whole body of the actor, from his breathing to his leg muscles, would become his main medium of artistic expression.

The Living Theatre, established by Julian Beck and Judith Malina, was the best known of the American 'environmental' companies; a travelling 'commune' of actors, whose first production in London (*The Connection* in 1961) was regarded as almost a triumph of naturalism, for it was assumed that they actually were the drug addicts of the script, but whose subsequent productions veered away from naturalism. In *Frankenstein* (London, 1971), the audience was surrounded by images of man's inhumanity to man. The Living Theatre actors would mingle with their audiences, argue with them, harangue and insult them, in an effort to break down normal restraints. Their demands were absolute and somewhat humourless. 'I demand everything,' said Judith Malina, 'total love, an end to all forms of violence and cruelty such as money, hunger, prisons, people doing work they hate.'

The Liquid Theatre, another company from the United

States, was less polemical in its approach. It interpreted environmentalism to mean encouraging the audience to feel new sensuous experiences. It specialised in feeling, touching and caressing the public to the strains of soft music. Richard Schechner of The Performing Garage was the most intellectually ambitious director of the American groups. A friend of both Grotowski and Brook, Schechner was concerned, first, to establish certain principles about the use of space within buildings used for theatre purposes, second, to evolve 'genuine' (as opposed to forcefully induced) forms of audience participation and, lastly, to consider the possible therapeutic use of drama. He rejected firmly the 'aesthetic' approach to the theatre. Drama's 'usefulness' consisted in awakening audiences to their surroundings, which might be political, or physical (as in the case of room dimensions)—or the significance of clothes. In a workshop session in Edinburgh (1974), he persuaded members of his audience to exchange clothes, right down to and including their pants, which must have meant overcoming a few inhibitions.

The influence of these groups permeated the fringe movement in Britain. In 1968, for example, the Freehold company was formed, whose leading director was an American, Nancy Meckler. The Freehold used some of the vocal and bodily exercise pioneered by Grotowski, evolving a disciplined, sound-movement theatre of its own. In *Antigone* (1969), the company chose not just to re-tell the Antigone story, but rather to illustrate certain elemental themes, such as the interchangeability of the dead Polyneices (representing all dead brothers), the kinship of Man and the struggle between social organisation and the love of freedom. Most of the Freehold's basic ideas were developed through group improvisations, but Stephen Berkoff's London Theatre Group (1969) and Roy Hart's company both developed along more authoritarian lines. Berkoff, best known perhaps for his realisations of Kafka's *The Trial* and *Metamorphosis*, was particularly concerned with carefully organised movement patterns, performed by the group in a style which was not quite dance, not quite army drill and involved some mime. Improvisation would have been out of place in his theatre, and probably out of step as well. Hart, an analyst, developed a method of increasing the range of the voice, remarkably successful in his personal case. He ran a small club in Hampstead to which everyone was invited to come and sing, cry, shout and bellow according to their means. He sometimes organised the choral effects into sung myths, such as his version of the *Bacchae*, and while his methods included improvisation (indeed encouraged it), his overall approach was conditioned by the somewhat messianic belief that full vocal ranges were the key to the liberation of the inner man.

In addition to such companies, there were also 'places' for environmental groups, usually unconventional buildings which were attractive for their architecture or 'free' atmosphere. One was in Liverpool, an old Church, the Blackie, converted into a project known as Great Georges, which invited visiting professional companies and encouraged the inhabitants of the somewhat run-down neighbourhoods nearby to participate in community get-togethers. Another was the Roundhouse in London, an old massive industrial building which Wesker chose originally to house his Centre 42 project; while others included the Oval House, the Arts Lab and various cellars or attics around London with names like Mum's Underground. Several companies toured around Europe with their environmental productions, nearly always stopping over at the Mickery in Amsterdam, the unofficial headquarters of many fringe teams. Jérome Savary, a director based in Paris with a multi-national (theatrical) company, visited Britain many times; with his version of Arrabal's *The Labyrinth* with its naked actor swinging over the heads of his audience, or the two gloriously anarchic productions of his Grand Magic Circus, *Robinson Crusoe* and *Scenes of Love and Death from Christ to Mao*. Another group which was based in France and included Americans and Britons in its numbers was les Tréteaux Libres. The environmental companies, which differed greatly in styles and qualities, encouraged fringe theatres to use their buildings imaginatively, to develop unconventional audience-actor relationships and to use sound in surprising (and not always cacophonous) ways.

2   Agit-prop

Environmental companies were not usually politically orientated, or, if they were, their inspiration came mainly from anarchism or a quasi-mystical Zen religiosity which had the incidental effect of being against all governments. There were also companies, however, who might have used Grotowski-inspired techniques but would have placed political action in the forefront of their aims. 'Agit-prop', a useful but loose word deriving from 'agitational propaganda', spans a range of political stances, in Britain mainly 'left-wing'. While few British companies advocated outright, violent revolution, in the traditional pattern of agit-prop, many called for revolutionary change without bombing or bloodshed—but also without those peaceful compromises embodied in the liberal idea of gradual evolution.

At one end of the scale, small companies like the Red Ladder (formerly Agitprop Theatre, founded 1968) went around community centres with plays about housing problems, exploitation by property developers and so on, casting over their documentary-based plays a red glow of Marxist commitment. Such teams used written scripts, usually in the style of Brecht, with popular songs and placards to inject a touch of entertainment. Much more sophisticated both in their political attitudes and in their dramatic techniques were two other politically orientated companies, the 7.84 company led by the dramatist John McGrath (founded in early 1972) and Joint Stock, which included two leading British directors, Max Stafford-Clarke and William Gaskill, and produced plays by leading writers, among them David Hare, Stanley Eveling and Heathcote Williams.

The distinguishing feature of both those groups was that they included writers, actors and directors who could have worked in the mainstream theatres, if they had wanted to. They chose to work in the comparative impoverishment of touring fringe groups in order to bring their political beliefs to sections of the population which might not otherwise visit the theatre. They also tackled plays in various styles. Arden and D'Arcy's *The Ballygombeen Bequest* (7.84, 1973) was an attack on the English absentee landlords in Ireland, based on an example of 'exploitation' and extended to cover the total English involvement in Ireland. A Scottish branch of 7.84 compiled a documentary about the exploitation of Scotland, concentrating particularly on Scottish oil; while *Fish in the Sea* by McGrath was an account of a workers' sit-in at a factory threatened by closure, which considered its effects both on the lives of the workers and their families, and its political repercussions. The stress in such plays was broadly rather than narrowly left-wing, supporting the workers against the bosses, the regions against the central government, the right to work (and to strike) as opposed to individualism and the competitiveness of the free enterprise economy.

Joint Stock shared similar beliefs, but picked a wider range of authors and productions. Some were austere and serious, such as David Hare's *Fanshen*, an account of how a Chinese village changed after the Mao-led revolution, the complexities of this change and the problems which arose. Others were scarcely political (Eveling's *Shivvers*, a comedy about how low a man can sink and the advantages of the lower depths), or closer to a pub music hall (*The Doomduckers' Ball*). A strong music-hall element, with cartoons and songs, also affected other companies, which used the genre to attack various Western governments. David Edgar wrote two such cartoon scripts for the General Will (a company from Bradford University, founded in 1971), attacking the then Tory government. Albert Hunt, another writer-director from Bradford, wrote two other cartoon 'documentaries' (which were not documentaries at all) *John Ford's Cuban Missile Crisis*, based on Kennedy's confrontation over Cuba, and *James Harold Wilson Sinks the Bismark*. There were many such cartoon-music-hall-inspired productions, from companies like Belt and Braces, and Hull Truck.

The populism of the British agit-prop companies provided a marked contrast with the intensity of some Off-off Broadway companies, whose minds and political outlooks were filled by the Vietnam war and its surrounding doubts about the American Way of Life. The visits of the La Mama company in 1967, of Chaikin's Open Theatre in 1967 and the Bread and Puppet Company in 1969 showed London audiences a forceful theatre launching general attacks against a range of American phenomena (its ad-mass outlooks, its neo-colonialism), beside which British fringe companies seemed somewhat parochial. They tended to be folksier, better-humoured (though not so funny) and more inclined towards documentary naturalism. Similarly, the *événements de mai* in

Paris (1968) provoked no equivalent student or other rebellion in Britain, a fact which was ruefully noted in Trevor Griffith's play, *The Party*.

3 Multi-media groups

Whereas the 'environmental' companies based their work upon flexible audience-actor relationships, the 'multi-media' groups produced events which involved amplified sound (usually rock music) and light shows, having the effect of imposing these elements upon the human relationships within the theatre. The contrast between the two genres can be illustrated by two productions of Sam Shepard's *The Tooth of Crime*, a story about two folk heroes (pop stars, prize fighters or what you will), one declining and the other ascending. In London, the battle between them was seen in terms of rock music (which Shepard had written) and both stars were basically singers, in spangled costumes, clutching microphones. Schechner's production (seen in Edinburgh, 1974) dispensed with the spots and the amplifiers and concentrated on the rhythms of half-spoken, half-sung speech, on intimate audience-actor contact (the public could move around the performing area) and was partly improvised. The London production belonged, in my terminology, to multi-media productions: the Edinburgh version to environmental ones.

Multi-media companies developed from pop-shows. If the leading West End examples turned out to be from Broadway and, disappointingly, such works as *Hair* and *Jesus Christ Superstar*, there were several fringe multi-media companies which tried to extend the range of their work beyond the average hilarities of pop festivals. Pip Simmons Group, strongly influenced by American rock groups, began as an ordinary play-producing fringe company, tackling production style, blending rock with music-hall slapstick, borrowing cartoon characters (such as Superman) and pop-art styles. It was also more politically orientated than other multi-media groups, in such productions as *The George Jackson Black and White Minstrel Show*. Founded in 1968, the Pip Simmons Group produced an off-shoot company, Nice Pussy, whose first production was again based upon rock, pop and ad-mass.

Other companies followed, the Welfare State (from Leeds) and the Moving Being. As pop styles changed (from, say, Rolling Stones music to that of Pink Floyd), these companies changed too, finding appropriate light effects to match. The abrupt spots selecting the lead singer from the rest of the group might be suitable for Stones music, whereas moving and slowly merging patterns of colour, like copulating organisms on the sea bed, were considered more appropriate for Pink Floyd. Not all companies, however, stayed with rock music: they found that amplified sound caused theatrical problems, among them how to prevent audiences from being blasted out of their seats and the actors from being upstaged by electronics. Some companies turned to a mixture of folk music and rock, as in the Celtic musical, *Pucka Ri* (1973), while others concentrated on forms of visual display, such as the Black Box Theatre. Black Box was a company formed in 1965 but which held its first performance-exhibitions in 1970. It would build large-scale images, of woods, streams, pools and fountains, using light projected through coloured glass as a means of changing the images and, sometimes, of telling a visual story (such as *Narcissus*, 1974).

4   The neo-Dadaists

Many fringe groups were more lighthearted than these summaries imply. Students with satirical revues joined the fringe circuits, which were gradually growing up around the country, involving university theatres, studio theatres connected to reps and independent fringe theatres. Among the professional or semi-professional fringe groups, small, basically non-political, pub music-hall teams sprang up, such as Ken Campbell's Road Show with such 'stars' as the incredible Sylveste McCoy, and competitions like the World Ferret-Down-Trousers Record. The Low Moan Spectacular (formed 1970) specialised in very funny and accurate parodies, of variety shows in a South American night-club (*El Coca-Cola Grande*) and Bulldog Drummond adventure stories

(*Bullshot Crummond*). The Low Moan Spectacular gained a cult following in Britain and the United States, a proper reward for their skill.

These two companies, however, were comparatively non-experimental. The distinctive feature of many fringe comedy and non-comedy teams was their re-discovery of the delights in Dadaism, in nonsense for its own sake and in the shock ramming together of unlikely images. The leading group here was The People Show (formed in 1965), which consisted of four main actors, Mark Long, Laura Gilbert, Mike Figgis and José Nava. The many productions of The People Show were usually improvised in part, but the structure was always determined in advance, usually a sequence of sounds and images, centred (not logically) around an atmosphere rather than a story. One show took place in a seedy, Graham Greene-type inn, with rain beating on a metal roof, a man eating himself to death, billiards played with crooked cues on a collapsing table and Guinness sucked through a ten-foot straw. The People Show risked much by their improvisations, lending an edge of daring to their work, much increased by their preparedness to shock audiences out of modesties and lethargies. In one show, Mike Figgis seemed to be masturbating on stage, but eventually drew out a lump of red meat from his guts, which he then ate.

There were other improvisation groups, among them Sal's Meat Market (formed in 1972) with two wise-cracking and inventive comedians, Hassett and Ratzenburger, Neil Hornick's Phantom Captain, Bruce Lacey's L'Ecole de l'Art Infantile and the John Bull Puncture Repair Kit. Most of their shows were planned in advance, but included areas where improvisation could take over. The key element in their work was a loose-limbed irreverence, borrowed half from the *Goon Show* or *Monty Python's Flying Circus* (two BBC programmes) and half from various *avant-garde* theatrical ideas, culled from Artaud and others. The real gap in the work of the neo-Dadaist fringe groups was in any real attempt to explore the idea of 'chance'.

'Chance' was after all the connecting link between improvisational drama (which depended, or should have done, on the actors reacting to stimuli from the audience) and Dadaism, based on the belief that chance governs all.

Various composers of music after the war (John Cage and Christian Wolff in the United States, Cornelius Cardew in Britain) used 'chance' as part of their 'methods', if this isn't a contradiction in terms. Cage believed that all sounds had value and beauty, as did silence, and that we restricted our appreciation of sound by trying to impose man-made patterns on it. We only listened to what we wanted to hear, not what was there, and by that means were shutting out the beauty of the world. Similar arguments might have been put forward for 'chance' drama, and at one period in the early 1960s, the Happenings movement veered in this direction, only to be distracted by politics. The neo-Dadaist fringe companies were rarely willing to risk random events from breaking up their shows. At one performance, several police cars came blaring past the theatre, hooters and sirens sounding, the blue lights visible through the partly covered windows of the theatre. The effect was instantaneous and dramatic. But the actors, although improvising, took no notice whatsoever. Their improvisation involved concentration, of shutting out the world around. Among composers, there was an attempt to open out the mind to the surrounding world. They would have delighted in the police sirens.

The four categories mentioned above were really fringe styles, alternatives which many different companies adopted sometimes for a few months or a year, sometimes as house styles. But the fringe also took on the function of the old little theatres, by providing places and companies which could tackle new (usually conventionally written) plays. Many fringe theatres were established around London and elsewhere in the country, of which the most notable and one of the first was Marowitz's Open Space Theatre. A pub-theatre movement began at the King's Head in Islington, which offered dinner and a show, at The Bush, at the Act Inn, the Lamb and Flag, the Orange Tree, the Pindar of Wakefield and the Playroom. Many of these pub-theatre managements were ambitious and quick to detect new fringe talents: Howard Gibbins at The Bush was one of them, with Brian Macdermott the founder of The Bush, and Charles Crockett. They brought such varied talents as Lindsay Kemp (the mime whose production, *Flowers*, transferred to the Regent Theatre in 1974), David Edgar (whose musical *Dick Deterred* was a noted satire on the Nixon-Watergate affair), Stephen Poliakoff and Sal's Meat Market to an area of West London without a theatre.

These fringe theatres were eager to produce new plays, if only because the Arts Council New Drama grants (which were not enough to compensate major rep theatres for producing new plays with all the risks entailed) were a valuable part of their income. Teams of playwrights formed small companies, of which the best known was Portable Theatre (founded in 1968, disbanded in 1972). The first production of Portable Theatre was an account of Kafka's life, based on his diaries and performed at the Arts Lab. David Hare interpreted these diaries as being about 'a young man freeing himself from the repressions of his bourgeois background'. This view was in a sense a typical one of the group, which came to include Snoo Wilson, Howard Brenton and Malcolm Griffiths, in that it was firmly anti-bourgeois. They had something in common both with the agit-prop companies and with the Angry Young Men of the 1950s. From their fringe origins, David Hare and Howard Brenton both graduated to rep and leading subsidised theatres, such as the Royal Court, while Snoo Wilson's *The Beast* was produced by the Royal Shakespeare Company at The Place in 1974. They were thus absorbed into mainstream theatre, forming a significant part of the Second Wave of new British dramatists, as John Russell Taylor obligingly dubbed them. They also collaborated on group-written plays, such as *Lay By* (about rape, prurience and the pornographic society) and *England's Ireland*, whose title is self-explanatory. But Portable Theatre was also prepared to tackle works by writers not normally associated with the group, such as Chris Wilkinson with his two savage satires on violence and pornography, *I Was Hitler's Maid* and *Plays for Rubber Go-Go Girls*.

David Halliwell, who started another play-producing and writing group, Quipu, was known as a dramatist before the formation of the company. His *Little Malcolm and His Struggle Against the Eunuchs*, a sad but funny account of a student rebel who dreams of leading a revolutionary movement against the establishment and becomes a fascist bully in miniature, was successfully produced in London in 1965, without a long run, although a film was eventually made of it. Quipu was the first lunchtime theatre club in London, founded in 1966, where short plays could be tried out, often with well-known actors who were appearing during the evenings in West End theatres. Through Quipu, Halliwell could also develop some of his own dramatic ideas, which included 'multi-viewpoint' drama, 'where the audience experiences the characters as they, the characters, experience themselves...and each other'. His first play in this style, *K. D. Dufford...*, 1969, was an account of a child murder, from many different angles, including that of the murderer, Dufford. It involved many devices, freezing the action, changing acting styles, switching from area to area of the stage to present different viewpoints.

Portable Theatre and Quipu were both formed more or less in accordance with the visions of their creators. They became noted for certain types of plays. Other play-producing theatres and companies had no such central outlook, but enjoyed a more catholic approach. At the Soho-Poly, Fred Proud and Verity Bargate produced a wide variety of plays, written by such writers as David Edgar and Cecil Taylor, and attracted star actors to lunch-time productions (such as Colin Blakeley). The Wakefield Tricycle Company (started by Ken Chubb and Shirley Barrie in 1972) began at the Pindar of Wakefield with productions of rare French plays (by Tardieu and others) and then, too, encouraged plays by new British writers. The great merit of the play-producing groups and theatres was that they kept alive 'orthodox' experimental theatre at a time when the fringe was in danger of being swamped by the 'unorthodox' variety, the environmental and multi-media companies.

The relationship of the 'fringe' to mainstream theatre was complicated. It did not usually share the stance of the little theatres, which always tended to look towards transfers into commercial theatre to justify their existences. Indeed there was a certain polarisation of taste, whereby fringe theatres attracted fringe audiences who would have disliked and avoided mainstream theatres. On the other hand, there were occasional transfers to the West End (say, of E. A. Whitehead's *The Foursome* from the Theatre Upstairs). The leading subsidised theatres, however, cast a benevolent eye towards their struggling fringe rivals. The Royal Court staged a *Come Together* season for fringe companies in 1970, while Peter Hall, when he took over the new National company in 1974, indicated that he wished the Cottesloe Theatre in the new National Theatre Building to be devoted to visiting fringe companies. Many reps used their studio theatres for fringe purposes.

There was also a complicated relationship between the fringe and society at large. The fringe catered for those who had at least acquired the taste for the unconventional, occasionally rebellious and underground worlds; but they were also prepared to take part in very worthy above-ground schemes. Ed Berman of the Inter-Action Group inaugurated a number of children's theatre schemes, among them a Fun Bus which visited playgrounds. Similarly, the Bubble Theatre Company, subsidised by the Greater London Arts Association, toured around London parks with productions staged in a kind of tent. But it was hard to reconcile the original, experimental, 'anything goes' role of the fringe with the social purposiveness, and this conflict (which rarely became an open battle) was also illustrated in the struggle for fringe grants from the Arts Council. If the fringe movement was to be genuinely independent, genuinely prepared to be radical or subversive or shocking, it could hardly expect to be subsidised by the State at the same time. And yet it was, a British compromise which may have watered down both the aggression of the fringe groups and tempered the loftiness of the establishment with a genuine concern for the young and the novel. There were signs in the early 1970s that the enthusiasm of the fringe (at its peak perhaps during the years 1967–72) was on the wane. The outstanding talents which emerged during this period became absorbed into mainstream theatre, while particular causes for political grievance (notably, even in Britain, the Vietnam war) had changed towards a general political discontent which could not be easily pinned down to any one issue. At best, the fringe was piece-meal theatre, seizing many different ideas and discarding them, almost too soon after trying them out. Too many fringe productions gave the impression of being instant art, soluble in cold water as well as hot. Despite the small grants and subsidies, the struggle to maintain little fringe theatres was unending, and managers and directors simply ran out of energy and money. By 1974, some leading British directors, finding conformism among mainstream theatres and tatty hopefulness among fringe ones, sought other territories where they could fundamentally re-examine the nature of their arts. Peter Brook was one—who staged *Orghast* at Persepolis in Persia and then, with the aid of a French Government grant, established a theatre research centre in Paris. Without such leaders, the British fringe seemed to settle down into a useful but scarcely *avant-garde* rut, of cheerful small shows, transient companies of different hues and new plays of varying merits.

Chapter 10

National aspirations

In 1963, Britain, having mainly been without a national theatre, found herself virtually with two. The officially titled National Theatre opened its first London season at its temporary home, the Old Vic, on 22 October 1963. The first production was *Hamlet*, starring Peter O'Toole and directed by Sir Laurence Olivier, its first artistic director. In the previous years, however, Peter Hall, who was appointed as artistic director of the Shakespeare Memorial Theatre in 1959, had rapidly established what was generally considered to be a national company, the Royal Shakespeare Company, with a permanent ensemble, two theatres (in Stratford and at the Aldwych, London) and the reputation of being the liveliest, finest company in Britain. If the National Theatre Company was the *de jure* national, the Royal Shakespeare Company could regard itself as being then the *de facto* one. Both companies expected new theatres, the National Theatre Company on a South Bank site which eventually settled on Princess Meadow downstream from Waterloo, and the Royal Shakespeare Company on the Barbican development near St Paul's Cathedral. Both companies either received or expected to receive grants to match their status, both acted as cultural emissaries abroad and as leading tourist attractions at home, and both drew their strength of appeal partly by calling on folk memories, the Royal Shakespeare Company from Shakespeare and Stratford, and the National from the glowing memories of the Olivier/Richardson Old Vic Company seasons in the last years of the war.

Why were these companies not amalgamated? National theatres, like marriages, stale with repetition: it suggests a cultural bigamy on the part of the State. There were attempts to unite the companies, during 1960–2, from which the RSC withdrew. The reasons for the failure to amalgamate are complex. The superficial reason was that the RSC, having just taken on the leases of the Aldwych and (for a season) the Arts Theatre Club, was unable to break from these contracts to join the NT project. But in 1959, Olivier had apparently invited Peter Hall to join him in working toward a National Theatre, and Hall refused, wishing to press ahead with his plans for the Shakespeare Memorial Theatre. It seemed not a decision based upon personal differences. Olivier and Hall collaborated happily on the planning and design of the new National Theatre building. Hall was appointed as Olivier's successor in November 1973 (with Olivier's approval) and they retained a warm and mutual respect. The fundamental cause for the separation was the general feeling that the two companies had 'evolved' differently in as much as they had evolved at all and that they were both on the verge of new challenges which amalgamation would have caused them to neglect.

The Stratford theatre, for example, possessed a long and honourable history before its metamorphosis into the Royal Shakespeare Theatre and company. Established by Frank Benson, a prophet of the modern repertory movement, in 1879, it was originally a summer festival theatre. Its old building, 'something of a Victorian monstrosity', was burnt down in 1926, which caused a more modern theatre to open in 1932. Sir Barry Jackson took over the Festival Season after the war, at a time when, according to Peter Brook, 'every conceivable value was buried in deadly sentimentality and complacent worthiness'. Jackson, then an elderly man, was very alert to this musty air of tradition and the need for radical change. Among his directors for the first season was Brook, whose astonishing *Love's Labour's Lost*, which broke away from the rather too poised exchanges of wit and achieved a youthful, flowing intoxication of spirits, was the year's great success and established Brook's reputation when he was only twenty. For the next few years the gaiety of this production dogged Brook: West End managers chose him to direct frothy insubstantial plays, such as Roussin's *The Little Hut*. Peter Hall saw this *Love's Labour's Lost* too, and ten years later, in 1956, he directed the same play for his début at Stratford. Jackson also introduced some young actors into the company, among them Paul Scofield, and, although Jackson retired in 1948, some residue of the changes which he had brought about was retained by his successor, Anthony Quayle. Jackson had sought for a permanent company, basically without stars; but his policy lost money. Quayle introduced stars into the Stratford seasons, cut down the number of productions each year, tried to improve their quality and launched a policy of tours abroad. In 1955, for example, Laurence Olivier and Vivien Leigh headed the Stratford company, while the touring company featured John Gielgud and Peggy Ashcroft. But Quayle, and his eventual co-director and successor Glen Byam Shaw, did not neglect the new talents discovered in Jackson's régime. Brook directed Olivier in a play previously considered intractable, *Titus Andronicus*, 1955, a success which in its physical power, its bloodthirstiness and sophisticated Grand Guignol anticipated *The Marat/Sade* and marked Brook's development from a brilliant young director of light comedies into someone who could be relied upon to tackle violence and tragedy as well. During the 1950s, the Stratford theatre rarely had even a semi-permanent company, but it regularly brought together established stars (Redgrave, Gielgud, Olivier, Ashcroft, Tearle and Wynyard) with up-and-coming ones (Burton, Scofield and Albert Finney). The touring companies visited Australia (1952–3), Canada and the United States (1953–4) and Russia (1958–9), by which time it had become the *de facto* national, the British way of returning visits from abroad by other national companies.

In contrast, the officially titled National Theatre had an erratic history indeed. The idea was originally proposed by a publisher, Effingham Wilson, in 1848, who afterwards received unexpected financial support from a brewer. A fund was started, but the scheme drifted into long periods of inertia, enlivened by the support (at different times) of Matthew Arnold, William Archer, Granville-Barker, Shaw and Winston Churchill. Several sites were considered and one actually bought, in 1937, opposite the Victoria and Albert Museum in Kensington. After the war, with the plans still on the drawing board, the LCC swopped this site for another one on the South Bank, where in 1951 the Queen laid the foundation stone. In 1952, this site too was changed to another one by the river. In 1949, the National Theatre Bill allowed the Government to pay up to a million pounds towards the project, a sum which was to be paid at the discretion of the Chancellor of the Exchequer. There were by this time many different authorities involved, including the LCC and the government, and the discussions still dragged on, with costs escalating and different ideas (such as a twin building housing an opera house and a national theatre) competing for acceptance. It was not until 1969 that plans were formally accepted on all sides and the building actually started. By this time, the costs had escalated, first to about £7½ million and then to £14 million. The opening of the National Theatre was planned for 1973, then 1974, when it was delayed once again and hit by a severe economic recession, which cast even the move into the new buildings in doubt. It opened in fact in March 1976.

In the meantime, however, a National Theatre company had been formed, and the impetus towards the company, as opposed to the building, really began in 1958, when Sir Laurence Olivier was appointed as trustee of the National Theatre. There were many hitches. On 9 December 1960, the Executive Committee of the Joint Council of the National Theatre presented a memorandum to the Chancellor of the Exchequer, Selwyn Lloyd, that the new National Theatre building should be built on the South Bank and opened in 1964, the quatercentenary of Shakespeare's birth. The company should employ 150 players and incorporate the RSC. In 1961, the Chancellor announced that he and the government could not support this scheme, on the grounds that it would cost more than the estimated £2,300,000; but this opposition was withdrawn, when the LCC offered to pay more than half of the estimated cost of the new building. This scheme for the new building was again dropped, and a temporary home for the newly formed NT company was found at the Old Vic, which was clearly too small for the size of the company originally envisaged. The RSC thus withdrew from the scheme.

The temporary home of the NT, the Old Vic, however, carried with it strong historical associations, first with Lilian Baylis who in 1912 had taken over a temperance music hall and transformed it into the first serious attempt to provide good drama, centred upon Shakespeare, at prices which the working classes could afford, and, second, with the great achievements of the Old Vic company (with Olivier and Richardson) during the Second World War. Although the Old Vic had fallen somewhat into decline during the 1950s, it had retained much of its almost symbolic appeal. John Neville and Richard Burton were the matinée idols of the early 1950s, and the last major achievement of the Old Vic management was to stage over several years the complete cycle of Shakespeare's plays. Olivier was regarded (rightly) as being one of the last, but the greatest, of the actor-managers. One important difference between the RSC and the NT was that between the temperament and reputations of its two leaders during the early 1960s.

Olivier was by any standards a star, a figure who towered above his comtemporaries in British drama. As he pointed out, he may not have been an ideal first director of the NT but he was the only one whose reputation alone could help to bring it into existence. The policy at the NT partly reflected his strengths and perhaps weaknesses. Oliver was somewhat unsure of the new wave of drama which had emerged since 1956, and so he appointed Kenneth Tynan as his literary adviser, a deliberately contrived blend of traditional skills with the new radicalism. Together, they sought for a wide range of drama, reflecting genres from abroad, styles in this country, so that the NT would provide in its repertoires something like a library of great drama. The play selection policy rarely expressed any prevailing outlook. Noël Coward's production of his *Hay Fever* offset William Gaskill's production of *Mother Courage* in the 1964–5 season. Although Olivier brought together an 'inner circle' of directors, mainly from the Royal Court, such as John Dexter and William Gaskill, who were later followed by Michael Blakemore, Jonathan Miller and Frank Dunlop, he tended not to aim for the consistent directorial approaches which, as we shall see, characterised the RSC. Between October 1963 and October 1974, no less than 41 directors were given productions at the NT, 25 of them directing only one play. Some directors came from abroad for specific productions, Zeffirelli (for *Much Ado* and *Saturday, Sunday, Monday*), Ingmar Bergman (for *Hedda Gabler*), Victor Garcia (for Arrabal's *The Architect and the Emperor from Assyria*) and Wekworth and Tenschert for a Brechtian *Coriolanus*. Among the 'inner circle' directors, Dexter tackled 13 productions, Olivier 9, Blakemore and Miller 6 apiece, and Dunlop 5.

Among the 'inner circle' directors, there was also a careful blend of outlooks. Dexter, who was responsible for many outstanding productions, was not someone like Brook whose approach could be quickly identified. Dexter possessed obvious talents for visual effects and organising mime or complicated stage movements: these were particularly evident in his productions of *The Royal Hunt of the Sun* (1964), *Armstrong's Last Goodnight* (1965), *A Bond Honoured* (1966) and *Equus* (1973) where he trained the actors to rear their heads and paw the ground as the horses which haunted the imagination of a boy, Alan Strang. His greatest quality, however, did not rest with these gifts, but in his sensitive grasp of the styles most appropriate for the selected plays. He allowed Olivier's performance to mould his production of *Othello* (1964), not attempting to cut the actor's vision to suit his directorial cloth. He directed equally well at the Chichester Festival Theatre where, in the beginning, NT productions were staged, often before transferring to the Old Vic: he understood the demands of the open stage as well as those of the proscenium arch. He could also be daring. There was no actual script for Shaffer's *Black Comedy* before the rehearsals began, just an idea and a few scenes which were rapidly brought together into a neat farce, conventional in structure though with an original idea, with Peter Shaffer re-writing the script to the very days before the opening. Dexter could be tough with his actors, but he also knew when to get out of their way, with the result that he stimulated them towards outstanding performances: Robert Stephens and Colin Blakeley in *The Royal Hunt of the Sun*, Albert Finney and Stephens in *Armstrong's Last Goodnight*, Alec McCowen and Diana Rigg in *The Misanthrope* (1973) and McCowen and Peter Firth in *Equus*. Without Dexter's pragmatic brilliance (shown to disadvantage in 'committed' plays, such as Griffiths's *The Party*), the record of the NT would have been worthy but without panache.

Olivier's best productions were those of standard classics, *Uncle Vanya* (1963), *The Crucible* (1965), *Juno and the Paycock* (1966), *The Three Sisters* (1967) and *Eden End* (1974). Blakemore was, like Dexter, an adaptable director, able to give leeway to his actors, to organise a complicated stage picture and to change his style radically according to each play. He was responsible for Peter Nichols's *The National Health* (1969, his first NT production), O'Neill's *A Long Day's Journey into Night* (1971) and the Hecht/MacArthur comedy, *The Front Page* (1972). The NT also invited leading directors from other British companies, such as George Devine and Lindsay Anderson (from the Royal Court), Clifford Williams (from the RSC), Peter Brook, Glen Byam Shaw and even Tyrone Guthrie, the elder statesman among British directors, who directed *Tartuffe* and *Volpone* in the 1967–8 seasons.

This 'mixed policy' outlook succeeded very well in the first four years of the NT's existence, when out of twenty-eight productions, all but six were critical and popular successes. The most common complaint then against the NT was that it was so difficult to get seats for their productions. During the second four years, they also presented twenty-eight plays, but nearly half of them were comparative failures. This, by normal commercial standards, would still be regarded as a good average, but the NT had set high aims for itself. In 1970–1, the NT hit a bad patch: Olivier was seriously ill, a West End season at the New Theatre which included Giraudoux's *Amphitryon 38* and Mitchell's *Tyger* was a disastrous financial flop, while some new plays at the Old Vic drew poor houses. There were also large cracks visible to the public eye in the structure of the NT organisation. Kenneth Tynan, for example, came into conflict with the NT Board, led by Lord Chandos, over Hochhuth's *Soldiers*, a historical play which put forward the view that Winston Churchill was responsible for the death of General Sikorski. The board vetoed this production, which Chandos described as 'a grotesque calumny on a great statesman'. About Tynan, Chandos commented, 'He's done good work for the theatre, of course, but he will take off like a guided missile.' This row surfaced in 1967, but continued to simmer for several years, and indeed the curious mixture of management personalities, with Tynan representing a 'romantic Marxism' and Chandos being an ex-Conservative cabinet minister, could scarcely have been expected to endure. There was another reason for the troubles of the NT in the late 1960s. The NT in its early days had taken over many members of the Royal Court company, with Stephens, Blakeley, Joan

Plowright and Frank Finlay among the actors, together with the Royal Court directors already mentioned. There was thus a nucleus of a permanent company. As the stars and the directors became famous through the NT, they drifted away to more profitable assignments, Dexter to the United States, Stephens to films. In an effort to recoup the lost fortunes of the NT, outside stars were brought into the company, among them Gielgud, Irene Worth, Edward Woodward and Paul Scofield, with the result that the company structure declined.

The key problems with the NT were perhaps these, that it had not evolved a company style, nor had it attracted the constant presence of stars. Its achievements represented the reverse side of these complaints, that it had tackled a wide variety of work with much success and that in its early days it had nurtured the growth of many actors and young directors who became stars. After the troubles of 1970–1, there came a change of management, with Sir Max Rayne taking over from Lord Chandos, another literary manager appointed to whom Tynan acted as 'consultant' and a new 'inner circle' of directors. The final stages of this re-shuffle came in November 1973, when it was decided that Olivier, whose health remained a matter of great concern, should not lead the NT company into the new theatre building. Peter Hall was appointed as his successor, a selection which was opposed by Kenneth Tynan and other members of the original NT team (with the exception of Olivier) on the grounds that Hall had not emerged from the company and that the company members of long-standing had not been consulted in his choice.

The RSC developed along different lines. Peter Hall was only twenty-nine when he was invited to become the artistic director of the Shakespeare Memorial theatre, and did not possess the settled reputation of an Olivier. He hadn't had time to acquire one. But he was known as an excellent director, from his Arts Theatre Club seasons in 1955–6, his West End production of the musical *Gigi* (which proved his versatility) and at Stratford his productions of *Love's Labour's Lost* (1957), *Twelfth Night* (1958), *A Midsummer Night's Dream* (1959) and *Coriolanus* (1959) with Olivier. He was also very ambitious, not necessarily on a narrow personal level, but to achieve a type of permanent company which he felt that Britain had always lacked. He was persuasive—the Stratford governors led by Sir Fordham Flower accepted what must have seemed an almost grandiose plan—and an outstanding administrator. He had lectured during the war in business management. Hall was the architect of the modern RSC, whose influence cannot be measured in terms of his best productions (such as *The Wars of the Roses*, 1963) or his exceptionally detailed interpretations of Pinter's plays. His first achievement, however, was to fire others with enthusiasm for his 'grand plan' for the Stratford theatre.

'The plan was radical and creative,' wrote Peter Brook in 1968, '…before the structure was ready he opened his grand project: suddenly the vast company, the immense repertoire, the constant output, the excitement, the disasters, the strain all came into existence….He was trying to create a living organism, where flexible imaginative conditions were related to flexible imaginative individuals in key positions.' In less rhetorical terms, this scheme meant the formation of a company which would overcome the normal difficulties of permanent companies by offering actors flexible contracts, so that they could take on work elsewhere, and by opening a London theatre (which turned out to be the Aldwych) so that they could be seen in the West End. The Stratford stage was to be re-designed: there was to be a change of approach towards Shakespearian productions; and there was also to be a bringing-together of various young directorial talents, among them Peter Brook, John Barton and Hall himself, with the veteran Michel Saint-Denis, to provide a ballast of experience. He also wanted almost to force the hand of the government, through the Arts Council, to give the company a substantial annual subsidy, which initially the company lacked.

Other young directors joined this group; Clifford Williams, David Jones, Trevor Nunn (who succeeded Hall in 1968), Terry Hands. The RSC was intended to be a company which was based upon the work of Shakespeare and his contemporaries, but also (through its London branch) concerned with contemporary drama too and the encouragement of new writers. The 'modern' attitude would illumine the 'past' and vice versa. Unlike the NT, a recognisable RSC style emerged during the early 1960s which was based upon its directorial outlooks, thus leading to the belief that the

RSC was a 'directors' theatre.

Trying to pin down this style is not easy: it was recognisable but hard to describe. It was based on perhaps four main aims, which can also be regarded as virtues: liveliness, social relevance, textual care and theatrical totality. By 'liveliness', I do not mean boisterousness or mere physical energy, although some RSC productions gave this impression. It was rather the search for a freshness of response, which Brook considered as the quality which distinguished the Immediate Theatre from the Deadly Theatre. The Deadly Theatre occurred when the theatrical styles were rigid and masked a lack of inner conviction or relevance:

> In France there are two deadly ways of playing classical tragedy. One is traditional and this involves using a special voice, a special manner, a noble look and an elevated musical delivery. The other is no more than a half-hearted version of the same thing. (Despairing of Imperial gestures, the young actor) wants to play his verse more realistically...but he finds the formality of the writing is so rigid that it resists this treatment. He is forced to an uneasy compromise that is neither refreshing, like ordinary talk, nor defiantly histrionic, like what we call ham (Peter Brook, *The Empty Space* 1968).

Escaping from the Deadly Theatre meant first the search for the inner truths of lines and weighing the usefulness of the formal verse structures. Hall once suggested that the greatest contribution which the RSC made to English theatre was to revolutionise the speaking of Shakespearian verse. Brook in *The Empty Space* quotes two studio exercises, one where he encouraged his students to speak the names of the dead after Agincourt in *Henry V* with that attitude of mind which we might use for a more recent tragedy (the list of the dead in Auschwitz), and another where he encouraged an actress playing Goneril in *King Lear* to speak the first lines praising and honouring Lear as if she really meant them. Actors were not encouraged to display their intentions prematurely, from their knowledge of the rest of the play, but as if the situation were happening 'now'.

The quest for liveliness could also mean shocking the audience, along the lines of Artaud, but more particularly, it was concerned with the search for a contemporary social relevance. Inspired by Brecht and Jan Kott's *Shakespeare Our Contemporary*, an influential work, the RSC directors were quick to point out that the political complexities of Shakespeare's plays did not belong to a remote society but were also related to our own. Struggles for power obviously still exist, so do lofty men like Coriolanus, scheming murderers like Macbeth, working-class revolutionaries like Jack Cade and political factions. Such parallels were easily drawn, but the stress on their existence helped to give a normal, everyday and contemporary flavour to stories which could so easily become accounts of the Downfalls of Kings. Sometimes, however, there were attempts to draw more specific analogies. When John Barton tackled *King John* (1974), he was struck 'by how much the play, written in 1594, is about England and us now. Our world of outward order and inner instability, of shifting ideologies and self-destructive pragmatism, is also the world of *King John*. Even the specific political issues have modern parallels, although I have never seen this fully emerge in performance.' Unfortunately Shakespeare's *King John*, as it was written, did not quite fit into Barton's plans, and so he introduced extracts from two earlier Elizabethan 'King John' plays and re-wrote passages of his own. The resulting work proved remarkably prophetic of Britain's entry into the EEC, of inflation and of the Wilson/Heath premierships: 'King Barton's *John*', as one critic dubbed it.

The search for social relevance could obviously get out of hand, but at the RS,C it was tempered by a concern for textual accuracy and scholarship. Barton had previously been a don specialising in Elizabethan speech and drama at King's College Cambridge. This scholarship did not necessarily mean a deadening pedantry but the use of literary research to illumine texts. G. Wilson Knight, for example, was one Shakespearian scholar whose books on Shakespearian imagery greatly influenced RSC productions. Wilson Knight had pointed out that Shakespeare's imagery was not a question of clever metaphors, but belonged to his understanding of universal patterns in life, shared by most Elizabethans. The key idea was that of hierarchy. Hierarchy meant an established order, derived from God's laws, which if broken led to anarchy. Just as the Sun was the King of the Heavens (with the Moon as his consort), so the King shed his benevolent rays upon the country beneath. The King could also be compared to the Eagle, to the Lion, or to Gold; but not to the Owl, or the Antelope, or to Silver, which had different symbolic meanings. The clearest statement of the hierarchical principle occurs in *Troilus and Cressida* (notably in Ulysses' speech in Act 1, Scene 3), a play which prompted one of Barton's best productions. Hierarchy is not an idea which appeals to modern societies. Since it seemed so important to an understanding of Shakespeare's plays, the RSC productions stressed its significance by, say, beginning plays with coronation scenes whether or not the texts demanded them, staging explanatory compilations about Kingship (*The Hollow Crown*, 1961) and by using the crown itself as a dominating symbol.

Another aspect on this emphasis upon scholarship was illustrated by the attempt to present plays in groups, believing that the way in which Shakespeare tackles a theme in one play might illumine another. Bringing the three *Henry VI* plays with *Richard III* into a shortened version of this cycle, *The Wars of the Roses* (1963), was an obvious choice: they were linked by the unfolding of history. In 1972, Nunn tackled a more ambitious project, the four Roman plays (*Coriolanus*, *Julius Caesar*, *Antony and Cleopatra* and *Titus Andronicus*): these plays were not written as a cycle, there was no continuous historical narrative and they were not written in the same period of Shakespeare's life. But Nunn argued that together they represented the growth and decline of a civilisation, and, more significantly, illustrated a Shakespearian vision of an ordered society which rejected unwisely the disciplined virtues which made it great. The Roman plays also illustrated another facet of the RSC aims, towards a certain theatrical totality, where the stage set would be illustrative of the underlying themes of the plays, sound and movement also intertwining to provide a sense impression of the play's meaning. Each Roman play at Stratford began with a parade of the ruling classes, though Shakespeare's plays began otherwise. By this means, Nunn illustrated the different types of rules, the cold military régime of Caesar, the sensuous indolence of Egypt, the barbarism of Titus's Rome. Similarly, in Barton's *Troilus and Cressida*, the Trojans and Greeks looked different: they represented different physical stocks as well as life styles. Sometimes, the programmes at the RSC seemed to swim with footnotes, providing the historical backgrounds to plays, and to Shakespeare, and to the events of the plot as they occurred in 'real life'.

These four aims/qualities also influenced the contemporary side of the RSC's work at the Aldwych and the short play seasons at the Arts Theatre Club and, later, The Place. The contemporary plays were often noted for their 'good' (verbal) writing, their literary qualities. Hall set the pattern here with his immaculately organised productions of plays by Pinter and the American dramatist, Edward Albee. David Mercer was another contemporary writer whose vaguely Marxist sympathies were often expressed in almost dandified language. Both Jeremy Brooks, an early literary adviser to the R SC, and Ronald Bryden, a later *dramaturg*, were particularly concerned with the literary merits of new scripts. They might choose plays, such as Peter Barnes's *The Bewitched* which offered the opportunity for much visual spectacle, but they were particularly impressed by qualities of language. Among the contemporary productions, there were also attempts to search for 'social relevance', most noticeable perhaps in Brook's *US* and in David Jones's productions of Gorky's *The Lower Depths*, *Enemies* and *Summerfolk* where the keynote was naturalism but where there were also implications about the nature of revolutionary situations of relevance to Britain. The search for 'theatrical totality' was particularly evident in Brook's *The Marat/Sade* and *A Midsummer Night's Dream*, and in certain productions by Terry Hands, such as *The Bewitched*.

The overall image of the RSC during the 1960s was the product of various directorial talents, which (like the qualities) at best complemented one another but which also ran the danger of toppling over into excess. The imaginative vision of Brook balanced the austerity of Hall, the textual care of Barton complemented the occasionally slapdash but very lively abilities of Hands and Clifford Williams. When Hall left the RSC, Nunn inherited the remnants of an established team, some of whom had already decided to go other ways, Brook to Persia and Paris, Williams to New York and *Oh! Calcutta!* Nunn was a young man (as Hall had been on taking over the theatre) whose previous experience with the RSC had shown his versatile adaptability. Facing a cutback in finance, he staged a highly successful production of *The Revenger's Tragedy* within a set designed for *Hamlet*: confronted by his leading actor dropping out before the opening of Mrozek's *Tango*, he took over the part himself. By this time, however, the company had grown to an extent which made the sheer problems of organising it, and financing it, arduous indeed, particularly for Nunn; the complaint directed against his work largely derived from the fact that he was trying to keep an operation going which had been the product of other minds. Critics complained that some new productions were conceived in memory of what had gone before, that the old qualities had become clichés and that the deadly habits castigated by Brook were re-emerging in the shape of RSC mannerisms. Nunn's production of *Macbeth* (1974) which featured an astonishingly powerful performance by Nicol Williamson, demonstrated these eccentricities: an overall style based on the Black Mass with an altar stage, an unnecessary coronation to begin with, a too deliberate funeral of Duncan (who in this production was blind) and a tendency to underline verbal images, so that Williamson actually snuffed out a huge candle during the speech which includes 'Out, out, brief candle!' Helen Mirren, who had been the sex goddess of the RS since *Troilus and Cressida*, played Lady Macbeth not so much as a hellcat but as a playboy's kitten. When this production transferred to the Aldwych, Nunn drastically transformed it—into what some regarded as the other RSC cliché, total Brechtian austerity. The coronation scene was scrapped, together with most of the Black Mass ritual. In its place, was a bare stage with a circle, actors standing around and banging thundersheets when required, and drifting on to the central acting areas when their presences seemed to be required by Shakespeare.

The RSC then, like the NT, struck a bad patch during the early 1970s. Like the NT, its productions during this time would not have seemed unworthy but for the glories which had gone before. Despite their different evolutions, there were other points of comparison between the two companies. Neither national wanted to be considered as a museum theatre. They were in this respect unlike the nationals from some other countries. They encouraged new drama and became associated with new writers (at the RSC, in addition to Pinter and Mercer, Livings, Rudkin, Griffiths, Arden and Stoppard were given productions; at the NT, Wood, Stoppard, Nichols, Hopkins, Spurling, Saunders and Griffiths were helped). If the RSC had no single star to match the presence of Olivier at the NT, they possessed a directorial star in Peter Brook and attracted to the company such names as Ashcroft, Scofield and Williamson. Both companies were also reluctant to be regarded as 'élitist' ones, a hard concept to define but which permeated their different views. There were attempts to make the RSC a 'democratic' institution, where small-part players could be cast for leading roles, and certain decisions were taken by group consultation. Nunn once stirred up a minor controversy by calling the RSC a 'left-wing' theatre. Both companies wanted to avoid being thought establishment-minded. Sometimes, as the critic Arnold Hinchliffe has suggested, the RSC wanted to criticise society so much that it presented a picture of sombre despair. Commenting on the RSC's work at Stratford, Aldwych and the Arts Theatre Club during the early 1960s, Hinchliffe wrote that *The Wars of the Roses*, *The Marat/Sade*, Middleton's *Women Beware Women*, Rudkin's *Afore Night Come* and the Brook/Scofield *King Lear* all 'suggest a view of the world as an existential nightmare, a world bereft of hope, gentleness and compassion'. The upper heights of British theatre were clearly fascinated by the lower depths of mankind.

A more sympathetic view to the work of the nationals might lay a different stress. Both companies offered humanistic outlooks: it was part of the spirit of the times perhaps. The new NT building (partly designed during the early 1960s) illustrates the dislike of pomposity, the concern for intimacy and human contact in the theatre. The auditoria were not intended to be places for mass audiences, but were deliberately kept small, so that no member of the audience should be further than 65 feet from the stage. The willingness to work in studio theatres—and the establishment of a Young Vic under Frank Dunlop—was another sign of a desire for warmth and a conversational contact with the public. Both nationals struggled to be open-minded, self-critical institutions, much concerned to make their work freely available to the public at large, while preserving a human scale to their ventures. Both companies were concerned to tour, not necessarily with massive star-spangled productions, but on a smaller basis, say, to schools with the RSC's Theatregoround venture.

But is it ever possible for national theatres not to be élitist? Does not their very situation (their grants, their buildings, their reputations) prevent them from being anything other than élite organisations? Is it not their job to set standards for others? A national theatre isn't a popular theatre necessarily. Most theatre-lovers in Britain would have felt outraged if, say, the *Carry On* team appeared at the Old Vic rather than the Victoria Palace. If the word 'national' doesn't mean popular or of the people, what does it mean? Is there a national culture distinct from the tastes of the people who make up the nation? Obviously not, and yet we accept the distinction between 'national' and 'popular' because it is useful. In a sense, we pay our nationals not to be 'popular', for if they were 'popular', as the *Carry On* team are popular, there would be no need for subsidies. Because we fear that popular tastes aren't enlightened enough to support those companies which we feel to be appropriate to our image as a theatre-loving nation, we pay the government to provide national theatres. National theatres can therefore never represent national tastes without ceasing to advertise themselves as nationals, for there are many types of popular theatre in rivalry, but only two companies to whom we have conceded the title national, confident that the Arts Council will take this adjective more seriously than perhaps we do.

The nationals exist because of a widespread view that something better-than-average should represent the British theatrical super-ego. This much is true of all national theatres. Other national theatres, however, are intended either to preserve cultural heritages more or less intact (the Comédie-Française, the Moscow Art Theatre) or to express some more or less 'official' point of view (Marxism and the

Berliner Ensemble). The British nationals were attempting to tackle tasks which were both more ambitious and less specific than these. The RSC was, at Stratford, committed to Shakespeare, Elizabethan and Jacobean drama; but it was determined to interpret these plays in a new, more modern spirit. The NT was not tied to Shakespeare, although his plays formed an important part of its repertoires, but it also wanted to present a world library of classic drama. Both nationals also wanted to be leaders in the production of new plays. They didn't forget the *avant-garde*. Both wanted to be dynamic companies, not just prestigious ones. Neither could resign itself to expressing one point of view: this would have been inappropriate in a varied and diverse society such as Britain. And so, in a sense, they had continually to define what 'better-than-average' meant. Year by year, they strove to present new and different ideals of excellence.

This attitude proved both to be the strength and weakness of the two companies. At best, when the nationals were confident of their ideals and knew where they were going, their work was exceptionally youthful and exciting: the RSC has won no less than sixty-six major national and international awards in fifteen years. But at worst, there were sudden crises of confidence and the productions could seem pretentious and striving after effect. In the early 1970s, faced by the transfer of leadership at the RSC from Hall's régime to Trevor Nunn's and (following a bad patch during Olivier's illness) from Olivier's régime to Hall's at the NT, considerable elements of self-doubt permeated the productions at the nationals which did not cast the enterprises totally into question but tarnished the buoyant confidence which had been engendered.

Chapter 11

Many roads, few maps

The outpouring of new British plays in the eight years which followed 1956 was distinguished by two kinds of revolt; technically, against the 'well-made play' and, emotionally, against the stuffiness of the 'British establishment'. The emotional revolt could mean almost anything, from a considered left-wing attack against a bourgeois, capitalistic society to the jibes against sexual hypocrisy, financial corruption and complacency which could come from almost any political or a-political direction. The 'second wave' dramatists were faced with a different situation. Unlike Osborne, they were surrounded by technical alternatives. They could write in the style of Brecht and no director would quail. They could write Absurdist plays without necessarily being accused of meaningless obscurity. They would write scenario, without formal dialogue, just hints for improvisational games; or gather together, as Barry Bermange once did, extracts from recorded street interviews, assembling them into a dramatic collage (*Darkness Theatre*, 1969). They could write for three basic types of stage—arena, thrust and proscenium arch—or for no formal stage at all. While it was perhaps true that their royalties from plays were shrinking, mainly due to the decline of the touring theatres, they could receive incomes from other sources, television, playscript paperbacks and commissions from the reps and the nationals.

But they were also faced with a common problem, how to transform their new opportunities into something equivalent to a dramatic 'culture'. Culture, an awkward word, has two contrasting (though complementary) meanings: it implies the nurturing of certain ideas, styles or genres, until they produce fine blossoms, and it also means the weeding out of the unwanted and irrelevant. Culture implies the search for values, and if there are no values which assume an importance beyond those of other possible aims, then a grey, undramatic sameness descends. Anything can happen, but nothing seems worth doing. Beyond that stage lies an un-selective anarchy. The dramatists had the job of trying to determine, both individually and collectively (though usually not as the result of formal collaboration) what values would predominate in the brave new world of the Second Wave.

While the burden of this task fell on the shoulders of the playwrights, the climate of social and popular opinion also necessarily played a large share in the selection process. The prevailing atmospheres had changed from the mid-1950s. The theatre, for example, was no longer an orphan strug-gling to survive in a world of mass media: it had become the favourite adopted son of the new establishment. Its more im-aginative projects therefore acquired a different aura. In-stead of being desperate gambles, glamorous because of the fundamental stakes for which they were played, they now too often seemed in the public mind to be the flights of fancy from directors securely resting on Arts Council grants. The right to fail, once boldly claimed by the Royal Court, was a privilege which could be too easily invoked. The experiments may have been equally worthwhile, but the public response to them was different. A Brechtian musical, which would have seemed challengingly ambitious in the tatty surround-ings of an old rep, might have the appearance of self-in-dulgent propaganda in the plush auditorium of the Bir-mingham Rep. Artaud became the excuse for shouting, nakedness and brutality which had ceased positively to shock, but merely negatively bored.

And the political climate had changed. Among left-wing dramatists, rebellious anger was no longer an interesting posture. The anti-establishment denunciations of the Angry Young Men during the 1950s had taken place against the background of an apparently secure Conservative govern-ment. For most of the 1960s, a Labour government was in power, and it was hard for left-wing writers to generate the same degree of self-righteous outrage against (say) the Labour government's tacit support for the American in-volvement in Vietnam, as had previously been aroused against Suez. They did their best. In Peter Brook's *US*, Glenda Jackson called for napalm in Hampstead to bring home to the British the 'truths' about Vietnam, a threat which was

received with quite stunning equanimity by London audiences who did not feel that either they or Brook could influence the war one way or another. Left-wing writers either
had to play the game of being more socialist than thou, at the
risk of isolating themselves from what was regarded as being
the normal vehicle of socialist change in Britain, the Labour
Party, or they had to opt out of radical political comment
altogether, coupling a rough general support for the government in power with (say) a concern for the alienated individual in times of social change.

There were variations on these attitudes. Some writers
might attack a hidden 'bourgeois élite' controlling the strings
of government (through the City, the Treasury, the Civil Service, the Freemasons or whatever), thus absolving the
Labour Party from blame. Others might resort to a Cas-
sandra-like gloom in which the downfall of civilisation was
predicted. In general, however, left-wing writers showed a
reluctance to attack the Labour Party and government
directly, though they might attack a System which somehow
existed above, beyond and surrounding the government.
The satirical attacks on the Labour Government (such as *Mrs
Wilson's Diary*, 1968) were more good humoured than the
previous attacks against Harold Macmillan and company.

This comparative reticence meant that there was a lack of
plays dealing with real, as opposed to spurious or diversion-
ary, political issues. There were many attacks against the
whole social system, laying the blame predictably on the
'public schools, the old boys network' and the other
favourite whipping posts of the left. One example was Peter
Barnes's *The Ruling Class* (1968), about the scion of a decadent
aristocratic family, the fourteenth Earl of Gurney, who
harmlessly believes that he is Jesus Christ until this gentle
madness is driven out of him, to be replaced by the violent
insanity of a Jack the Ripper: as a dangerous madman, the
Earl takes his seat in the House of Lords and could not be
distinguished from the other dangerous madmen. Barnes's
wit, his verbal fluency, his delight in madness, horror and
coups de théâtre were very exciting, but there were those who
wondered if he had not chosen a hackneyed (but unconvincing) target, and overstated his case. The problem with the
House of Lords is not that peers are sadistic monsters, or

even decadent aristocrats; but possibly that they can frustrate legislation from an elected government.

Barnes, in a sense, delighted in baroque exaggeration. He was much influenced by the Jacobeans. His two short plays, *Leonardo's Last Supper* and *Noonday Demons* (1969), were Gothic comedies, while his adaptation of Wedekind's Lulu plays (*Lulu*, 1970) revealed a similar taste for humorous *Sturm und Drang*, handled with great delicacy, verve and narrative skill. The problems really came when he tried to direct these fantasies towards political comment and (though usually obliquely) towards contemporary themes. *The Bewitched* (1974) was an account of the decline of the Spanish Hapsburgs, concentrating on the epileptic and deformed Carlos II whose inability to sire a successor led to the War of the Spanish Succession. But Barnes believed that the decline of the Hapsburgs held lessons for other waning civilisations, including perhaps our own. To prevent the audience from relaxing into the past, he jolted them up with anachronisms. The *auto-da-fè* was preceded by a re-written version of the song, 'That's Entertainment'. Certain scenes were written in the styles of French farces or musical comedies. But the general message, when it came, proved to be very general and rather banal. National declines are caused by the very fact that ruling classes exist. ''Twill make a desert o' this world Whilst there's still one man left t' give commands And another who'll obey them.' This blanket condemnation of all authority seems to me about as unreal a political statement as it is possible to write, for it obviously sweeps away all governments, all laws, all social structures and makes no distinction between types of limited authority and Absolute Power.

The looseness of left-wing attacks was also revealed by the differing ideas about the 'bourgeoisie', which was sometimes considered to be with some precision the 'ownership' or 'entrepreneurial' classes, but more often was held to apply to a range of manners and habits connected with a variety of British customs from Oxbridge to cricket. On occasions, the left-wing seemed to advocate ethnic hatred as a pre-requisite for revolution. But even if we consider the more limited definition of the bourgeoisie as the ownership classes, unselfcritical contradictions abounded. The 7.84 fringe company, for example, derived its title from the statistic that 7 per cent of the British population owned 84 per cent of the country's wealth. This figure was gleaned from the *Economist*, an apparently impeccable, even right-wing source, and was originally based upon government supplied statistics. As it stands, it implies a shocking concentration of ownership. But the 7.84 company failed to point out that the statistic was based upon pre-tax income, thus ignoring two points—the re-distributive effect of taxation, where income could be taxed very heavily (up to 95 per cent) at certain levels, and second, that family incomes were usually registered under one name, the husband's. Furthermore, the word, ownership, can have two distinct meanings, 'consumption' or 'the power to control'. It is obviously ridiculous to suggest that 7 per cent of the population live in 84 per cent of the houses or eat 84 per cent of the country's food. To that extent, the figure is meaningless. But if we suggest that 7 per cent of the population have the power to control how the other 84 per cent live, then clearly the figure is too optimistic or too pessimistic, according to one's political beliefs. A very much smaller percentage controls the governmental decisions of the country, or runs the unions, or the nationalised industries, or the major private industries. These are obvious points, but they tended to be overlooked by some writers who pursued a neo-Marxist logic, in which 'ownership' equalled wealth equalled money equalled power equalled bourgeois class interest.

Money was regarded as the weak link in this chain, being 'just' a symbol, although it could be used as the 'pander' through which the bourgeoisie exploited the poor. Some writers gave the impression that if money could be done away with altogether, an age of pristine innocence would reign. To accept that money could be good or bad according to its usage was a concession to pragmatic capitalism which would have thrown the mechanistic logic out of gear and, in the early 1970s, some writers seemed to be welcoming rampant inflation as a means of bringing about the downfall of the social system. 'National interest?' jeers the young comedian-rebel in Trevor Griffiths's *The Comedians*, 'Up yours, sweetheart!' With such attitudes, the Left fragmented into groups—the 'moderates', the social democrats, the Marxists, the Maoists and WRPs—and an atmosphere of academic confusion reigned, in which the targets attacked often seemed curiously chosen. In one of the better and more pointed plays, *Brassneck* by David Hare and Howard Brenton (1973), there was a barely concealed attack on the development scandals surrounding the careers of John Poulson, T. Dan Smith, Alderman Cunningham. Hare and Brenton presented a colourful picture of bribery and corruption in local councils, with night-club revelry and secret societies (such as the Masons) thrown in, while contriving to miss the precise political reforms (registration of business interests for councillors and MPs, open council debates, community involvement at all levels of development planning) for which many harassed politicians were striving.

But it is a negative form of criticism to mourn the debates which didn't get launched, rather than to consider those that did. Among left-wing dramatists, in addition to the attacks on the bourgeoisie, there were three topics which prompted serious, concerned, though not always sombre, plays: the difficulties of staging revolutions particularly in Western 'so-called' democracies, the alienation of the individual in capitalistic societies and in times of social change, and the possibility of a more fundamental form of human corruption beyond alienation into something equivalent to original sinfulness.

Two of Trevor Griffiths's major plays, *Occupations* (1971) and *The Party* (1974), are concerned with problems in the way of revolution. Griffiths, a Marxist, took the 1920 Fiat Strike in Italy as the subject for his first major play, *Occupations*; a fascinating theme which involved a conflict between the Marxist theoretician, Gramsci, and a visiting agent from the USSR, Kabak. Gramsci's cause was that of the striking workers and he saw this action as the first stage in a wider revolution which would culminate in the overthrow of the capitalistic system. But he needs the support of the Soviet government. Kabak, pursuing the ends of Soviet nationalism, is prepared to compromise with Western capitalism; and he frustrates Gramsci. Revolutions can only succeed through the solidarity of the working-class movement, fired by a purist sense of mission. But is it possible in diverse societies to obtain this solidarity? In *The Party*, Griffiths considers the behaviour of a random assortment of left-wing intellectuals and non-intellectuals at the time of the *événements de mai* in Paris, 1968. They are all sympathetic to the cause of the Paris students and the other revolutionaries; but they each have different reasons for not actually helping them—a drunken writer? because revolutions have to be a spontaneous revulsion against the bosses—a Trotskyite from Glasgow? because the revolution hasn't come from the industrial working classes—an economics don? because he is looking to the Third World as the area where the revolution will begin—and a television producer, in whose flat the debate takes place? because he feels emotionally impotent.

Griffiths connects the failure to take part in revolutions with certain types of emotional corruption, which are themselves the product of the capitalistic system. Kabak, for example, behaves grossly towards women: he ignores the fact that one mistress is dying of cancer, while demanding the sexual attentions of her maid with all the arrogance of a feudal aristocrat insisting on the *droit de seigneur*. In *Sam, Sam* (1972), he contrasts the behaviour of two brothers, one who stays loyal to his working-class background and the other who struggles and competes to rise above it. The competitive brother is 'successful' though corrupted, the other is not. In *The Comedians* (1975), Griffiths considers the nature of stand-up comics, contrasting those who use their comedy to illuminate the society around them and those who are merely catering to the prejudices and fantasies of their audiences. At times, Griffiths seems to be asserting that all hang-ups and unhappinesses are the product of the social system which, if it were changed, would leave everyone happy.

C. P. Taylor, however, who is also a committed socialist, was not prepared to indulge in this kind of wishful thinking. Taylor, a Glaswegian, was brought up in the Labour movement and his childhood was spent among the slums of the Gorbals district. Unlike Griffiths, he is prepared to be sceptical, even about his own political beliefs. 'The first thing that a play has to be about...' he once wrote, 'is people: their relationships to one another and to the society they live in.' Political attitudes only form a part of this general texture of relationships and polemical stances can often conceal the true nature of human needs. Taylor's plays, at best, are social comedies of manners, very funny and telling, and often set within the left-wing environment in Glasgow which he knows so well. *Allergy* (1966) was about the love-life of a young man who runs a revolutionary paper with a tiny circulation. *Bread and Butter* (1966) was about a couple whose lives reflect the changes in Glasgow since the early 1930s, while *The Black and White Minstrels* (1972) concerns a left-wing writer (and his friends) who has got involved with a struggle to evict his tenant, a black girl, without wishing to evict her or to do anything else which would compromise his principles.

Griffiths and Taylor are both extrovert writers, the former open in his commitments and direct in his methods, the latter buoyant in good humour, scathing of hypocrisies and ironically self-aware. There was a more introverted vein, however, in much left-wing writing which focused upon the anxieties of the age and, in particular, on personal 'alienation'. To Griffiths, alienation primarily meant unsatisfactory sex in bed, soul-destroying submission to capitalistic bosses at work. To David Mercer and David Storey, two Yorkshire writers, the problems of alienation were more complex, leading to schizophrenia, loss of 'roots' or to a perpetual (and self-perpetuating) madness.

The central characters in several of Mercer's plays (Morgan in *A Suitable Case for Treatment*, 1966, Peter in *Ride a Cock Horse*, 1965, Link in *After Haggerty*, 1970, and Flint in *Flint*, 1970) are isolated men, retarded, eccentric or mad, although they could be regarded as protecting themselves from the insanities of the outside world. In his filmscript, *Family Life*, Mercer followed the arguments of R. D. Laing, by presenting 'madness' as an essentially sane escape from the pressures of a nagging and enclosed nuclear family. The sanest of his heroes is Bernard Link, the theatre critic in *After Haggerty*, who as his name suggests is trying to hold things together, his associations with the past (and particularly his stubborn and reactionary father), East and West (via his lectures on British theatre), even the theatre which seems likely to fall apart into the mindless anarchy of a Living-Theatre type of fringe production. Unfortunately, the strains on the Link are so powerful that he is kept taut, silent and incapable of taking decisions, a fact of which the aggressive mistress of the flat's former tenant, Haggerty, is all too aware. Anyone can impose upon Link, simply because he is unable to tell them to go away. He withdraws into drink and compromises, but finally rebels against his father.

Morgan and Flint are, in their different ways, both rebels. Morgan wants to stamp his individual mark upon everything, from his mother's sheets to the flower-bed at the mental hospital. Flint is an agnostic vicar, lecherous and human, whose presence, constantly rubbing against the rock of the Church, produces not only the fire of scandal but a literal fire as well. But his unconventional behaviour is not essentially destructive. He may burn down the odd church, but he also reminds those who come into contact with him of their primary duties, not the preservation of custom but the Love of Man. *Flint* is an amusing, witty and optimistic play; but dominating Mercer's vision, and most fully expressed in *Duck Song*, 1974, is the sense of Western society collapsing under its own internal pressures. The only proper response for the individual is to rebel or retreat. Reform or political commitment to specific parties (Mercer has described himself as a communist without a party) merely adds to the overall madness.

The central character in David Storey's first play, *The Restoration of Arnold Middleton* (written 1959, produced 1966), is very much like a Mercer hero: he is a provincial schoolmaster, brought to the brink of madness by family pressures and heroic longings but who (after a breakdown) miraculously recovers. Mercer's plays, however, were usually written in short scenes, changing from place to place, usually connected by monologues, witty (if gag-ridden) and somewhat televisual. Storey was primarily a naturalistic writer, whose best plays were constructed somewhat in the style of Chekhov, as portraits of societies revealed through certain central events, such as an anniversary (*In Celebration*, 1969), the erection of a wedding marquee (*The Contractor*, 1969), the behind-the-match behaviour of a rugby team (*The Changing Room*, 1971), the return of a rebellious child (*The Farm*, 1973) or a day in the life of an Arts College (*Life Class*, 1974).

With this wider canvas and Chekhovian technique, Storey illustrated clearly how social frustration spreads, from generation to generation, from work to family, from teacher to student. The only alternative to such frustration is occasionally provided by team efforts, rugby or the erection of the marquee. The merit of Storey's plays comes in his social detail, particularly revealed by his capacity to sustain many different characters on stage, each contributing to the overall sense of atmosphere and 'texture'. *The Contractor* is not just concerned with the efforts of a business man, Ewbank, to impress his daughter and her husband with his professional skill. His firm specialises in marquee erection. Surrounding Ewbank and his family are the workers and their problems, the gentilities of society and the disillusion of the young. Territorial rights within the family circle matter in *The Farm*, while the sense that a technological society is about to replace the vague and waffling culture, expressed by the tired teachers and bored pupils, dominates *Life Class*, where the central event is an attempted rape on a model which the art lecturer is unable to stop. Storey's plays rarely contain 'messages', except by implication, but they are detailed studies of social environments, lovingly realised on stage by the director, Lindsay Anderson. Over these studies, is a wash of pessimism: work has lost meaning and purpose, families are embittered.

Even more pessimistic than Storey's plays, although on a smaller scale, are those of E. A. Whitehead (*The Foursome*, 1971; *Alpha Beta*; 1972; and *The Sea Anchor*, 1974) who followed Storey into detailed naturalism but chose themes of marital disputes and the lazily vindictive maltreatment of women, who were capable of being vindictive in return. The men dream of absurd heroisms, such as crossing the Irish Sea from Liverpool in an open boat, with no lifebelt, a defective radio and no capacity to swim. They either die (as in *The Sea Anchor*), survive to discover that these gestures mean nothing, which is another form of death, or back away from the challenge. Their normal, non-heroic lives are grubby; a round of drunkenness, work drudgery and crude sex.

Behind this pessimism, which was shared by writers other than Storey and Whitehead, we can perhaps detect one 'value', expressed by some in the Second Wave—a certain determination not to be fooled by hopes and promises. Whereas Arnold Wesker's plays contained heroines like Beatie who is seized in *Roots* with a life-enhancing vision, such characters in the left-wing drama of the late 1960s were rare and would have been considered naïvely created. Wesker himself expressed a personal disillusion with an optimistic vision of the future in *Their Very Own and Golden City* (1965). The negative side to this commendable 'realism' was the feeling of predictable and 'unfocused' despair. The open boat on the Irish Sea will never arrive. The lecturer's disillusion in *Life Class* becomes sadly repetitive. Depression becomes a stock response to all circumstances, its causes cannot be analysed, its effects decline into a paralysing negativism.

The writer with the bleakest vision of all was Edward Bond, the most technically ambitious dramatist of the Second Wave, who was rarely 'experimental' in the sense that he rarely tackled a style of writing for which there were no sound precedents, but who was not afraid to attempt difficult, unusual tasks and to seek the fresh impact through the familiar form. His plays can be sombrely naturalistic (*The Pope's Wedding*, 1962, *Saved* 1965), or blackly farcical *Early Morning*, 1968), or grimly, amusingly epical (*Narrow Road to the Deep North*, 1968), or historical problematical (*Bingo*, 1974) or literary reconstructional (*Lear*, 1971) or almost any other combination from Polonius's comprehensive catalogue. Within this variety, Bond retained certain distinctive stylistic features: one was his pointed, austere and polished language, and another was his use of violent images.

Violent scenes have always formed an important part of Western drama, from the tearing apart of Pentheus to the deaths, battles and suicides in Shakespeare's plays. Fifty murders a day are on average screened on television. In Bond's case, the violent scenes have a powerful reality to them, which shocks us out of a casual acceptance of violence. In *Saved*, a baby is stoned to death: a scene which caused a furore in 1965 and led to the prosecution of the English Stage Company, which to evade the censorship laws had transformed the Royal Court into a theatre club. In *Narrow Road*, a tyrant is executed and dismembered, while his attendant priest disembowels himself. In *Bingo*, a wandering girl is whipped to a state of madness, then hung. In *The Pope's Wedding*, a recluse tramp is murdered, while in *Early Morning*, cannibalism, inbreeding and every type of deviation, plausible and fantastic (mainly fantastic) are assembled into one black farce indictment of Victoriana. These violent scenes provoked two contrasting reactions: one was that Bond simply likes blood (*Saved* was described by one critic as a 'psychopathic exercise') and the other was that Bond hated cruelty so much that he was determined to bring home to his audiences the full horror of it. *Saved* was thus considered by Bond's supporters to be an indictment of violence, whose point would have been lost if the scenes had failed to shock. This view I happen to share, and indeed the most tragic scene of all perhaps is the last one, without violence, where a family sit together, carrying on meaningless, gum-chewing activities—happily forgetful of the baby's murder. Violence in *Saved* is shown to be the consequence of social deprivation, of the bored lovelessness of the characters' lives, and in Bond's best plays, the cruelty and horror are 'natural' consequences of the situations given and the arguments provided. Is Basho, the *haiku* poet in *Narrow Road* who opts out of all social action, even that of protecting an abandoned child, less cruel than his opposite, a tyrant who governs the state brutally but with a rough justice? Why does the young husband in *The Pope's Wedding* fear and hate the tramp his wife protects? Why does society in *Bingo* turn the helpless wandering girl into a wastrel, then an 'enemy' and finally a victim?

In *Bingo*, Bond asked of Shakespeare the question which used to be demanded of God. How could Shakespeare, who was so wise and sensitive, have tolerated living in a world where there is so much misery? How could he have maintained that deceptive air of generosity, when he was supported and protected (in return for some help on his behalf) by a system which threw starving peasants off their strips of land, mutilated and killed lost girls and piked the heads of rebels on city walls? Dispossession, greed and cruelty is in the air that Bond's Shakespeare breathes. It was in London with the bear-baiting and in Stratford, where Shakespeare attempts a retirement, having set aside a nest egg for his old age in the form of land and rents. It is even in the local pub where he listens to an aggrieved Ben Jonson, who loathes Shakespeare's eminence but needs a loan. It is above all in the scaffold where the tortured girl hangs. Despair creeps over Shakespeare, with the leadenness of a slow death. He has (in his own opinion) done nothing with his life, but pile up money to buy off his fear and guilt. One step separates him from suicide: it is quickly taken. In Bond's *Bingo*, Shakespeare buys a phial of poison from Ben Jonson and kills himself.

Whether Shakespeare actually died like that does not matter. Bond dots his play (and the introduction) with historical references, but *Bingo* is really about *a* Shakespeare, not *the* Shakespeare, someone, that is, who had achieved more in his lifetime than anyone else could claim and was still brought to realise that his supreme talents could not touch nor alter the society in which he lived, except negatively, by helping the system he hated. Bond's argument is an extreme extension of that voiced by Brecht; that private virtue, private heroism, private morality is not enough: even Shakespeare was corrupt because he lived in a corrupt society, and was therefore suicidally unhappy, and impotent. Only political action to change that society is worth considering. In his introduction, Bond writes about a Goneril society, capitalism rampant and destructive, where money seems to be the cause, not just the effect, of man's inhumanity to man.

Often the logic of Bond's plays (Marxist in essence) seems to be strangely Christian—or rather 'strangely' for those who vaguely associated Bond with the devil. His argument is that without a common concern and love for all mankind, the hands of men, however noble, are stained with blood. Their so-called achievements cannot disguise the Mark of Cain. Bond also shares with the Christians a vision of man's evil tendencies, though without expressing the prospect of a redeeming force. Bond is a puritan, grim, unyielding and lacking a natural warmth, though he can be witty and light-hearted: the dramatic weaknesses of his plays are those of puritanism, a tendency to lose his craftsmanship on occasions within hell-fire visions and too obvious statements of ideals. The peasant's representative in *Bingo* is one example of this habit, who is saddled with several didactic speeches. His introduction to *Bingo* underlines the moral of the play. Only total democracy will free mankind from the tyranny of repressive governments, but total democracy will only work if men themselves renounce their cruel tendencies. Since men show little sign of doing so, the Goneril society thrives—but is also doomed.

Bond's vision is austere, but he could be criticised for

building his political cases from extreme examples. Baby-stoning is not common in South London. To blame money for the Goneril society is like damning clocks for the ageing process. His inventive and powerful plays were least convincing when they strove to present political arguments. If we contrast plays by left-wing writers in the country with the work of Athol Fugard, the South African, the British playwrights often seemed to be suffering from a bad attack of 'politics in the head', which became as common a complaint as 'sex in the head'. Fugard's plays launched no direct attacks on the Vorster government: they display as much sympathy with the down-and-out South African whites as with the oppressed blacks, and for this reason, Fugard has sometimes been criticised for being too sensitive, liberal and tolerant. But it is hard to imagine more powerful indictments of apartheid in its different aspects than those provided by such plays as *Statements* (about the working of the Immorality Act) (1972), *Sizwe Bansi is Dead* (about the pass laws) (1973) and *The Island* (about a South African penal colony) (1974). The restraint, which can partly be attributed to the fact that Fugard wished to work in South Africa with his small multiracial drama group near Port Elizabeth, only adds to the power. In such plays as *The Blood Knot* (1960), *Hello and Goodbye* (1965) and *Boesman and Lena* (1969), Fugard extends his criticism of the apartheid system towards other victims of an oppressive régime and is concerned with those who live in a twilight world, the nonentities, the whites who have lost status, the drifters and social outcasts. Fugard knew exactly what he hated and morally loathed about the society in which he lived: his political comments were precise, his feeling unforced, his awareness of human potential lost and wasted, lent a tact and dignity to his writing. Also, his political cause was a just one: he did not have to rake around for excuses to attack the capitalistic society. Extreme examples of the fears and hatreds bred by the apartheid system littered most streets.

I have used the term left-wing so far to cover a whole range of social and political stances, from neo-Marxism, to near anarchism, to a liberal concern for the individual in a world of mass pressures, to a condemnation of materialism and a hatred of the bourgeoisie. We could add to this list the apocalyptic anarchism of Heathcote Williams, whose first major play *AC/DC* (1970) is a fantasy of schizophrenia, obsessed with power struggles, and whose *Remember the Truth Dentist* (1974) is a full frontal assault on Western 'death culture' in favour of a Zen- and sperm-orientated 'Mongolian clusterfuck'. Williams's language has an almost Biblical intensity. Indeed Blake and the Bible were two important literary influences on his style, and he spurts out aphorisms and commandments like a generous one-armed bandit. He was an expert graffiti writer in North Kensington. Unfortunately, his didactic brilliance also leaves the impression of prophetic insanity, and critics are divided as to whether his plays are those of a mystic or a madman. They gave him the benefit of the doubt with *AC/DC*, which won four awards, and reversed their decision with *Remember the Truth Dentist*. Also verbally brilliant, and much saner, were the plays of Charles Wood, whose best-known works (*Cockade*, 1963, *Fill the Stage with Happy Hours*, 1966, *H*, 1969, and *Veterans*, 1972) combine a lively wit, an acute sense for social hypocrisies, a talent for richly idiomatic dialogue and an inventiveness in constructing solo scenes. His overall control over a play, however, can be unsteady. He tackled an ambitious play for the National Theatre about the Indian Mutiny, *H*, based on the career of the Christian warrior, General Havelock. While there were many excellent ironies and contrasts—between, say, the Christian general whose beliefs drive him towards most unChristian and bloodthirsty acts and the professional soldier without such holy fervour who behaves more humanely—*H* lacked a tight, overall form and rambled unduly.

These writers, dissimilar in so many respects, shared certain general assumptions, that society is rotten and needs to be radically transformed, that the individual is the victim of social circumstances, that the forces of the establishment are there to be opposed and that British history has been particularly notorious for the suppression of the working classes. Were there no dramatists to assert the reverse? There were no 'patriotic' playwrights in an overt sense, although social criticism need not necessarily be regarded as unpatriotic. Several dramatists continued to work with the conventional form of middle-class, drawing-room comedies

and dramas: William Douglas Home was the most successful
of them, with *The Reluctant Peer* (1964), *The Secretary Bird* (1968)
and *At the End of the Day* (1973). Anthony Shaffer, Peter
Shaffer's twin brother, continued the West End tradition of
small-cast 'hit' mystery plays, with *Sleuth* (1970), while John
Chapman was among several highly successful writers of sex
farces. These popular writers provided no sort of retort to
the left-wing dramatists, except that of ignoring them. Commercial hits were mainly a-political, although Home sometimes smacked out left and right at all politicians, while seeming ultra-conservative in style himself.

The most technically accomplished of the new popular
dramatists whose commercial success sometimes distracted
from the recognition of his real skills and insights, was Alan
Ayckbourn, who learnt his crafts at a small theatre-in-the-
round in Scarborough and would polish his plays there
before the seemingly inevitable transfers to the West End.
Ayckbourn has kept to the themes of traditional domestic
comedies (mistaken identities, class differences, marital and
love confusions), handling them with great tact and ingenuity. His main plays (*Relatively Speaking*, 1967, *How the
Other Half Loves*, 1969, *Time and Time Again*, 1971, *Absurd Person
Singular*, 1972 and *The Norman Conquests*, 1974) all start from
comparatively simple ideas, which take unexpected turns
and are developed ingeniously. He contrasted the behaviour
of two couples, one upper- and the other lower-middle-class,
in *How the Other Half Loves*, dividing the stage for this purpose.
Three Christmases with three other class-assorted couples
were the subject of *Absurd Person Singular*; while in *The Norman
Conquests* he attempted the most technically daring scheme of
all. *The Norman Conquests* were three full-length plays, all concerned with the same weekend in a small country house, with
the same time-span, but set in different rooms. The action
of one play continues on stage, while the other two are supposedly happening simultaneously elsewhere in other rooms.
If this sounds too much like a crossword puzzle, it was
Ayckbourn's skill that the characters seemed funny and convincing, original creations who were not just being pushed
around to suit the technical requirements of the author.

Apart from Ayckbourn, whose comedies would rightly
have been successful any time over the past fifty years for

they are based on good construction, tightly written dialogue and firm characterisation, there were other comedy writers who followed Mortimer in sketching out the decline of the British middle classes. Alan Bennett, from the original *Beyond the Fringe* team, constructed several amusing variations on the shabby and country genteel, in *Forty Years On* (1968), set in a decaying private school, *Getting On* (1971), about the waning idealism (and growing tolerance) of a middle-aged Labour MP, and *Habeus Corpus* (1973), about a doctor struggling with Hove and his sexual instincts. Peter Nichols also delighted in satirising the social nuances of the middle classes (as in *Chez Nous*, 1974), although he also chose wider social themes, such as the health service in *The National Health* (1971) and *The Freeway* (1974), which were both distinguished by his bright and perhaps over-witty dialogue. But Nichols's originality was perhaps best revealed by two more personal plays, *A Day in the Death of Joe Egg* (1967), about his experiences in coping with his spastic child, a 'mere vegetable', and *Forget-Me-Not-Lane* (1971), about growing up during the war, a time of amateur concert parties and rationing, and his problems with his father.

In addition to the social satirists, there were the 'professional sceptics', notably Tom Stoppard, Stanley Eveling and several less well-known writers of comedies, John Spurling and Paul Ableman among them. Almost as a matter of course, it seemed, they were intent upon casting doubt on the assumptions popularly held. Stoppard delighted in a sense of private irrelevance. The characters of his main plays (Rosencrantz and Guildenstern in *Rosencrantz and Guildenstern Are Dead*, 1967, George in *Jumpers*, 1972, and Henry Carr in *Travesties*, 1974) are all outside the swirl of events, lost and uncomprehending. The audience invariably knows more than they do—and they are thus figures of fun. But Stoppard cleverly reverses our normal expectations in that they are not exactly fools: they have no way of knowing what will happen to them, and Stoppard gains our sympathy for their ignorance. We are all, the feeling runs, equally lost, at the mercy of forces outside our knowledge and control. In *Travesties*, the hero is an ex-consular official in Zurich in 1917, a time when James Joyce, Tristan Tzara (the Dadaist) and Lenin were all undertaking epoch-changing work. But Henry Carr, the official, knows nothing about them, except from rumours and chance meetings: he is concerned with his great performance in *The Importance of Being Earnest*, an amateur production managed by Joyce. Carr hates Joyce, whom he sues for the cost of a pair of trousers. The world is changing around Carr, but all he can see is his lost trousers and an amateur production.

Stoppard uses the theme of irrelevance as a launching pad for his dazzling literary pastiches—variations on chance themes in *Rosencrantz and Guildenstern Are Dead*, abstract philosophising in *Jumpers*, and styles and ideas of 1917, in *Travesties*. After three or four plays, however, this harping on irrelevance can seem irrelevant in itself. Is Stoppard suggesting in *Travesties* that men are always poohsticks, drifting aimlessly beneath the bridges of Time, in which case he could have chosen a more startling poohstick (such as Lenin himself)? Or is he simply pointing out that, from different angles, history changes colours and shapes, a familiar point but one which, in a world full of dogmas, is worth a stress or two?

Stoppard's plays sometimes seem to be tending towards the multi-viewpoint drama of David Halliwell, without going quite that far. John Spurling, like Stoppard, casts doubt upon the knowability of life's events and has borrowed from Halliwell some multi-viewpoint techniques. In *MacRune's Guevara* (1969), he writes about a dramatist, Hotel, who lives in a room previously occupied by a Scottish artist, MacRune. MacRune, a Marxist, was an admirer of Che Guevara and has scrawled pictures about Guevara's revolutionary exploits all over the walls. Hotel, whose political views are right-wing and establishment-minded, is an admirer of MacRune: in deciphering the sketches, he tries to reverse their political content. And so we have three possible views of Guevara—his exploits as they have been recorded as happening, MacRune's interpretation of them and Hotel's understanding of MacRune's interpretations. The truth? That lies perhaps somewhere in the mixture, not 'factual' nor 'absolute' truth, but a shifting climate of thought which has its own intangible reality.

This sort of chronic scepticism, though valuable, can become a bad habit, in that ideas are always being formulated, only to be dismembered. In a sense, scepticism as a habit is the reverse side to absolute belief: one side asserts that we know nothing, the other—that (through Christianity, Marxism, Buddhism or whatever) we can discover the Secrets of the Universe. Stanley Eveling, a moral philosopher by trade, is more sophisticated in his understanding of philosophical stances. His witty and irreverent comedies play around with ideas, generating a schoolboy sense of fun while maintaining an underlying seriousness. The fundamental existence, upon the surface of which the ideas bubble, is drab, sad and futile: a world of abortions, suicides and 'lower depths'. Eveling, however, takes this apparently gloomy material and transforms it into the stuff of intellectual farces. In *Caravaggio, Buddy* (1972) a potential suicide recalls his past life, and those of other lives, in the moments between switching on the gas oven and oblivion. In *Shivvers* (1974), he considers all those attitudes associated with the 'lower depths'—the married man craving for limitless orgies, the priest who believes that he can see God better from down below, the prostitute who regards all such fantasies as part of her trade. Eveling's plays, however, were perhaps most successful when his delight in ideas did not distract him too much from his equally energetic pleasure in writing funny plays. *Union Jack and Bonzo* (1973) contains few 'ideas', in the sense of philosophical arguments, but it is a wonderfully funny Boy Scout murder story, where the ghost of Baden-Powell presides in shock but not always silence over many dirty deeds at the annual camp.

To 'balance' the often austere, serious but (to my mind) bleak and somewhat unrealistic views of the left-wing dramatists, the Second Wave produced dramatists working in traditional genres (Ayckbourn), sceptics and light-hearted writers of social comedies. The Second Wave writers are, I would have thought, no less skilful than the Anger and After men. On the contrary, their innate talents profited from the earlier technical discoveries. A young writer, like Christopher Hampton, can choose from many alternatives: he can write a neat 'bourgeois' comedy (*The Philanthropist*, 1970) which also burlesques the genre, or a social epic (*Savages*, 1973) about the destruction of the Brazilian Indians where the hero is a Western sceptic, or a domestic drama (*When Did You Last See My Mother?*, 1966) or a historical-biographical account of the relationship between Verlaine and Rimbaud (*Total Eclipse*, 1968). David Hare, a committed left-wing writer, can choose between writing very neat comedies (such as *Knuckle*, 1974, which sees Home Counties/stockbroker life through the eyes of a Dashiel Hammett thriller) or austere Brechtian accounts of the way in which a Chinese village, Long Bow, changed under the impact of the Maoist revolution (*Eanshen*, 1975). Talent, technical alternatives, opportunities, skill and resources: the Second Wave dramatists possessed these qualities and chances. Why then did the feeling grow during the early 1970s of failure, of lack of excitement, so that even the successes brought with them an air of *déjà vu*? Had we all(and critics in particular) become too jaded and sophisticated? Or were certain standards imperceptibly dropping? What element, if any, was missing?

The ingredient lacking is perhaps best defined by that mysterious word, authenticity, which I mentioned in the first chapter. Judged by purely literary standards, *Look Back in Anger* and *O What a Lovely War!* were both clumsy plays, but they had a certain power to speak directly to their audiences—because they expressed certain deep-rooted feelings, which had not quite been stated before and which lay in the backgrounds of our minds and hearts. They seemed, to use an unashamedly moral word, 'honest' plays—though perhaps only in their time and to those audiences. To go on repeating these statements, however, dressed up in ever more elaborate disguises, seems less than honest, rather like cashing in on a good racket. Many left-wing plays of the late 1960s and early 1970s left the impression of merely re-stating what had been said many times before—without the 'honesty' of a Wesker, without the 'urgency' of an Osborne. The same qualities apply to a-political plays: the late 1960s produced few plays quite to match Pinter's *The Caretaker* in its direct statement of a situation which most people could recognise as belonging (under however heavy a masking) to their own lives.

Having generalised thus far, I will wander still further into the thickets of assertion. It may be in the nature of the theatre that it derives its 'authenticity' from a consideration of the various 'transactions' which govern our lives. Because the theatre is not 'real life', we can contemplate alternative ways of living without necessarily committing ourselves. The key to these alternatives lies in the nature of social transactions. Human beings, I would suggest, have a need for self-realisation, for developing their talents and their natures to the fullest practicable extent: this search for self-realisation is what we term 'freedom'. But we know that we cannot be completely free because we live in a society and our 'freedom' would or might impinge upon the freedom of others. And so we deliberately limit and extend our freedoms in association with others: 'this is my territory and you must not trespass', with its corollary, 'these are the boundaries of my territory beyond which I must not trespass'. Marking out the limits of personal freedom are what I term transactionalism: transactions are mutual pacts and they are expressed in a whole variety of phenomena, from money systems to law to marriages to codes of sexual behaviour.

Altering transactions, because they seem unfair or too limiting on personal freedoms or too loosely defined, seems to me the habit which dominates much of our lives; but altering transactions profoundly is something which can provoke great upheavals, from wars and revolutions to nervous breakdowns. We are putting aside pacts on which our lives have previously been based to formulate new ones, with which others may not agree and which may not indeed work. To avoid the tragedies which could occur when the old transactions are broken and the new ones not accepted, we try out the changes in game form—through fiction and the theatre. Theatrical authenticity derives from understanding the old transactions, appreciating the need for change and speculating intelligently about new alternatives; and finally, by finding appropriate technical means through which this vital debate can be transformed into a full statement, using the rich language of drama. Its reward is not necessarily social change, although this may well come, but a deeper human appreciation of the situation with which it is concerned.

Chapter 12

Climate and language

Over the past thirty years, British theatre has changed rapidly and profoundly; but many of these changes cannot be assessed simply in terms of individual plays, productions, writers and companies. They are really changes of theatrical 'climate', by which I mean something more than a fashion and less than revolution. One such change came with the abolition of stage censorship; another with the swing away from 'universal' themes towards 'topical' ones—and from 'formality' to 'informality'—and from deliberately 'class-structured' theatres to 'community' or 'class-less' ones. The theatre system as a whole changed, together with its methods of financing, which in turn led to problems and opportunities which had not existed in the early 1950s. These climatic changes cannot be taken in isolation, neither from each other nor from the general development of the theatrical language.

If we try to isolate them, we run into problems, for individually they seem less significant than they were collectively. Was, for example, the abolition of the office of the Lord Chamberlain's Examiner of Plays (the censor) a non-event? It can be regarded as such for several reasons. By 1968, the year of abolition, censorship had lost much of its original force. Apart from the fact that the censors had become more liberal in outlook (tolerating some swear-words and glimpses of nakedness), there had been for years an easy way of dodging censorship altogether. The theatre club system had developed during the 1950s and early 1960s, to exploit that shadowy area of the law where two principles overlapped—the preservation of public decency and the protection of home privacy. Clubs were regarded as private property, whereas the theatres were public premises. Provided that the clubs were not run as brothels and that they were genuine 'membership' clubs, almost any theatrical display could be presented in them. The major changes of taste concerning (say) stage nakedness had taken place before censorship was officially abolished: in the Soho strip clubs and such events as the Theatre of Cruelty season. Furthermore, the restrictions on public theatres did not end with the abolition of censorship, for managements could still be prosecuted under various Vagrancy Acts for 'obscenity'. If the theatre was relatively 'free' before abolition and still to some extent 'restricted' afterwards, then what was the value of abolition at all?

Getting rid of the censor meant, first, the end of a certain paternalistic control over the theatre, enshrined in an archaic office. Before abolition, the theatre had been in a category apart from other public media (such as newspapers and public meetings) in that plays had to be vetted in advance of production. All public media were subject to the Vagrancy laws, but only the theatre (and the film industry, whose censorship laws were to some extent derived from those of the theatre) had to present certain guarantees and receive certain licences before production could take place. This meant that improvisatory plays were, by definition, banned, not because they were 'obscene', but because they couldn't give guarantees in advance (together with scripts) as to what they would be about. Furthermore, the object of censorship was to remove affronts to public tastes, or those considered to be 'public' by the censor. But there was a significant theatrical movement, expressed by Artaud and formulated by Brook, that shock was necessary to the theatre. It woke people up. Hence, the aims of censorship and those of certain sections of the theatre were in direct conflict, not about the right to stage sexy plays, but about 'shock' and improvisatory freedom.

Nor was it easy to defend censorship, for the codes of public behaviour had changed. The definition of such words as 'obscenity' and 'the tendency...to deprave and corrupt' really required the background of an essentialist philosophy, in this case Christianity, because it is only if you know what virtue means, that you can legislate against vice. Lord Chief Justice Cockburn, whose definition of obscenity was retained by British courts, had formulated this definition in 1868, against a background of a prevailing Christian culture. A century later, could legislators rely on a public norm, based upon Christian beliefs? And, if not, how could they define such words as obscenity? 'To define pornography or obscenity precisely,' wrote Alma Birk, chairman of the British Health Education Council, 'has proved beyond the wit of man. Maybe we should stop trying.' In 1968, we stopped doing so through the office of the Lord Chamberlain's Examiner of Plays.

Many feared that the abolition of censorship would open the floodgates to a tidal wave of pornographic plays. Its actual effects were far less extreme. While some sex shows were very successful (*Oh! Calcutta!* and *Pyjama Tops*), impresarios quickly discovered that nakedness on stage did not necessarily lead to instant fortunes. *The Council of Love* (1970), with a full-scale orgy and blasphemy to boot, lost money. If abolition did not lead to a wholescale rape of the West End by sex shows, it did, however, contribute to a change in attitude which might have been of greater consequence. The question of censorship overlapped with another issue. Should the theatre attempt to 'set standards'?

The overall impression from plays and productions immediately following the war is that there was a theatre continually trying to set standards. The standards may have been moral, ranging from the stoicism of Whiting's heroes, to the acceptance of destiny in Eliot's plays, to the difference between good husbands and faithless lovers in Greene's and Rattigan's plays, to the proper behaviour of scientists in Charles Morgan's. Writers on all levels were prepared to chip in with sturdy defences of traditional values. The standards were not, however, always moral. They were also fashionable, social and orientated towards certain class outlooks. Drawing-room sets were clapped on opening nights by audiences who had dressed up for the occasion. Fashionable designers, such as Oliver Messel, were as well known as fashionable beauties, male as well as female. The West End retained traces of Edwardian dandyism: going to the theatre was a formal experience, and legitimate theatre (for which one dressed up) contrasted with the less legitimate varieties (such as music halls and touring nude revues) where one did not.

During the late 1950s, attacks were launched against these

standards. The drawing rooms became kitchens, the elegant Oxbridge actors became rough regional ones. The dramatists of the early 1950s aspired to preserve, or conform to, certain literary standards, such as the well-made play, poetic language and sentences of dialogue constructed grammatically and completed. By the late 1950s, there was a much freer and more conversational use of verbal language, while the old rules were bent in all directions until many broke. Critics, like George Steiner, deplored the backing away from old literary standards which they regarded as fundamental to drama. These were not just changes of verbal style. There were fundamental issues involved, for (as we have seen) the origins of the well-made play derived from the attempt to express certain universal principles. Eliot considered that his main task as a dramatist was to stress the universal principles which were latent (though buried) beneath society drama. Universality was considered to be the test of a play's worthiness. Sir Barry Jackson was proud of his boast that no play produced at the Birmingham Rep would not have been equally worthwhile staging in twenty years' time. He would have disdained mere topicality. At the time of Munich, the Birmingham Rep was playing *The Wooing of Anne Hathaway* by Grace Carlton.

Partly under the influence of Brecht, partly through the new satirists of the early 1960s and partly through the direct and topical attacks launched by Osborne and others, this emphasis on universality diminished, to be replaced by topicality. Even when writers tackled 'universal' themes, they did so to prove their modernity. John Bowen's version of *The Bacchae* (*Disorderly Women*, 1969) contained hidden references to contemporary drug culture. The Freehold's version of *Antigone* was orientated towards Vietnam; Fugard's treatment of the same legend (in *The Island*) commented upon South African laws. Shakespeare was our contemporary.

If 'universality' influenced the construction of plays (as it did, through such moral ideas as 'hubris' which in turn affected the way in which dramatists handled 'crises'), so too did 'topicality', often in the opposite direction. A certain loose-limbed immediacy of effect took over, where plays might be strung together roughly as 'documentaries', where 'crises' were avoided and so were 'universal' statements, parcelling up the meanings of plays into tidy final scenes. The pessimism of the late 1960s partly consisted of a refusal to pretend that problems could be easily solved, a fair enough attitude but one which led to deliberately irresolute final scenes. In general, for example, the old three-act 'well-made' plays were replaced by two-act plays, with one interval. This change was partly a matter of convenience: it can be irritating to be dragged away to the bars twice in an evening, though some may not find it so. But the three-act plays followed the pattern of a classical syllogism. The first act stated the major premise, the second the minor, and the third the conclusion or resolution. By dropping an act, the logical pattern was also set aside. Similarly, as Alain Robbe-Grillet once said about novel writing, modern authors refused to be Gods to their characters. They stopped pretending (or pretended that they had stopped pretending) that they knew everything about them. At best, this led to a certain open-mindedness and lack of censoriousness, unless the characters were members of the bourgeoisie (in which case they were often held to be beneath contempt): at worst, it led to a vagueness of characterisation in which it was impossible to tell what the characters were like at all.

Thus, the swing against stuffy bourgeois standards resulted, first, in a proletarian fashion, and then steadied into a sort of classless image. The actors of the early 1960s (such as Albert Finney, Alan Bates, Kenneth Haigh, Tom Courtenay and John Neville in his 'Alfie' disguise) who were tough and virile and had made their reputations in regional or 'working-class' plays, were followed in the late 1960s by actors with a more classless, introverted and perhaps older style: David Warner and Ian McKellen among the younger actors, Frank Finlay, Alec McCowen and Edward Woodward among the older ones. A similar trend is detectable among actresses. The 1950s was an age of theatrical *grandes dames* (Dame Edith Evans, Dame Sybil Thorndike), of *grandes cocottes* (Kay Hammond, Googie Withers) and of the *ingénues* (Geraldine McEwan, Dorothy Tutin, Maggie Smith and Claire Bloom). The early 1960s brought a different class image: Barbara Ferris, Barbara Windsor and Rita Tushingham were (to retain the French symmetry) *gamines* or even *grisettes*. The actresses of the late 1960s and early 1970s were certainly not *cocottes*, *grandes* or otherwise, nor *gamines*. They were poised, assured, classless women, usually conveying the impression of being independent of men: Diana Rigg, Glenda Jackson and Janet Suzman.

These are rough generalisations: Albert Finney and Claire Bloom did not stop working or suddenly fall out of fashion when David Warner and Diana Rigg came along. Nicol Williamson, passionate introversion personified, did not drive John Neville into sheep-farming. But there was a tendency towards the classless actor, which had its merits and its weaknesses. A view prevailed that Britain had been, and perhaps still was, a uniquely class-structured society: classlessness was an attempt to escape both from snobbery and inverted snobbery. But there was a vagueness about what constituted the class system. To an anarchist, such as Heathcote Williams or Ion Alexis Will (who collaborated with Ken Campbell on *The Great Caper*, 1974), a bourgeois was anyone who paid his or her debts, worked hard and tried to maintain a nuclear family. To a Marxist, owners and entrepreneurs were naturally members of the bourgeoisie. To writers who were not 'left-wing', being middle-class was a natural state of mind referring to certain aspirations, such as the desire to be well-spoken and well-thought-of, to own one's own house, to have some control over the education of one's children, to have a responsible job with opportunities for advancement and to be in a position where personal choice was important.

It was extremely hard to opt out of all the possible ramifications and definitions of the class system without becoming a non-person. The classless characters of the 1970s were often those who merely responded to events, who stood aside from all kinds of involvement and who sometimes seemed to be revelling in irrelevance. Bernard Link in Mercer's *After Haggerty* (played in London by Frank Finlay) was afflicted with continual strains and constant indecision. Someone like Dysart in Peter Shaffer's *Equus* looked in on other people's emotions from outside, being incapable of feeling them for himself. The anguish of being classless (of losing one's roots) became as popular a theme during the late 1960s almost as the pain of being downtrodden. This was the negative side of classlessness, the positive being the refusal to condescend or to kow-tow, the attempt to communicate with all people on a more or less equal footing and the detestation of jingoism. Negatively, classlessness might mean the refusal to admit of any values whatsoever on the grounds that they might incriminate one. Positively it could mean that the classless person acknowledged the subjective limits to his scheme of values and thus sought not to impose these values on others. The abolition of censorship could even be regarded as a decision in favour of classlessness.

This was not just a personal attitude. It became enshrined in the theatres we built and the programmes they offered. The reps, for example, usually strove to provide 'mixed' programmes, with plays selected to appeal to different sections of the public in turn. Thus, the programmes might alternate between a farce, a thriller and a play like *The Tempest*, with pop concerts and chamber music on Sunday nights. This variety could be valuable, in preventing cultural snobbery; but it could lead to a situation where no type of experience was considered more valuable than any other. The effort to contact all sections of the community also affected the ancillary activities of the reps, the theatre-in-education programmes, studio productions or (at its most spurious) the attempts to drum up trade by (at one theatre) praying very publicly at the local church. There were again positive and negative sides to these community activities. Positively, actors acquired a range of talents (from schoolteaching to staging pub music halls) which they would not have gained through the old commercial system or with 'prestige' companies: negatively, these new talents were often accompanied with superficiality, the belief that if their performances had succeeded in the classroom or pub, they had done their job as actors. Social work of this sort also strained some actors who were neither accustomed nor trained to undertake it, but felt guilty if they did not.

The new theatres stressed the 'classless' image. Tiered theatres, for example, with balconies and circles were considered to be class-orientated theatres, for they separated the rich people in the stalls from the poorer ones in the upper circles. To seat audiences in single fan-shaped auditoria around thrust or arena stages was considered more democratic. Peter Cheeseman once wrote that, forms of theatre differ in their techniques of performance, but also philosophically and even politically in the relationships implied in the human structure of the environment they create. People form the partial or total background to the action presented in a thrust or arena stage, each spectator can see almost the entire audience, the drama is played out in a space cleared in the middle of the community.

But there is more than an element of hypocrisy in such views. To suggest that one is only part of a community if one happens to be continually watching other members of the audience is rather like suggesting that you can only be in love if you're staring at your beloved. There are better arguments for arena stages. Furthermore, tiered theatres do not necessarily mean class-orientated theatres. To get as many people as possible into a town theatre occupying a small land space, architects have to design tall buildings, with many seating levels. To cut out balconies and circles in some town theatres simply means that you are reducing the seating capacity of these theatres, which is scarcely the way to make going to the theatre more democratic or egalitarian. By deliberately avoiding tiers, you are also distorting the economics of the theatre, because with smaller audiences less money can be recovered through the box office. Hence, many new theatres became increasingly dependent upon State subsidies, which is perhaps the least egalitarian way of financing a theatre for it is subject to no kind of popular choice.

Members of the Arts Council, and its officers and their panels, usually react strongly against the suggestion that they are connected with some kind of élitist institution. They point out that State help is given in response to local initiative, which in turn is often prompted and spurred by public demand. They represent no particular political or cultural view. They are rather united by the general belief that a civilised society requires strong patronage for the Arts and that the Arts Council is the institutional means through which this end can be realised. If the 'balanced pattern for patronage', called for by Sir William Emrys Williams, failed to materialise, this was not the Arts Council's fault, but that of the local authorities, unions, industry and private benefactors who failed to respond to the challenge. The Arts Council, with the rise of its government grants which began dramatically in 1964, simply stepped in where they had feared to tread. Furthermore, in one respect State subsidies have had the effect of allowing theatres to be more egalitarian: they have kept seat prices low.

Nevertheless, I do not see how the Arts Council can avoid the charge of being an élite, however enlightened their officers, however wise the appointments to the various panels, however cleverly the Drama panel represents a cross-section of theatre opinion. Comparatively few men control the division of comparatively large sums of money, on which the majority of theatres depend for their survival in Britain. The Arts Council itself, a body of some twenty persons of whom the Chairman is directly appointed by the Minister of the day, can overrule the standing officers (of whom three are concerned particularly with the theatre)— and on occasions has. The standing officers are advised by the unpaid members of the panels: there are thirty-odd members of the Drama panel, ranging (in 1973–74) from Peter Oliver of Oval House, representing the community fringe, to Trevor Nunn of the Royal Shakespeare company. There are various sub-committees. Thus, about fifty men control in effect the disposition of State money to theatres around the country. This is not *so* much of an élite, perhaps, as that represented by Prince Littler Consolidated Trust in the early 1950s, but it is nevertheless an élite; and while I am inclined to feel that power (like money and muck) is not good unless it be well spread, the fact that the Arts Council is an élite worries me less than the fact that it pretends not to be one.

Elites usually have to justify their position, and defend it, by providing standards which are arguably higher than those of popular and commercial art. The attempt to discover and express high standards, belonging to whatever moral, social, religious, aesthetic or political schemes of belief, is an inseparable part of being (or belonging to) an élite. These values can be attacked by alternative groups, who in turn wish to claim recognition as being the new or up-and-coming élites. The Arts Council, however, doesn't wish to be involved in this sort of conflict about values, and therefore to some extent it disguises its élitist position by seeming helpful to every deserving case. 'State support...without State Control.' Unfortunately, decisions have to be taken and, in the absence of a perceptible scheme of values, they are usually taken in the spirit of the less controversy the better. Thus, many of the resources devoted to art in this country have been spent either on establishing institutions (such as some major reps) or maintaining them on substantial annual grants, in the belief that if these enterprises are kept going, something interesting in the way of art must, by the law of averages, emerge.

'Classlessness' in short has also influenced the style of patronage. As with classlessness on other levels, it has its good and bad aspects. Its good side is revealed by the very presence of major civic theatres around the country, each tackling a wide range of work in a non-pompous way. Its bad side is that it can offer something like 'packaged theatre' as we talk about packaged holidays—in other words, short production periods leading to three-weekly runs so that neighbourhood audiences can appreciate a variety of plays in competent productions. Culture teeters towards bureaucracy, and since these two words are not normally associated with each other, perhaps I should explain them further. To my mind, the essence of culture lies in a certain respect for one's work, a desire to do it (in all aspects) 'better', which in the theatre also involves a respect for other people. Artists may be very difficult to live with, but in their desire to find exact statements for the experiences which they feel, they are affirming the importance of honest relationships. Bureaucrats, on the other hand, are trying to do without relationships, to place the contact between individual and individual on an over-formalised basis, to money shuffled across a counter, to age and parents on a form, to height and weight in a description. Bureaucrats may be easy to live with, for they demand nothing more from one than a few easily compiled facts, half one's attention, a little time and a lot of instant obedience. They may protect one from the disasters of illness, unemployment and poverty; but if one is living in a society which has the feeling of bureaucracy, then one's contacts with other people become merely mechanical—and to compensate, private fantasies become increasingly necessary to wear out the days.

Slipshod artists are half-way to becoming bureaucrats, because they have stopped bothering about whether their language exactly matches what they wish to say. They are slipping what looks like a play or a production across the counter, confident that the public will accept it as having some sort of meaning, as a standard document and what is to be expected, and cease to make that effort to invest this transaction with true understanding. Every age has its form of bureaucratic art. Our problem is that with centralised patronage which ducks away from value judgments, with a repertory system (including many admirable managements and companies) which normally pursues 'mixed' programmes and settled production routines, with entry into the acting profession severely (and not unwisely) controlled by Equity and with the decline of other methods of financing the theatre, we may easily smother the inspirational impetus even with good intentions.

This thought brings us back to the Auden quotation, that the prime duty is 'to maintain the purity of the language'. Kenneth Tynan has said that from a critic's point of view the history of twentieth-century drama is that of a 'collapsing vocabulary'. By this, he may have meant that the old rules governing play-writing and productions are no longer acceptable and that we have yet to discover new rules which are equally valid and useful. Much the same point has been made about music. My view is much less apocalyptic. The 'vocabulary' of the theatre has surely greatly increased over the past thirty years. Shaw found it technically difficult to present working environments in his plays: since Wesker, Henry Chapman, Peter Terson and the arrival of other dramatists for whom the study of working environments provides the stuff of drama, this deficiency has ceased to exist. Since British theatre began to accept the influences of Wedekind and Brecht, it has been possible to break up the old Unities of the well-made play which inhibited the treatment of certain wide-ranging themes. Since the abolition of censorship, the restrictions which prevented the dramatic realisation of certain sexual subjects have disappeared. With the arrival of environmental theatre, the lecture-hall relationship which raised the actor on to a podium and confined his public to passive onlookers, is no longer obligatory, thus opening out the prospect of a more flexible, conversational idiom. With the arrival of different forms of Absurdist drama, it is no longer necessary for writers to feel hamstrung by syllogistic logic. They can also employ the associative logic of dreams, the iconoclastic anti-logic of Dadaism, allegorical logic and childlike (if not childish) nonsense. And so on. One striking feature of these various vocabulary developments is that they have not been accompanied by a Tower of Babel situation, with many different companies speaking different vocabularies, each foreign to the other. The vocabulary has grown without bursting into fragments.

But vocabulary is only one component of language, the other main ones being syntax, form and pattern. My feelings here are less sanguine, I mean the way in which one theatrical impression is related to another, usually within some form of dramatic logic, not necessarily syllogistic. If we compare individual scenes from Brecht's best plays with those many Brechtian Epic plays (documentaries and the like) from British writers, we rarely find detailed and satisfactory construction of scenes from British plays which even grope towards the standards set by Brecht. There are two common faults: an unwillingness to carry through the argument of a scene towards its logical conclusion and an eagerness to snatch up a superficial logic usually at the expense of a more pervasive, complicated, internal reasoning. Brecht was able in, say, *Mother Courage*, to maintain several different points of view within each scene: British writers rarely do so. The scenes in British plays tend to be shorter. It is now comparatively rare in modern British drama to find a scene which unfolds over twenty minutes or more, involving (say) six characters of equal dramatic weight. Characters can be compared to orchestral instruments. They have their own tonal colourings, their melodic lines, their own 'voices', which ought to contribute to a rich overall effect. When they do not, this is equivalent to poor or sparse scoring in music. There was a tendency at one time to allow a central character, perhaps a Jimmy Porter anti-hero, to run away with scenes, in long rhetorical speeches.

As with syntax, so with form. Here too we find common

clumsinesses. The first is that 'formalism' (rather than form) which imposes itself obtrusively upon the play's content. At one time, nearly all Royal Shakespeare Company productions seemed to start with a coronation, usually with a slow march to music by Guy Woolfenden. Among Brechtian plays, the formalism was a ballad every ten minutes or so: among naturalistic plays, it was a bit of naturalistic pottering about, showing how people normally work, whether or not these work patterns had any direct relevance. Formalism can be a denial of form for it distracts us from the internal life of a play (which should provide its own form) by superimposing an irrelevant design. But at least formalism recognises the need for form, even when it amounts to a tacit admission that the director or dramatist cannot discover what the form should be. There was also, however, an almost philistine disregard for form, particular among some fringe companies, who seemed to believe that form was a bourgeois invention, antagonistic to the spontaneous good humour of the working classes.

In the contemporary use of pattern, the situation is different. Many traditional delights have survived, among them the Edwardian pleasure in neat phrases, aphorisms and epigrams. We have many very witty writers, among them Mercer, Stoppard, Ayckbourn, Hampton and Marcus. On another level, we have many designers and directors who delight in spectacular visual effects, from the gymnasium setting and swinging trapezes of Brook's *A Midsummer Night's Dream* to the glowing Aztec sun in *The Royal Hunt of the Sun*. Some Edwardian techniques have been lost, notably in the use of flying ballets and stage music, but some compensation can be found in the more sophisticated usages of lighting, stage areas, props and stage 'textures', including the use of such contrasts as steel with fur. If showbusiness musicals have declined in number and quality, the use of music in straight drama productions has become much more sophisticated. The Royal Shakespeare Company productions in particular use music for Shakespearian plays, which far outstrips the obligatory trumpets (for battle scenes) and violins for dances, which used to be so monotonous a feature of their productions in the 1950s. The electronic music of Brook's *King Lear*, the elaborate vocal effects, Weillian tunes, evoca-

tive sounds and small ensembles of other productions have
added many incidental delights to the Royal Shakespeare
Company's work. Similarly, although the elaborate stage
dances of 1950s musicals are rare, the use of mime and dance
in fringe productions (such as those of the now disbanded
Freehold company and Lindsay Kemp's troupe) has become
much more familiar. There are many directors (where there
used to be only a few) who can handle complicated stage pictures, with mime and precise groupings. The Guthries and
Helpmanns of the other years have left good successors in
the Dexters, Hands, Blakemores and Eyres of today.

These crude generalisations about the changing nature of
the theatrical language also miss out what is perhaps the
most important element: the way in which our minds as
theatregoers and as members of the profession can be seized
by certain images and productions which afterwards act as
touchstones of excellence. Peter Brook in *The Empty Space* has
said that he is haunted by certain theatrical memories—of
Winnie, buried up to her waist and then to her neck, in
Beckett's *Happy Days*, the four soldiers and the dangling corpse against a winter landscape in Arden's *Sergeant Musgrave's
Dance*. Perhaps the greatest achievement of British theatre
over the past thirty years is that it has provided so many of
these experiences, at least for me. I am haunted by the
spotlit, chattering Mouth and the shadowing, sceptical figure
in Beckett's *Not I*, by the lonely woman dragging her wagon
and her daughter beating the drum in *Mother Courage*, by the
oblique threats against Stanley in Pinter's *The Birthday Party*
and Donald Pleasance's shuffling evasiveness as Davies in *The
Caretaker*, by the loneliness, violence and poverty of Bond's
Saved, by that extraordinary change of mood and atmosphere in the second act of *West Side Story*, Max Wall's sly
masochism as a comedian, Lindsay Kemp's stillness as Devine
in *Flowers*, Olivier's Shylock and Othello, the mad scenes in
The Marat/Sade, Wolfit's Lear, Kani and Ntshona in Fugard's
Sizwe Bansi and *The Island*—and so on, sometimes by whole
productions (Barton's *Troilus and Cressida*, Nunn's *The
Revenger's Tragedy*, Dexter's *The Misanthrope*), sometimes by
fleeting impressions (Olivier's hat-bending grandfather in
Saturday, Sunday, Monday). These productions have not, of
course, originated in Britain always, but this to my mind does

not matter. We have been able to see and to experience them, thus retaining an awareness of the potential which lies within the theatre, its emotional rather than technical potential: in short, its authenticity.

If there is a connecting link between these different impressions, it is that they all seemed to me to be exact statements of particular experiences couched in precise language. As experiences they might be disliked or found painful, but they could not be mistaken for statements about something else: they could not easily be misunderstood. The gap between individual and individual within the theatre had thus narrowed almost to nothingness. We were gripped by a unity of experience, which has nothing to do with uniformity of outlook, but only with the sheer pleasure of shared understanding.

Index

Regional and suburban theatres are listed under their towns or districts, thus—Stratford-upon-Avon, Shakespeare Memorial Theatre. London theatres are listed by their names, thus—St James's Theatre.